D1458003

An Unsettling God

"This republication from Brueggemann's *Theology of the Old Testament* is important and compelling; important because it focuses like a laser on the very heart of Hebraic faith and practice—the interactive partnership between God, world, and humankind; compelling because, as Brueggemann masterfully demonstrates, our full engagement in this partnership is nothing less than a 'life-or-death matter in our society that has too long been uncritically committed to a path of death.' For those who want to begin at the beginning in the daring enterprise of theological reflection, there is no better place to start than by heeding Brueggemann's summons to encounter Israel's surprising God."

Samuel E. Balentine
Professor of Old Testament
Union Theological Seminary-PSCE

"An unsettling God? 'An unsettling Walter Brueggemann,' some of my students would say. He keeps making them see things in the Old Testament that clash with what they have been told about God, and making them reframe and expand their understanding of God as the Bible describes God. He does that in these chapters from the heart of his *Theology of the Old Testament*. It is unsettling experience but a constructive one."

John Goldingay
David Allan Hubbard Professor of Old Testament
Fuller Theological Seminary

An Unsettling God:

The Heart of the
Hebrew Bible

WALTER BRUEGGEMANN

Fortress Press

Minneapolis

AN UNSETTLING GOD
The Heart of the Hebrew Bible

Cover image: Mikhail Larionov's "Rayonist Composition: Domination of Red (1912-13)" © 2009 Artists Rights Society (ARS), New York / ADAGP, Paris; digital Image © The Museum of Modern Art/Licensed by SCALA / Art Resource, NY.
Cover design: Paul Boehnke
Book design: PerfecType, Nashville, TN

Library of Congress Cataloging-in-Publication Data

Brueggemann, Walter.
 An unsettling God : the heart of the Hebrew Bible / by Walter Brueggemann.
     p. cm.
 Includes bibliographical references and index.
 ISBN 978-0-8006-6363-6 (alk. paper)
 1. God—Biblical teaching. 2. Bible. O.T.—Criticism, interpretation, etc. I. Title.
 BS1192.6.B76 2009
 231.7′6—dc22
                              2009011355

Manufactured in the U.S.A.

For Tia

Table of Contents

Acknowledgments

I am glad to express my thanks to Neil Elliott at Fortress Press for initiating this project of a revision of my work, and for his patience in bringing the project to fruition. It is appropriate that I dedicate this book on "partnership" to Tia Foley. She has been my partner in the completion and publication of a number of my books over a period of seven years. In more recent days we have entered into the fuller, deeper partnership of our life, and I am grateful to her on all counts.

Walter Brueggemann
September 8, 2008

Preface

It is an exciting time to be studying the Old Testament. The general crisis of our society and the sense of displacement that is widespread among us constitute an invitation to return to the old and deep resources of faith that continue in the present with compelling authority. In some ways the Old Testament strikes one as ancient, odd, and remote from us. But in other ways it is clear that the Old Testament offers categories of interpretation and guidelines for life that are rich and contemporary in their force. The present volume is an attempt to articulate some of the categories of interpretation and guidelines for life that could make a difference in our present social context.

The big idea of this book (that echoes the big idea of the Old Testament) is that the God of ancient Israel (who is the creator of heaven and earth) is *a God in relationship*, who is ready and able to make commitments and who is impinged upon by a variety of "partners" who make a difference in the life of God. Such a notion of *God in relationship* that pervades the Old Testament is both a stark contrast to much classical theology that thought of God only in God's holy self, and to the modern notion of autonomy whereby God and human selves as well are understood as isolated and independent agents who are only incidentally related to each other. The view taken here is that such relatedness is intrinsic to existence and definitional for all agents, including the agency of the God of ancient Israel.

This suggests that the defining category for faith in the Old Testament is *dialogue*, whereby all parties—including God—are engaged in a dialogic exchange that is potentially transformative for all parties . . . including God. This constitutes a conviction that God and God's partners are engaged in mutual talk. That mutual talk may take a variety of forms. From God's side, the talk may be *promise* and *command*. From the side of the partners, it may be *praise and prayer*. The Old Testament is an invitation to reimagine our life and our faith as an on-going dialogic transaction in which all parties are variously summoned to risk and change.

The reason for this study—and like current study of the Old Testament—is that we live in a time and circumstance that require fresh articulation of faith. It is clear that some of the older, widely accepted categories of interpretation are no longer adequate or satisfying for either faith or intellect. There have been many attempts to reduce biblical faith to a single normative idea. But two things strike one. First, the variegated reality of the text allows for no single dominant idea. Second, the Old Testament is not reducible to "ideas," but in fact features transformative interaction that may be reenacted and replicated in many performances of the text, whether in study, prayer, or public worship. That is, ours is a time when it is imperative to pay attention to the complex, dynamic, and fluid character of the faith of ancient Israel, with a recognition that fixity is not a quality of serious reality. The dynamism of recent psychology and of contemporary physics witnesses to reality that is in process and in on-going transformation. When we are freed of static categories of interpretation that are widely utilized among us, we are able to see that the articulation of God in the Old Testament partakes exactly of the qualities of complexity, dynamism, and fluidity that belong to the post-modern world. While such an open and thick articulation of faith may be threatening to some and may require unlearning by us all, it is evident that such a fresh perception of God in the Old Testament goes a long way toward letting this God be a contemporary partner in a world that is open and in process. Thus the work of this book is to offer an exposition of the faith of ancient Israel that connects to the dialogic world in which we now find ourselves.

The issue of dialogical faith is particularly important in our present societal context. Our society is now tempted to solve societal (and therefore personal) problems by old, predictable remedies. These remedies often seek to reduce solutions to power or to technology or to more commodity goods. Thus political threat is countered by more military power. Thus problems of illness or aging are managed by more technology. Thus loneliness is overcome by more commodity goods, whether cars, new information technology, or beer. What we know, however, is that the most elemental human issues—social and personal—do not admit of such resolution. The reason is that human persons in human community are designed for serious, validating relationships that call for mutual care and responsibility; no amount of power, technology, or commodity can be substituted for relatedness. Thus Israel's great confession of faith is that at the bottom of reality there is the fidelity of a holy God who seeks relatedness with appropriate partners. Study of the Old Testament, when done on a sustained basis, consists in changing the agenda from the categories of modernity (knowledge, technology, commodity) to interactions that make for genuine, sustained creatureliness in the world of the creator God. This book is an invitation to think about and enact that changed agenda.

As I have thought about *God and God's partners*, I have focused on four such partners that are evident in the Old Testament, partners that continue to be front and center in our contemporary world.

1. There is no doubt that God's first partner is *Israel as the chosen people of God*. Israel emerges in the text through God's call to Abraham (Gen 12:1-2), through the emancipation of the slaves from Egypt (Exod. 15:1-18), and through the covenant made at Sinai so that this people will be a "priestly kingdom" among the nations (Exod. 19:6).

There is no doubt that Israel as God's chosen people is a complex and difficult claim on many counts. For example, this designation of a special people introduces into the core of the tradition the "scandal of particularity," the conviction that God may take sides in quite concrete ways in the world, so that many peoples are "not chosen." Second, the idea of Israel's chosenness is a complicated issue for the Christian tradition, for the claim of Christ's ultimacy lives in some tension with the claim of Israel. Christians continue to struggle with such an issue. Third, there is no doubt that the theological claim of Israel as God's chosen people is made more complex by the contemporary state of Israel that both makes theological claims and operates by the force of *Realpolitik*. Fourth, at the very edge of the Old Testament there are hints that this same God may in the end select other chosen peoples as well (Isa. 19:24-25; Amos 9:7). What becomes clear is that our more-or-less settled judgments about this matter must be rethought in careful and disciplined ways.

Alongside such reality, it is useful to recognize that Israel is peculiar in its practice of interpretation that, in the hands of the rabbis and the on-going tradition, has refused the kinds of settled interpretation to which Western thought is always tempted. Jews historically have refused "final interpretation" (by being open to continued dialogic interaction), and have been victims, in the twentieth century, of an attempted "Final Solution." Thus much work remains to be done to see how the "scandal of particularity"is related to the unbearable violence against Jews in the twentieth century. It is clear in any case that "final interpretation" is a step toward "final solution."

2. The same dialogic dynamics makes it possible for the Old Testament to offer quite fresh images of *human personhood*. It is by no means an accident that our contemporary understanding of human personality largely derives from Sigmund Freud who was a Jew who understood, from the ground up, that human persons are a designed for dialogic interaction as a way of processing complex and conflictual personal and interpersonal reality. Much of what has developed in recent psychological theory is derived from that great insight of Freud and from the Old Testament model of engaged conversation. The book of Psalms, with its emotional and liturgical extremities of praise and lament, is a primer on human character and human relationship. Indeed, it is an easy case to make that what have become popular "Twelve Step Programs" are seeded in Israel's ancient practices, for such dialogue is an indispensable antidote to modern pathologies of conformity, denial, and despair. The dialogical character of human personality resists both authoritarianism that imagines that full control can be exercised over human life, and autonomy that imagines that individual persons can go it alone. The twin practices of authoritarianism and autonomy are practiced together in a consumer society, autonomy as a pursuit of commodity but under the aegis of authoritarian economics in which everything is measure by productivity.

The faith of ancient Israel endlessly pondered the question, "What is Man?" (Ps. 8:4). It understood, moreover, that human persons are "fearfully and wonderfully made" (Ps. 139:14) and so cannot be "settled" in any modernist scheme that seeks to put a lid on the irascible yearning for freedom in community. Attention to the interpersonal dynamics practiced in ancient Israel is worth the effort, for the sense of healthy humanness imagined there is a response to a glaring deficit in our contemporary world.

3. The God of Israel is confessed to be sovereign over *the nations*. This is not an easy case to make in the modern world of autonomous national states. Much modern thought has solved the problem by leaving God to be engaged with individual persons, and letting the public sphere of life be "might makes right." But of course the Old Testament is unwilling to leave any part of life—including international life—outside the scope of God's dialogic engagement.

The great temptation of modern national states is to imagine independent autonomy without answering to anyone. There is, moreover, no more blatant example of such arrogant autonomy than the recent unilateralism of the United States that has conducted policy on the assumption that it could do anything it wanted, that it owed nothing to the other nations, and that there was no compelling moral limit to aggressive acquisitiveness.

But arrogant national states, all the way back to ancient Egypt and ancient Babylon, have assumed the same. The faith of ancient Israel, especially voiced in prophetic oracles, asserts that there are God-given, God-enforced limits and lines of accountability that curb and chasten raw power. A study of this dimension of Old Testament faith poses exceedingly difficult questions about the governing limits of God in internal affairs:

- Could it possibly be that South African apartheid reached its limit because such brutality was beyond the limit of God?
- Could it be that the fall of the Soviet Union occurred because the power of the state outran what could be borne in the world of God?
- And if one entertains such thought, then one may ask, What are the limits that are non-negotiable even in terms of US power?

Study of this topic invites engagement with the prophetic rhetoric of the Old Testament that knows that the entire political enterprise has a theological dimension to it that cannot be disregarded. Such thinking is reflected in the language of the church that prays regularly, "Thine is the kingdom and the power and the glory." The terms of the prayer, faithful to the Old Testament, are political in a way that places all other political claims in question. Study of this topic must resist "silly supernaturalism," but may nonetheless take seriously the claim of God that renders all other claims as penultimate.

4. With the current accent upon the environment and a sense of the ecological crisis, it is urgent that *creation* as God's partner should be a topic of study. We have tended, in the modern world, to reduce "creation" to "nature," and regarded it as a given on its own terms; the recovery of the language of "creation" will serve to refer the world back to the creator who has ordained into the world limits, and order, and fruitfulness. It will make a difference if and when we are able to recognize that all creatures—beavers, radishes, ore, birds and lilies, oceans—are creatures of the creator who relate to God in terms of obedience and praise. Recently, I saw a beautiful sight in our town when the sun shone brightly on every ice-covered tree and bush. Without being romantic about it, it was not difficult to imagine that the

trees and bushes in their beauty were enacting praise to their creator. Nor is it difficult to imagine that creaturely life that has been distorted (by combat, by neglect,
by abuse) is alienated from the creator and yearns for a restored relationship. Such
a view is an important challenge to our usual reductionism that sees the world as a
collage of commodities for our use, enjoyment, and exploitation.

When we consider God in relation to God's partners, it is clear that we are
not engaged in an ancient, esoteric question. Rather, we are at the edge of the most
crucial contemporary issues. The study of the Old Testament is an opportunity to
rethink, from the ground up, the most demanding issues before us and particularly before the younger generation that must live with our crisis into the coming
years. Concerning these four partners, we will have to ask:

- how chosenness is maintained without idolatrous hardening;
- how human persons in dialogic modes can resist authoritarianism and
  autonomy;
- how nation-states can be understood in terms of penultimate answerability;
- how creation can be re-embraced as a living organic connection, limited
  and sustained by the creator.

In all of these dimensions, partnership is a summons away from modernist misconstruals, from theological naiveté, and from spiritualization that shuns the hard
work of interaction. In fact this menu of partnership may suggest, in a more or
less programmatic way, an agenda for our common work of interpretation that is
a life-or-death matter in a society that has been too long uncritically committed
to a path of death.

The burden of my argument is to recognize that *Israel* (with its ideological temptation), *human persons* (with the seductions of authoritarianism and
autonomy), *nation-states* (with an imagined ultimacy), and *creation* (tempted to
mechanical reductionism) are to be understood in a dialogical way.

The God of the Bible, of the Old Testament, is a God *in relation.* That in turn
means that God's sovereignty is governance-in-relation, marked not only by power
but also by fidelity and infidelity. This recharacterization of God is enormously
important, because it requires that God be acknowledged as agent; the agency
of God is decisive for the life of the world. But Enlightenment reductionism—in
the wake of classical theology—has worked long and hard to expel *agency* from
religious reflection. Without agency, however, there can be no partnership. Thus
God as agent in partnership is a God who is always impinged upon, who is capable
of a range of emotional engagement, and who is seen in Israel to be capable of

remarkable interventions. Such a God cannot be reduced to code or formula, but requires rendition in narrative and song and oracle; God, in the discourse of Israel, is always an originary character not to be slotted in any of our familiar categories.

To stand before the Old Testament as a student is a demanding place to be. There is, however, no better place to be if one wants to engage the most critical, elemental questions facing us. I am glad to offer this guideline for study and anticipate a rising generation of readers who will go boldly into this tradition that has revolutionary, subversive, and constructive consequences.

These chapters are a revision of materials from my book of 1997, *Theology of the Old Testament*. I am pleased to republish this material because I believe that the notion of "partnership" as a theological datum is of acute importance in a technological society that refuses the interaction championed in this textual tradition. This large model of interactionism, a peculiarly Jewish insight in a modernist Enlightenment culture, moves in many directions in the text and touches many dimensions of faithful imagination. Thus I suggest that the notion of "partnership" that I have exposed provides important grist for critical reflection that concerns both the faithful practice of the church and larger public issues of humanness that pervade our society.

I am glad for a host of dialogic partners, some more severe than others. Along with Neil Elliott, I am grateful to Tia Foley who prepared these material for republication and to Richard Blake who patiently did the library work so essential to my own work. Finally, I am grateful to the company of dialogic companions who engage in resistance and subversion in the pursuit of an alternative world that is strange and new, always again, in the goodness of God.

Abbreviations

AB	Anchor Bible
AnBib	Analecta biblica
BASOR	*Bulletin of the American Schools of Oriental Research*
BJS	Brown Judaic Studies
BZAW	Biehefte zur *ZAW*
CBQ	*Catholic Biblical Quarterly*
FRLANT	Forchungen zur Religion und Literatur des Alten und Neuen Testaments
HTR	*Harvard Theological Review*
Int	*Interpretation*
IRT	Issues in Religion and Theology
JBL	*Journal of Biblical Literature*
JSOT	*Journal for the Study of the Old Testament*
JSOTSup	Journal for the Study of the Old Testament—Supplement Series
OBT	Overtures to Biblical Theology
OTL	Old Testament Library
SBT	Studies in Biblical Theology
VT	*Vetus Testamentum*
VTSup	Vetus Testamentum, Supplements

WMANT	Wissenschaftliche Monographien zum Alten und Neuen Testament
WW	*Word and World*
ZAW	*Zeitschrift für die alttestamentliche Wissenschaft*

YHWH as Dialogical Character

1

T he word *God* is of course generic so that it can be (and has been) construed in any number of directions. In one direction, that of popular spirituality, "God" can be rendered as a vague force or impulse that tilts toward goodness. This direction is as ancient as Gnosticism and, in contemporary thought, can readily drift toward New Age religion. In the opposite direction, that of much classical Christian theology (of a scholastic bent or of a popular understanding of classical theology), "God" can be understood in terms of quite settled categories that are, for the most part, inimical to the biblical tradition. The casting of the classical tradition in a more scholastic category is primarily informed by the Unmoved Mover of Hellenistic thought and affirms, as the catechisms reflect, a God who is omniscient, omnipotent, and omnipresent, a Being completely apart from and unaffected by the reality of the world. There clearly are a variety of other options for the articulation of "God" on a spectrum that runs from New Age vagueness to classic settledness.

YHWH as Active Agent

But of course, "God" as rendered in the Bible—and most particularly in the Christian Old Testament—does not conform to either the temptation of vagueness or the temptation of settledness. In contrast to both of these interpretive alternatives, "God" as rendered in the Old Testament is a fully articulated personal agent, with all the particularities of personhood and with a full repertoire of traits and actions that belong to a fully formed and actualized person. Such a particular person cannot settle for vagueness because the particularity has a history and an identity that remain constant over time. Such a particular person cannot accept a fixity as reflected in some forms of classical tradition, because this particular person possesses all of the dimensions of freedom and possibility that rightly belong to a personal agent. To be sure, such a rendering of God suffers all of the problematic of the scandal of particularity, as this God is embedded in the interpretive memory of ancient Israel. Thus it is common to be embarrassed about the anthropomorphic aspects of this God, so embarrassed as to want to explain away such a characterization or at least to transpose it into a form that better serves a generic notion of God. There is a common propensity, in order to deal with the embarrassment, to reduce the agency of God to "force" or "impulse," and classical theology prefers to substitute aseity for the engagement of the personal. All such embarrassments, however, fail to do justice to the scriptural tradition. Beyond that, they fail to match the rich theological, religious, and pastoral resources that are available only through the personal and the interpersonal. While such a personal rendering of God may strike one as primitive or as supernatural, it will be clear in what follows that the personal dimensions of YHWH and the interpretive memory of ancient Israel—with all of the dimensions of faithful and less than faithful interaction—is fundamental to faith and therefore cannot be explained away or transposed into any other categories.

"Common Theology" Transposed

YHWH as the God of Israel did not emerge in a vacuum, but in the old, rich theological tradition of the ancient Near East. It is clear that in its articulation of Israel, Israel both appropriated from that ancient Near Eastern tradition and transposed what it appropriated into its own distinctive articulation.[1] The extent to which this was a process of *borrowing* or *transposing* depends upon one's view of the *commonality* of Israel's religion to its cultural context or one's conviction about the *uniqueness* of Israel's faith. While the data are not completely supple, the decision about commonality or distinctiveness to some great extent depends upon the impulse of the interpretive and the milieu in which the interpreter works.

Morton Smith articulated a "common paradigm" of ancient Near Eastern religion around six theses, and his articulation has been taken up by Norman Gottwald.[2] That paradigm operates, according to Smith, with these convictions:

1. There is a "High God" who is the generative power behind all natural and human phenomena.

2. That High God is active in the world, in nature, in history, and in society. This activity eventuates in a moral order in worldly reality, a moral order sanctioned through the legal and administrative organs of society.

3. That High God is presented in terms of natural and human analogues, so that "anthropomorphic" articulation is already present in the "common theology."

4. The High God is known to be powerful, just, and merciful. The divine power is in the service of justice. It is evident that the crisis of theodicy is inchoately present from the outset in this common theology.

5. This High God is peculiarly and definitively connected to a particular people or region. Thus the ambiguity of "universal" and "particular" is present from the outset. This also means that some contractual notion of covenant is definitional for the common tradition.

6. The High God is interpreted and represented by human agents who claim authority to voice divine purpose and will.

The accent in this common tradition is upon the sovereignty of God. There is no doubt, moreover, that Israel's doxological tradition—in turn taken up by the prophets—fully affirms the singular sovereignty of YHWH.[3] And while that sovereignty is primally directed toward Israel, there is no doubt that YHWH's rule and purpose extends beyond Israel to all reality.

The Old Testament is theologically interesting and demanding, however, precisely because it is not willing to settle for the common theology; it undertakes what Norman Gottwald terms a "mutation" of the common theology.[4] One can articulate that distinctive theological bent in the Old Testament in order to discern the ways in which YHWH is unlike the other gods of the ancient Near East. But one cannot explain how that has come about. Thus a comparative study that asks about the history of religion can go only so far. Then, in terms of the text itself, one falls back on human imagination of a constructive kind or on revelation. And even if one is shy about speaking of "revelation," if one is theologically

serious, one can entertain the possibility that human imagination of a constructive kind is led by a revelatory intrusion. In any case, with reference to Exod 3:1-9;
19:1—24:18; 34:6-7, Israel's own text attests that the distinctiveness of YHWH
in the tradition of Israel is the result of YHWH's generous self-disclosure, first to
Moses and then through Moses to Israel.[5]

Norman Gottwald has lined out in one mode what is differentiated in
YHWH when compared to the common theology of the ancient Near East.[6] He
notices first that YHWH's claim is unitary and uncompromising, thus on the way
to monotheism (mono-Yahwism).[7] Second, that single God Israel knew to be the
sponsor and advocate of a certain polity, namely, a covenantal Torah that pertains
to the practice of political, economic power and to the organization of society.[8]
From that, Gottwald draws two conclusions that are important for our discussion.
First, a focus on Exod 34:6-7 indicates that YHWH's propensity toward YHWH's
special people is laden with issues concerning steadfast love, that is, covenantal
reliability: "The most that is asserted is that YHWH is acting true to 'his' nature
when forgiving sin and when punishing sin. . . . The ambiguity about forgivable
and unforgivable sins noted in the liturgical formulation of Exodus 34:6-7 finds
various 'answers' in the way that YHWH is represented as forgiving and punishing sins in the course of 'his' generations-long dealings with Israel."[9] Second, the
authorization of human agents as representatives of YHWH, in the tradition of
Israel, concerns the authority of Moses, the articulator of the Torah at Sinai, and
the ongoing interpretive work of Levites in the practice of Torah.

Given these several dimensions of mutation, we may judge that the distinctiveness of "God" in Old Testament tradition concerns YHWH's deep resolve to
be a God *in relation*—in relation to Israel, in relation to creation, in relation to
members of Israelite society and of the human community more generally. The
power and sovereignty of YHWH is a given in the Old Testament that is rarely
called into question. What is readily and often called into question in the text is
the character of this God *in relation*, a defining mark of YHWH that requires a
radical revision of our notion of God. The overriding indicator of God in relationship is covenant, which sometimes is understood as a unilateral imposition on the
part of YHWH and at other times as a bilateral agreement.[10] It is precisely because
the covenant is articulated in so many variations that we are able to conclude that
covenantal relatedness makes it impossible for this God to be settled, static, or
fixed. This God is always emerging in new ways in response to the requirements
of the relationship at hand. This God is fully engaged in interaction with several
partners and is variously impinged upon and evoked to new responses and—we

may believe—to new dimensions of awareness and resolve. Because so much of the faith of Israel is "talking faith" in liturgy, oracle, and narrative, we may say that YHWH is a party to a dialogic exchange that never reaches closure. Rather, like any good dialogue, YHWH is engaged in an interaction with YHWH's partners that always pushes to a new possibility, that makes demands upon both parties, and that opens up fresh possibilities for the relationship. To be sure, in any particular utterance from YHWH's side, there may be an accent of finality. The wonder, however, is that after any such cadence of finality, there is always another text, another utterance, and another engagement.

It is clear that such a defining covenantal transaction—dialogic and interactive—caused YHWH to be impinged upon both in terms of emotive possibility and in terms of public performance.[11] Thus the text exhibits YHWH's reach, ever again, to various zones of agony and ecstasy; that emotional range is recurringly matched by policy initiatives of judgment and restoration that regularly run beyond the present situation.

One can speculate whether YHWH is so fully committed to relationship that there is something held back of sovereignty or whether, as in Job 38–41, YHWH's sovereignty will eventually prevail and trump relatedness. Such speculation, however, runs against the grain of Israel's readiness to situate YHWH in an ongoing dramatic transaction in which everything is at stake in the moment of interaction. As in all serious relationships, it is futile to speculate about grand outcomes when everything is at risk in the crisis of exchange. Thus while the character of YHWH reflects the common theology, Israel's own peculiar articulation of God takes YHWH's readiness to relate—with all of its problematic—as definitional. There are immense ramifications from this defining claim for Christian theologies of incarnation and immense pastoral resources in our culture milieu that is dominated by technology that wants to rob all interrelatedness of its thickness. Israel's sense of YHWH is definingly thick.[12] Its tradition attests to a thick relationship that renders the defining character of the biblical text as "strange and new."[13] Clearly such an interpretive propensity cannot be reduced to the fixity of scholasticism or to the vagueness of New Age spirituality.

Jewish Probes of the Dialogical

Entry into the Old Testament does not require Christian readers to deny their Christian confession. It does, however, require them to recognize the complexity of reading the Old Testament as Christians, and an attempt to take the text, as much as possible, without imposing Christian readings.[14] Beyond that, however, I suggest that a Christian reading of the Old Testament requires, in the present time, a recovery of the *Jewishness* of our ways of reading the text.[15] Whereas a recurring Christian propensity is to give closure to our readings and interpretations, it is recurringly Jewish to recognize that our readings are always provisional, because there is always another text, always another commentary, always another rabbinic midrash that moves beyond any particular reading. Jewish reading knows that "final readings" are toxic and eventually lead to "final solutions." Reading in ways that refuse finality causes our dialogic way with the text to be commensurate with the substance of the text, namely, YHWH's dialogic transaction with YHWH's several partners.

We may identify three Jewish interpreters who have contributed most to our understanding of dialogic reading. Foremost is Martin Buber, whose dialogic understandings are at the center of his philosophic thought. This concern is evident in his most popular work, *I and Thou*.[16] But beyond that best-known work, the matter of dialogue permeates Buber's thought. In his daring insistence upon religious (as distinct from philosophic) categories, Buber proposes that there is an "ontology of the between" in which subjective agents have an encounter marked by an intense immediacy. While Buber's rhetoric tilts in the direction of mystical encounter, there is no doubt that he is primally informed by the deepest claims of the Hebrew Bible in which the meeting of subjective agents is given a historical casting. From the initial encounter of the burning bush in which YHWH gave (and did not give!) the divine name, YHWH has been a confrontive, engaged agent in the life of Israel and in the life of the world. While Buber will insist that YHWH is always "Thou"—and does not entertain the thought that Israel may be the "Thou" for YHWH's "I"—it is clear that the "Thou" of YHWH is not only generative for the "I" of Israel; even as "Thou," YHWH is impinged upon by the "I" of Israel, called to account, and pushed in new directions. Buber stops before he goes further. In my judgment, however, it would be congruent with his work to entertain a provisional reversal of roles, so that on occasion YHWH might be the "I" authorized by Israel's "Thou." I think, for example, of Ps 22:3, wherein YHWH is "enthroned upon the praises of Israel." If Israel did not engage in doxology, YHWH's throne—and therefore YHWH's governance—would be diminished. It is for this reason that Israel's doxologies begin with a vigorous summons to praise.[17] There is much at stake for YHWH in Israel's doxology! This is beyond Buber's articulation but not incongruent with it.

Second, Franz Rosenzweig is Buber's close companion in insisting upon the dialogic character of faith. Rosenzweig's mode of expression is dense and enigmatic, but the direction of his thinking is clear enough. The creator God enacted creation as a monologue.[18] The monologue is transposed into dialogue when the "I" of creation answers back. The "I" who answers back to the "Thou" of God does not do so willingly, however, but prefers to hide. Rosenzweig clearly alludes to the narrative of Genesis 2 and 3 in this judgment, though the text is not cited: "To God's 'Where art Thou?' the man had still kept silence as defiant and blocked Self. Now, called by his name, twice, in a supreme definiteness that could not but be heard, now he answers, all unlocked, all spread apart, all ready, all-soul: 'Here I am.'"[19] It is when the answering "I" hears that dialogue ensues, the dialogue that is on God's terms. And when one asks about hearing and obeying, the focus is upon commandment:

> The answer to this question is universally familiar. Millions of tongues testify to it evening and morning: "Thou shalt love the Lord thy God with all thy heart and with all thy soul and with all thy might." Thou shalt love—what a paradox this embraces! Can love then be commanded? Is love not rather a matter of fate and of seizure and of a bestowal which, if it is indeed free, is withal only free? And now it is commanded? Yes of course, love cannot be commanded. No third party can command it or extort it. No third party can, but the One can. The commandment to love can only proceed from the mouth of the lover. Only the lover can and does say: love me!—and he really does so. In his mouth the commandment to love is not a strange commandment; it is none other than the voice of love itself.[20]

The commanding imperative of God is the voice of "I": "God's 'I' remains the keyword, traversing revelation like a single sustained organ note; it resists any translation into 'he'; it is an 'I' and an 'I' it must remain. Only an 'I,' not a 'he,' can pronounce the imperative of love, which may never be anything other than 'love me!'"[21] Rosenzweig understands the entire drama of the dialogue with the focus upon the reception of divine command. The only appropriate response to "Thou shalt love" is "I have sinned."[22] And the "I have sinned" is in turn answered by the divine word, "I forgive." Thus the dialogue is undertaken, while the "Thou" of God retains the initiative: "But here it really must do so. God does not answer the soul's acknowledgment, its 'I am thine,' with an equally simple 'Thou art mine.' Rather he reaches back into the past and identifies himself as the one who originated and initiated this whole dialogue between himself and the soul: 'I have called thee by name: thou art mine.'"[23] Rosenzweig goes on to assert that "prayer is the last thing achieved in revelation," the completion of the exchange.[24] Thus the answering "I" plays a decisive role in culminating the dialogical transaction.

Like Buber, Rosenzweig casts his rhetoric in quite personal terms. In reading the Old Testament it is clear that we must extrapolate from the deeply interpersonal transaction to public issues, for it is the same dialogic sovereign creator who presides over kingdoms and empires. The issue with all of the partners is the same. Finally it is the "I" of YHWH who will preside over public as over intimate transactions:

> For thus says the Lord GOD: I myself will search for my sheep, and will seek them out. As shepherds seek out their flocks when they are among their scattered sheep, so I will seek out my sheep. I will rescue them from all the places to which they have been scattered on a day of clouds and thick darkness. I will bring them out from the peoples and gather them from the countries, and will bring them into their own land; and I will feed them on the mountains of Israel, by the watercourses, and in all the inhabited parts of the land. I will feed them with good pasture, and the mountain heights of Israel shall be their pasture; there they shall lie down in good grazing land, and they shall feed on rich pasture on the mountains of Israel. I myself will be the shepherd of my sheep, and I will make them lie down, says the Lord GOD. I will seek the lost, and I will bring back the strayed, and I will bind up the injured, and I will strengthen the weak, but the fat and the strong I will destroy. I will feed them with justice. (Ezek 34:11-16)

Even the powers will learn, soon or late, that YHWH holds the initiative to which response must be made:

> It is I who by my great power and my outstretched arm have made the earth, with the people and animals that are on the earth, and I give it to whomever I please. (Jer 27:5)

> You shall be driven away from human society, and your dwelling shall be with the wild animals. You shall be made to eat grass like oxen, you shall be bathed with the dew of heaven, and seven times shall pass over you, until you have learned that the Most High has sovereignty over the kingdom of mortals, and gives it to whom he will. (Dan 4:25)

Thus Rosenzweig situates the entire drama of faith as a dialogic exchange in which (a) YHWH's preeminence is unmistakable, but (b) in which the answering partner has a decisive role to play.

Third, Emmanuel Levinas follows after the work of Buber.[25] While there are important distinctions between them, the general direction for Levinas, as for Buber, is dialogical. Levinas insists that face-to-faceness creates a generative openness for both parties, whereas the attempt to circumscribe in rigid ways the interaction leads to a closed totality that is authoritarian and is eventually given over to violence. While an ethical concern is surely central to Buber, Levinas is much more explicit in his judgment that the *face* of the *other* is itself a *commandment* that evokes an engaged response of obedience. Thus every usual understanding of "ontology" is interrupted by such engagement. It is this interruption by "saying," moreover, that is the defining issue for faith that is recast as *utterance and response*, as *command and obedience*, as *confession and forgiveness*, as *petition and attentiveness*, all the interpersonal ways of Jewishness that resist reductionism.

When we take seriously the way in which Buber, Rosenzweig, and Levinas have cast the argument, it is unmistakable that faith is a dialogic transaction that refuses closure, but that insists upon serious engagement that has commandment at its center. In the exposition that will follow in this volume, we will see that that serious engagement of *command and response, failure and restoration*, is a recurring theme in every sphere of the horizon of faith.

God in Pathos

We may take one further step in articulating the categories through which we will understand "God as partner." The general dialogic, relational quality of covenantal faith was given special and focused attention by Abraham Heschel in his exposition of YHWH's pathos.[26] While the notion of pathos, especially lined out by Heschel, may be taken specifically as the capacity of God to suffer, in fact the implication of Heschel's work is much broader. It concerns the engagement of YHWH with Israel and with the world, and therefore YHWH's vulnerability and readiness to be impinged upon. The particular focus of Heschel on God's hurt in the traditions of Hosea and Jeremiah makes abundantly clear that the God of Israel is unlike the God of any scholastic theology and unlike any of the forces imagined in any of the vague spiritualities available among us. The peculiar character of this God is as *available agent* who is not only able to act but is available to be *acted upon*.

I may mention two derivative studies that are primally informed by the work of Heschel. On the one hand, Kazo Kitamori has poignantly written on God's pain.[27] Special attention may be given to his appendix concerning Jer 31:20 and Isa 63:15. Kitamori notes how discerningly both Luther and Calvin, without any sentimentality, were able to take notice of God's pain. The articulation of that pain, moreover, required the poetic imagination of ancient Israel to speak in terms of bodily upset and consternation, resisting any attempt to permit this God to float off as an ephemeral spirit. The God of dialogic engagement is fully exposed to the realities of life in the world that we might most readily term "creaturely," except that those realities are, on the lips of the poets, the realities of the *creator* as well.

It is obvious that this line of reasoning, so characteristically Jewish, has immense implications for Christian theology. Jürgen Moltmann, informed by the work of Heschel, has forcefully carried the issue of God's vulnerability in Christian theology:

> It was Abraham Heschel who, in controversy with Hellenism and the Jewish philosophy of religion of Jehuda Halevi, Maimonides and Spinoza which was influenced by it, first described the prophets' proclamation of God as *pathetic theology*. The prophets had no "idea" of God, but understood themselves and the people in the *situation of God*. Heschel called this situation of God the *pathos of God*. It has nothing to do with the irrational human emotions like desire, anger, anxiety, envy or sympathy, but describes the way in which God is affected by events and human actions and suffering in history. He is affected by them because he is interested in his creation, his people and his right. The *pathos* of God is intentional and transitive, not related to itself but to the history of the covenant people. God already emerged from himself at the creation of the world "in the beginning." In the covenant he enters into the world and the people of his choice. The "history" of God cannot therefore be separated from the history of his people. The history of the divine *pathos* is embedded in this history of men. . . .
>
> Abraham Heschel has developed his theology of the divine *pathos* as a *dipolar theology*. God is free in himself and at the same time interested in his covenant relationship and affected by human history. In this covenant relationship he has spoken of the *pathos* of God and the *sympatheia* of man, and in so doing has introduced a second bipolarity.[28]

Moltmann has considered the way in which classical Christian theology has asserted the *apatheia* of God. It has done so by acknowledging the suffering of the Son in which the Father does not participate. Moltmann has shown, against that propensity, that in Trinitarian thought the Father as well as the Son suffers:

To understand what happened between Jesus and his God and Father on the cross, it is necessary to talk in trinitarian terms. The Son suffers dying, the Father suffers the death of the Son. The grief of the Father here is just as important as the death of the Son. The Fatherlessness of the Son is matched by the Sonlessness of the Father, and if God has constituted himself as the Father of Jesus Christ, then he also suffers the death of his Fatherhood in the death of the Son.[29]

Moltmann's statement is completely congruent, in the categories of Christian theology, with what Heschel had already discerned in Israel's prophets. The God of Christians, understood in the midst of God's revelation to ancient Israel, is a God deeply at risk in the drama of fidelity and infidelity in the world.

The Speech of Dialogical Fidelity

Because we are dealing with texts and because the dialogic transaction of God and God's partners concerns the sayable, we may consider particularly the modes of speech through which this dialogic engagement is transacted in the text. George Steiner has notably observed: "It is the Hebraic intuition that God is capable of all speech-acts except that of monologue which has generated our arts of reply, of questioning and counter-creation."[30] Very much scholastic theology has reduced God to a monologue. And very much fuzzy spirituality has eliminated speech altogether. Against such disembodied silence or against scholastic authoritarianism, however, Israel's covenantal speech is emphatically an antiphon between the God who *speaks* and the partner who *answers* or, conversely, the partner who *speaks* and the God who *answers*. Insofar as the community of biblical faith is a cultural linguistic community with well-established and well-disciplined practices of speech, we may in turn imagine how the partners practice the dialogue of faith.

We may begin with a consideration of Israel's practice of speech as it is addressed to God and take Israel's speech as a model for dialogic fidelity that may be practiced by all of God's partners.[31] We may take it as a truism—an important truism—that Israel's dialogic approach to YHWH is through praise and lament. If we appeal to Rosenzweig's formulation, we see that praise and thanks are primary but that lament functions as a crucial countertheme in the dialogue:

Praise and thanksgiving, the voice of the soul, redeemed for harmony with all the world, and the voice of the world, redeemed for sensing and singing with the soul. . . . All thanksgiving unites in the dative; thanksgiving gives thanks for the gift. By offering thanks to God, one acknowledges him as the giver and recognizes him as the fulfiller of prayer. The individual *qua* individual could not soar higher than the prayer of the individual, the individual lament. The fulfillment lay beyond except that, insofar as it occurred within the soul of the individual, the prayer was, as ability to pray, already its own fulfillment. All prayer, even the individual lament, subconsciously cries out for the coming of the kingdom, the visible representation of what is experienced only in the soul's holy of holies. But the kingdom does not come in revelation, and the prayer thus remains a sigh in the night. Now fulfillment is directly there. The kingdom of God is actually nothing other than the reciprocal union of the soul with all the world. This union of the soul with all the world occurs in thanksgiving, and the kingdom of God comes in this union and every conceivable prayer is fulfilled. Thanks for the fulfillment of each and every prayer precedes all prayer that is not an individual lament from out the dual solitude of the nearness of the soul to God. The community-wide acknowledgment of the paternal goodness of God is the basis on which all communal prayer builds. The individual lament out of the lonely depths of dire need is fulfilled by the very fact of wrestling its way out, by the soul's being able to pray. But the congregational prayer is fulfilled before ever it is prayed. Its fulfillment is anticipated in praise and thanksgiving. The congregational thanksgiving is already the fulfillment of that for which it is possible to pray communally, and the coming of that for the sake of which alone all individual pleas can dare to approach God's countenance with the compelling power of community: namely of the kingdom. Communal confession and praise must precede all communal praying as its fulfillment.[32]

In praise and thanks, the partner cedes its life over to God in all and gratitude.[33] Praise is the exuberant abandonment of self and the glad ceding of self over to the one addressed in praise. The patterned doxology of Israel, given succinctly in Psalm 117, consists in a *summons* to praise and an inventory of *reasons* for praise of YHWH that recites variously YHWH's past miraculous actions or YHWH's recurring characterization of fidelity and attentiveness.[34] It is clear that such doxological utterance is designed to enhance and magnify YHWH at the expense of other gods; it is also clear that such utterance, offered in unqualified loyalty, is a performative act whereby the rule of God is enacted and embraced. The response to YHWH in such praise runs all the way from stately enthronement psalms (Psalms 96–99) to the pastoral mood of Psalm 103 that concerns YHWH's reliable readiness to forgive (vv. 9-14) and YHWH's attentiveness to the reality of limit and fragility (vv. 15-18).

Israel's dialogic speech moves from the large sweep of praise to the specificity of thanksgiving, exhibiting Israel in a posture of glad gratitude. As Claus Westermann has shown in his category of "psalms of narrative praise," the articulation of thanks tells of a previous need of the human speaker, the remembered petition of that need, and the transformative intervention of YHWH in response to the petition.[35] Thus Israel's speech testifies to the entire drama of human need and human response under the rubric, "I called" (Ps 116:4) and "You delivered" (116:8). Such glad affirmation attests Israel's gratitude is appropriately accompanied by a thank offering (payment of vows; see 116:14-18), thus making clear that the dialogic exchange is both verbal and material.

The performative effect of praise and thanks is to portray a world that is concrete in need and abandonment but in which YHWH is featured as the defining character. In praise Israel responds to YHWH's generosity. In thanks Israel responds but also recalls Israel's own initiative in the utterance of petition. The initiatory petition of Israel is in fact located in an already established tradition of YHWH's fidelity and attentiveness.

The other pole of Israel's part in dialogic faith is lament, complaint, protest, and petition (the very petition remembered in songs of thanksgiving).[36] In a most elemental way, the lament is a cry of need in a context of crisis when Israel lacks the resources to fend for itself. The petition is an acknowledgment of such need and a turning to YHWH, who is recognized as an agent capable of rescue and transformation.[37] But lament, when it becomes complaint and protest, may also be more than an eager, desperate statement of need. It may also be an utterance that voices betrayal and abandonment, and therefore disappointment in the God who has left the speaker bereft. Such utterance dares to call into question YHWH's fidelity, so that the utterance may also be an accusation wherein Israel's prayer shades over into the forensic language of accusation.

The repertoire of *praise-thanks* and *lament-complaint* bespeaks Israel as a fully engaged dialogic partner who plays a role vis-à-vis YHWH in which a profound drama of fidelity and infidelity is regularly performed. Such covenantal-interactive utterance is not governed by the laws of conventional logic, and therefore Israel as utterer can move easily from one posture of address to another, the important point being the full range of postures vis-à-vis YHWH. The dialectic of lament (complaint) and praise (thanks), when appropriated in Christian tradition and transposed into christological formulation permit the faithful church to utter the loss of Friday crucifixion in lament (Ps 22:1) and to voice the wonder of Sunday resurrection in exuberant doxology. Thus the church, in its attempt to continue to "perform" the "mystery of faith," takes up the dialogical practice that is a staple performance in ancient Israel. It is enough that the dialogic utterance of Israel (echoed by the church) walks fully and honestly into the reality of *abandonment* and walks boldly and buoyantly into the wonder of *restoration*. This dialogue with YHWH is attestation to the crisis of fidelity that is the recurring subject of faith, for faith addresses the God who "for a brief moment abandoned," the God who in "everlasting love" restores to new life (Isa 54:7-8).

It is no surprise to notice that the utterances of YHWH are commensurate with the utterances of Israel. The two partners are indeed engaged in recurring subject matter that concerns both of them critically. YHWH's foundational utterance in the Old Testament is promissory speech that "gives life to the dead and calls into existence the things that do not exist" (Rom 4:17). YHWH's promissory speech is indeed performative in which YHWH *does* what YHWH *says*. At the outset, YHWH's utterance to Abraham is a promise (Gen 12:1-3) that is fleshed out in Genesis 15 and 17, and subsequently reiterated to his son and to his grandson (Gen 26:3-4; 28:13-15). In the completed tradition of Israel, that promise is seen to be fully enacted (Josh 21:43-45). The divine promise is crucial to the slave community in Israel (Exod 3:7-9) and again to David and David's heirs (2 Sam 7:1-16). The promises, inescapably, contain an imperative of alignment with YHWH, so that even the great promise to the slaves in Egypt already has the Torah of Sinai in purview.

It is most remarkable (and often noted) that the great Vesuvian cluster of promises in the Old Testament occur in the exilic prophets; it is in the abyss of abandonment that YHWH speaks an originary word that generates new possibility in Israel, a possibility that was nowhere on the political horizon of the sixth-century displacement.[38] Thus the great promissory utterers of YHWH in the tradition of Isaiah, Jeremiah, and Ezekiel generate new possibilities. Belatedly, moreover, we are able to see that the Book of the Twelve also culminates in Haggai, Zechariah, and Malachi in promise, a promise to which the hagiographer refers in 2 Chr 36:22-23.[39] The outcome is that both the culmination of the Christian Old Testament in Mal 4:5-6 and the conclusion of the Hebrew Bible in 2 Chr 36:22-23 bespeak a divine promise that is to be enacted in the historical process. The promissory utterance of YHWH, whereby YHWH has solemnly pledged new possibility, serves, whenever performed, to place the entire narrative of Israel (and of the world) under the future-generating utterance of YHWH.

The promissory speech of YHWH whereby YHWH initiates and participates in dialogue is matched in divine utterance by speeches of judgment in which
YHWH recognizes the failure of the relationship and summons the partner to
account for the default.[40] The harsh rebukes of the *indictment* and *sentence* leads
YHWH's utterance into juridical categories of innocence and guilt. In the utterance of YHWH, of course, the fault is unfailingly with the partner, just as the fault
in Israel's protest is predictably with YHWH.[41]

We may, without pursuing the point, observe that YHWH's utterance, not
unlike the utterance of Israel, is preoccupied in a rendering of a failed relationship (divorce, alienation) and the startling renewal of the relationship.[42] One sign
of this startling renewal is the recurring covenantal formula, "I will be your God
and you shall be my people," a formula that occurs just at the null point when the
relationship had been exhausted.[43] Mutatis mutandis, it is clear that these recurring patterns of divine speech serve well the Friday-Sunday form of the Christian
mystery, for the *speech of judgment* is about the *abandonment of Friday* and *the
promise* is about the inexplicable *wonder of Sunday*.

While the actual dialogic practice of YHWH and YHWH's partner is more
complex than this might suggest, this identification of four speech practices suggests a notable symmetry between the partners about the relationship:

- *Praise* is Israel's appropriate utterance toward the God who makes
  promises.
- *Protest* is Israel's appropriate utterance toward the God who offers juridical
  rebuke.

Or one may reverse the symmetry:

- *Promise* is the divine utterance that becomes the trigger for Israel's *praise*.
- *Speech of judgment* becomes the venue for Israel's *complaint*, as the two parties adjudicate fault for a dysfunctional relationship.

The continuing outcome of such a rich, complex, and thick dialogical transaction is a lively relationship in which all parties are capable of candor, in which all
parties are available for new possibilities, and in which all parties are addressed and
summoned to engagement and invited to respond. It is no wonder that the God of
the Old Testament is cast as a *person*, for it is only the *personal* and the *interpersonal*
that make possible the kinds of interaction that are generative of new transformative possibility. Every attempt to move away from the embarrassing particularity
of the interpersonal entails a costly loss of that transformative dimension of faith.

Scholastic temptations in theology tend to freeze the relationship and to stifle its dynamism. Vague spirituality tends to compromise the sharp over-againstness that is generative of newness. This dialogic faith does not aspire to settlements and final formulations, though it may come to some of those (that remain provisional) through the transaction. What counts is the *performance*. The performance continues to extend the transaction into all kinds of new situations, and is capable, always again, of surprise and innovation.[44]

Regulation via Imagination

What we have in the biblical text is a *human* document, a product of daring, evocative human imagination. But serious readers of this text of human imagination regularly are recruited, in the process of being addressed, to the conviction that what is surely daring artistic human imagination is, at the same time, an act of *divine revelation*. There is something different here that insists always on being "strange and new." What is *revealed* here is a Holy One who is undomesticatedly available for dialogic transaction; and because of dialogical transaction, what is *revealed* here, as well, is mature personhood that is commensurate with the undomesticated fidelity of the Holy One: "until all of us come to the unity of the faith and of the knowledge of the Son of God, to maturity, to the measure of the full stature of Christ" (Eph 4:13); "It is he whom we proclaim, warning everyone and teaching everyone in all wisdom, so that we may present everyone mature in Christ" (Col 1:28). I cite these texts (with their use of the word "mature" [Greek *telos*]) not to tilt the discussion in a christological direction, but to notice that the fully formed human person, in this relationship, is one who is engaged in the dialogical transaction of faith and obedience. Well before this particular epistolary formulation, Israel had understood that "maturity" as a creature concerns life congruent with the creator God. I judge, moreover, that Israel would further claim that the same "maturity" (completeness, Hebrew *tam*) may well pertain to every partner of YHWH, every creature—human, nonhuman, Israel, nations—for the creator God summons all creatures to maturity.

The reason I stress that the biblical testimony is revelation-as-human-imagination is that the text tradition fully delivers on adequate partners for YHWH, partners who are capable of sustained dialogic transactions of fidelity. Israel, in its formation and transmission of the text, found itself drawn out beyond itself into this always lively, redefining transaction. And while the framers and transmitters of the textual tradition lived a quite concrete human life—of family and sexuality, of money and property—they also understood that life in faithful intentionality was a performance of an ongoing transaction that caused it to be different in the world. Beyond its own performance, moreover, it also imagined (was led by the spirit to imagine) that all other creatures are also partners of the same God and so recruited into the same dialogic transaction. Thus Israel could construe the life of sea monsters and birds and creeping things as YHWH's creaturely partners (see Ps 148:7-10). And it could in like manner discern Nebuchadnezzar as "servant of YHWH" (Jer 25:9; 27:6) and the unwitting Cyrus as "YHWH's messiah" (Isa 45:1). It could imagine in the sweep of its performance that all of life is drawn into this dialogic transaction.

The commensurability between *dialogic God* and *dialogic partner* is well articulated by Jürgen Moltmann. In his thoughtful discussion, Moltmann has contrasted the apathetic God and the God capable of pathos. Then he extrapolates:

> In the sphere of the apathetic God man becomes a *homo apatheticus*. In the situation of the *pathos* of God he becomes a *homo sympatheticus*. The divine *pathos* is reflected in man's participation, his hopes and his prayers. Sympathy is the openness of a person to the present of another. It has the structure of dialogue. In the *pathos* of God, man is filled with the spirit of God. He becomes the friend of God, feels sympathy with God and for God. He does not enter into a mystical union but into a sympathetic union with God. He is angry with God's wrath. He suffers with God's suffering. He loves with God's love. He hopes with God's hope.[45]

The human person stands alongside YHWH in engagement with the tribulation and wonder of the world. In the exposition that follows in this volume, we dare to imagine as well that YHWH's other partners are also drawn into the same dialogic structure of *friendship*, *wrath*, and *hope*. There is of course a great deal at stake in this dialogic interaction of God with God's partners. The religious temptation to dissolve the dialogue into an authoritarian monologue is matched by the temptation to self-authorizing autonomy. Both authoritarianism and autonomy are temptations that are everywhere around us. The offer of technological solutions to relational problems is an encompassing temptation among us. Continuing attentiveness to this textual tradition is an affirmative reminder that our God-given, God-engaged creatureliness is of another ilk. It is not too much to conclude that the future of the world depends upon the continued performance of this dialogue that resolvedly refuses closure and buoyantly offers newness. ▬

Israel as YHWH's Partner

2

YHWH has acted toward Israel in ways that are defining for both YHWH and Israel. YHWH saved Israel, YHWH promised to Israel, YHWH led Israel, YHWH commanded Israel. YHWH is committed to Israel in freedom and passion.

In the testimony of the Old Testament, Israel becomes the key partner to YHWH and the subject of the testimony. In these ancient texts and in its ongoing life in the world, Israel is indeed an oddity and a mystery, because Israel is a theological phenomenon that has concrete sociopolitical embodiment and is expected to live differently in a world of power.[1] This odd combination of the theological and political realms is definitional for Israel, and therefore Israel is an inassimilable public entity in the world. Whatever else may be said of Israel, in the end Israel in these texts must regard itself Yahwistically. That is, in some impenetrable way, Israel's existence is referred to and derived from YHWH. Israel will not be discerned in these texts without reference to YHWH. But it is equally odd and noteworthy that YHWH will not be discerned in these texts without reference to Israel.[2]

We may organize our reflection on this primal partner of YHWH under rubrics that are in a general way historical, except that the canonically construed "history" of Israel is theologically paradigmatic.[3]

YHWH's Originary Love for Israel

Israel's existence is rooted in YHWH's inescapable, originary commitment to Israel. According to biblical testimony, there was a time when Israel did not exist. Israel came to exist because of the decisive, initiatory action of YHWH. It is certain that there were ethnic or sociological antecedents to Israel, but as a community, as a sociotheological entity, Israel came to exist in the world of the Near East because of the sovereign, free action of YHWH.

This action of YHWH—this inexplicable, irreversible commitment of YHWH—is rendered in two distinct narratives: the stories of the ancestors (Genesis 12–36) and the Exodus-Sinai narrative revolving around Moses (Exodus 1–24).[4] In these two very different narratives, YHWH in sovereign power speaks, and by promissory decree evokes Israel into existence. In Gen 12:1-3 YHWH addresses barren Sarah and failed Abraham, and issues a summons, command, and promise. In Exod 3:7-10 YHWH addresses bondaged Israel and issues a promise that is subsequently matched by command (cf. Exod 20:1-17).

These two dissimilar versions of initiation no doubt reflect very different circles of tradition. They are, nonetheless, agreed on the main points. The people that became Israel are themselves without hope, possibility, or future. The sorry situation of these people, barren and bondaged, is dramatically transformed by the sovereign utterance of YHWH. No ground or rationale is given for the utterance of YHWH, but because the utterance is on the lips of the Holy One, the utterance must be accepted, embraced, and obeyed by Israel.[5]

Thus from the outset there is something odd, enigmatic, and inexplicable about Israel's origin and continued existence. James Robinson is correct when he writes: "For the wonder that Israel is, rather than not being at all, is the basic experience of Israel in all its history."[6] It is important to remember that as Israel pondered and spoke about its existence, it offered no explanation for its existence. What appear to be explanations are in fact articulations of wonder, awe, astonishment, and gratitude, all addressed back to YHWH.

Israel characteristically uses three verbs, love (*'ahab*), choose (*bahar*), and set one's heart (*hashaq*) to express its awareness that its existence as a people in the world is rooted only in YHWH's commitment.

The first verb is love (*'ahab*).[7] YHWH is the one who loves Israel, who loves what was not-yet-Israel, and who by the full commitment of YHWH's self causes Israel to be. We may identify three clusters of uses of the term in this context of YHWH's generative inclination toward Israel. Deuteronomy is the theological tradition that ponders in most sustained fashion Israel's election by YHWH: "It was because the LORD loved you and kept the oath that he swore to your ances-tors, that the LORD has brought you out with a mighty hand, and redeemed you from the house of slavery, from the hand of Pharaoh king of Egypt" (Deut 7:8; cf. v. 13); "the LORD your God turned the curse into a blessing for you, because the LORD your God loved you" (Deut 23:5). This testimony is impressed not only with the sheer grace of YHWH's love for Israel, but by the recognition that this love of YHWH has singled out Israel, who is treated by YHWH as no other is treated.

Second, the prophet Hosea, ostensibly out of personal experience, articulates YHWH's love for Israel like no other love: "The LORD said to me again, 'Go, love a woman who has a lover and is an adulteress, just as the Lord loves the people of Israel, though they turn to other gods and love raisin cakes'" (Hos 3:1); "When Israel was a child, I loved him, and out of Egypt I called my son" (Hos 11:1). The first of these texts voices the undeserving status of Israel in relation to YHWH's love. The second uses the verb with reference to the initiatory event of the exodus rescue.

Third, in the midst of the crisis of the exile, when Israel has ample ground to imagine that YHWH's love for Israel is spent, the verb reemerges among the poets of the exile:

> I have loved you with an everlasting love;
> therefore I have continued my faithfulness to you. (Jer 31:3)

> I give Egypt as your ransom,
> Ethiopia and Seba in exchange for you.
> Because you are precious in my sight,
> and honored, and I love you,
> I give people in return for you,
> nations in exchange for your life. (Isa 43:3-4; cf. 48:14; Hos 14:4)

These latter statements attest to the durability and resilience of YHWH's love for Israel, and therefore Israel's capacity to continue in life and in faith, in extreme circumstance.

A second verb, choose (*bahar*), is regularly cited to speak more frontally of election, whereby Israel is given a special role and relation as having received a nomination or appointment by decree of the sovereign. This term *chosenness* has been treated in scholarship as peculiarly problematic in a perspective that yearns for universal religion.[8] In such a context, peculiar chosenness is an embarrassment and a scandal—the scandal of particularity. It is to be noted, however, that the specificity of Israel's chosenness evokes no embarrassment or need for explanation in Israel's own self-understanding. Israel accepts and relishes its specialness. Again, it is Deuteronomy that most fully attends to this verb and to its importance for Israel's self-presentation:

> For you are a people holy to the LORD your God; the Lord your God has chosen you out of all the peoples on earth to be his people, his treasured possession. (Deut 7:6-7; repeated in 14:2)

> And because he loved your ancestors, he chose their descendants after them. (Deut 4:37)
>   Yet the LORD set his heart in love on your ancestors alone and chose you, their descendants after them, out of all the peoples, as it is today. (Deut 10:15)

The latter two uses refer in particular to the ancestors, linking the communities of Genesis and Exodus.

The same term is used in a retrospect by Ezekiel: "On the day when I chose Israel, I swore to the offspring of the house of Jacob—making myself known to them in the land of Egypt—I swore to them, saying, I am the Lord your God" (Ezek 20:5). The term resurfaces in exile, in order to assert YHWH's continuing valuing of Israel in a peculiar way: "But now hear, O Jacob my servant, Israel, whom I have chosen!" (Isa 44:1).

The third term, set one's heart (*hashaq*), is used only twice, again in Deuteronomy, in texts I have just cited: "It was not because you were more numerous than any other people that the LORD set his heart on you and chose you—for you were the fewest of all peoples" (Deut 7:7); "yet the LORD set his heart in love on your ancestors alone and chose you" (Deut 10:15). The first of these texts concerns the community of Moses; the second, the ancestral community. But what is most important is that the verb *hashaq* has strong, passionate emotional overtones (cf. Gen 34:8; Deut 21:11). The term bespeaks a lover who is powerfully in pursuit of the partner, perhaps in lustful ways. Thus YHWH's commitment to Israel is not simply a formal, political designation, but it is a personal commitment that has a dimension of affection and in which YHWH is emotionally extended for the sake of Israel.

We may notice that two texts use all three verbs, love (*'ahab*), choose (*bahar*), set one's heart (*ḥashaq*), in extraordinarily powerful assertions:

> For you are a people holy to the LORD your God; the LORD your God has chosen you out of all the peoples on earth to be his people, his treasured possession. It was not because you were more numerous than any other people that the LORD set his heart on you and chose you—for you were the fewest of all peoples. It was because the LORD loved you and kept the oath that he swore to your ancestors. (Deut 7:6-8)

> Yet the LORD set his heart in love on your ancestors alone and chose you, their descendants after them, out of all the peoples, as it is today. (Deut 10:15)

These two texts serve different functions. The first is to assert a powerful "either/or" against other inhabitants of the land. The second is to contrast the particularity of Israel over against the universal governance of YHWH. Both state YHWH's peculiar commitment to Israel, and Israel's peculiar identity vis-à-vis YHWH. In both cases, the peculiar commitment of YHWH and the peculiar identity of Israel are offered as grounds from which appeal is made for serious, radical, concrete obedience.

Israel's Covenantal Obligation

The theme of obedience in these same texts moves us to a second aspect of YHWH's inexplicable originary commitment to Israel. The initiatory act of love, rescue, and designation is made by a sovereign who in this act of love does not cease to be sovereign. Therefore this relationship, marked by awe and gratitude for inexplicable generosity, brings with it the expectations and requirements of the sovereign who initiates it. The common rubric for this sovereign expectation is "covenant." YHWH designates Israel as YHWH's covenant partner, so that Israel is, from the outset, obligated to respond to and meet YHWH's expectations. As covenant partner of YHWH, Israel is a people defined by obedience.

A great deal of scholarly energy has been spent on the matter of covenant, and a student of Old Testament theology needs to know a bit about that scholarly discussion.[9] In the older critical scholarship from the nineteenth century, it was assumed that the covenant did not become a working construct in Israel until the emergence of ethical monotheism in the eighth and seventh centuries B.C.E., under the aegis of the Deuteronomic tradition. Then in the middle of the twentieth century, under the impetus of George Mendenhall and Klaus Baltzer, it was argued that covenant was an early and constitutive notion in Israel.[10] Most recently, led by Lothar Perlitt, E. Kutsch, and Ernest Nicholson, scholars have returned to the older critical position.[11] Be that as it may, Israel's theological self-presentation is not constrained by such critical judgments, but presents itself from the outset as YHWH's covenant people.[12]

If we take Israel's self-presentation as the proper subject for interpretation, scholars still have made important distinctions concerning YHWH's covenant with Israel. Thus it can be argued that the covenant YHWH made with Abraham is one of divine initiative that is unconditional, and the covenant made with Israel at Sinai is one of human obligation.[13] Or the matter may be expressed thus: the covenant may be unilaterally established by YHWH (with the verb *qum*, "establish") or it may be bilaterally agreed to (with the verb *karat*, "cut").

Conditional and Unconditional: A Misleading Distinction

Different accents are made in different texts out of different traditions and in response to different circumstances. On the whole, however, in my judgment it is futile and misleading to sort out unconditional and conditional aspects of YHWH's covenant with Israel. The futility and misleading quality of such an enterprise can be stated on two quite different grounds. First, even the covenant with the ancestors of Genesis includes an imperative dimension (Gen 12:1; 17:1).[14] Israel, as YHWH's covenant partner, is expected to order its life in ways that are appropriate to this relationship. It is unthinkable that the God who is holy, glorious, and jealous, who is the Creator of heaven and earth, will extend self in commitment without such an expectation. Second, if this relationship is indeed one of passionate commitment, as it surely is, it is undoubtedly the case that every serious, intense, primary relationship has within it dimensions of conditionality and unconditionality that play in different ways in different circumstances. The attempt to factor out conditional and unconditional aspects of the covenant is an attempt to dissect and analyze the inscrutable mystery of an intimate, intense relation that, by definition, defies all such disclosure. YHWH is all for Israel, and that includes both YHWH's self-giving and YHWH's intense self-regard.

A student of Old Testament theology must ponder this issue with some care. It is my judgment that the attempt by scholars to identify the conditional and the unconditional in this relationship is rooted in Paul's effort to distinguish the gospel of Jesus Christ from its Jewish counterparts, whereby Paul claimed for Christian faith the "gospel beforehand" in Abraham (Gal 3:8) and assigned to his Jewish opponents "Moses and the law." That same false distinction then showed up in the Pelagian controversy in the history of Christian doctrine; now, in a "therapeutic society," it issues variously in cheap grace and works righteousness.

All such distinctions betray the character of this covenant, which is at the same time utterly giving and utterly demanding. I suggest that E. P. Sanders's term *covenantal nomism* is about right, because it subsumes law (Greek *nomos*) under the rubric of covenant.[15] By inference, I suggest that grace must also be subsumed under covenant. Covenant is the larger, working category through which this witness understands its life with YHWH, which entails a full relationship of self-giving and self-regarding in which embrace of commandment (in obedience) and embrace of love (in trust) are of a piece. To forgo the umbrella notion of covenant and to sort out cleanly "grace" and "law" is a distortion of the way in which the Old Testament speaks about this relationship. Such a false distinction may serve on the one hand to remove grace from the expectant, insistent relationship of covenant, or it may serve to reduce covenant simply to law. Either maneuver is a distortion of the testimony and self-understanding of Israel.

Such a distinction does incredible mischief to Jewish-Christian relationships, and comparable mischief in self-discernment about persons in community. (That is, grace and law as twin aspects of covenant become competing issues of entitlement and responsibility, when in fact both belong inescapably to a workable covenantal existence.) Israel was to respond in love to the self-giving love of YHWH. As in any serious relationship of love, the appropriate response to love is to resonate with the will, purpose, desire, hope, and intention of the one who loves. It is for that reason that the traditions of Deuteronomy, without apology or qualification, understand that Israel's proper response to YHWH's inexplicable love is obedience, to do the purpose of the One whose love has made its life in the world possible.

The evocative, forming, summoning power of YHWH, which gives life to Israel, puts Israel under profound and unqualified obligation to YHWH. When we try to give substance to that obligation, it is clear that the testimony of Israel is diverse and variegated. Israel's obligation to YHWH is to be fully responsive to, complementary to, and in full accord with the character of YHWH, so that the way in which obligation is understood is commensurate with the way in which YHWH is construed. In sum, the obligation of Israel to YHWH is to love YHWH. Thus, the first commandment:[16] "You shall love the LORD your God with all your heart, and with all your soul, and with all your might" (Deut 6:5);

"The Lord your God you shall follow, him alone you shall fear, his commandments you shall keep, his voice you shall obey, him you shall serve, and to him you
shall hold fast" (Deut 13:4).

Love is a dense term. Clearly it is a covenant word that means to acknowledge
sovereignty and to keep one's oath of loyalty, on which the covenant is based. But
such a political dimension to the term does not rule out an affective dimension, in
light of the term *set one's heart* (*ḥashaq*), which we have already considered. At the
core of Israel's obligation to YHWH is the desire to please YHWH and to be with
YHWH (Pss 27:4; 73:25). This dimension of desire and joy is what, in the best
construal, keeps Israel's obligation to YHWH from being a burden. At its best, this
obligation is not a burden, but is simply living out Israel's true character and identity, for Israel lives by and for and from YHWH's freedom and passion. This same
dimension of desire has permitted the reading of the erotic love poems of the Song of
Solomon as a reflection of the affective commitment between YHWH and Israel.[17]
Thus we may focus the obligation of Israel around a yearning devotion for YHWH;
but with that focus we must recognize that the enactment of that obligation takes
many different forms, depending on time, place, circumstance, and perspective.

In the exploration of this obligation, I will first thematize the material around
the topics of hearing and seeing, and then I will draw two extended conclusions.
It is recognized that in the Deuteronomic-covenantal-prophetic traditions, Israel's
obligation is to listen as the sovereign YHWH, through many interpreters, issues
commands: "Hear, O Israel: The Lord is our God, the Lord alone" (Deut 6:4).
Thus one aspect of Israel's obligation is to hear and to respond by doing (cf. Exod
24:3-7).[18] Less recognized is a second perspective on obligation, stemming from
the tradition of tabernacle-temple-Priestly tradition: that Israel is to see, to look on
the splendor and beauty of YHWH (see Exod 24:11). These two accents together,
one in the tradition of Deuteronomy and the other in the Priestly traditions, eventuate in a hermeneutical program of proclamation and manifestation, which in
turn may be understood in Christian tradition as word and sacrament.[19]

The Obligation to Listen and to Do Justice

Israel is to "listen" to the command of YHWH and to respond in obedience. While
the commands in the tradition concerning listening are many and varied, we may
say in sum that Israel's obligation is to do justice. Israel is a community put in the
world, so the testimony suggests, for the sake of justice. The justice commanded by
YHWH, moreover, is not the retributive justice of "deeds-consequences" wherein
rewards and punishments are meted out to persons and the community according

to conduct. Rather, Israel understands itself as a community of persons bound in membership to one another, so that each person-as-member is to be treated well enough to be sustained as a full member of the community. In its articulation of justice as its principal obligation, Israel is acutely alert to sociopolitical differentiations and is aware that the strong and the weak, the rich and the poor, live differently and need to be attended to in different ways. It is not belated ideology to recognize that Israel's covenantal-prophetic sense of YHWH's justice does indeed have "a preferential option for the poor" and the marginated. This preferential option that is mandated to Israel is rooted in YHWH's own practice and inclination, so that in the practice of justice Israel is indeed to imitate YHWH.[20] Thus, in Deut 10:17-18, YHWH is one who "loves strangers": "For the LORD your God is God of gods and Lord of lords, the great God, mighty and awesome, who is not partial and takes no bribe, who executes justice for the orphan and the widow, and who loves the strangers, providing them food and clothing." As an immediate consequence, Israel is enjoined to do the same: "You shall also love the stranger, for you were strangers in the land of Egypt" (v. 19). This act toward strangers is understood as a way to "fear YHWH," for the next verse makes the connection: "You shall fear the LORD your God; him alone you shall worship; to him you shall hold fast, and by his name you shall swear" (v. 20).

In the hearing tradition of Israel, there are many and differentiated commands: some are conservative in order to maintain social equilibrium, and some are downright reactionary to protect status quo advantage. Without denying any of this, it is evident that Israel's most characteristic and theologically intentional practice is to attend to the needs of those too weak to protect themselves. In the tradition of Deuteronomy, these too weak are characteristically "widows, orphans, and resident aliens" (cf. Deut 14:29; 16:11, 14; 24:19-21; 26:12-15; Isa 1:17; Jer 7:6; 22:3; Zech 7:10).

It is clear that in these most radical injunctions, understood as Israel's covenantal obligations, the wealth and social resources of Israel are understood not in privatistic or acquisitive ways, but as common resources that are to be managed and deployed for the enhancement of the community by the enhancement of its weakest and most disadvantaged members. This linkage between Yahwistic obligation and commitment to the well-being of the marginated, while especially featured in the covenantal traditions, is also present on the horizon of the wisdom teachers:

Those who oppress the poor insult their Maker,
but those who are kind to the needy honor him. (Prov 14:31)

Those who mock the poor insult their Maker;
those who are glad at calamity will not go unpunished. (Prov 17:5)

This specific and radical command to do justice is to characterize the whole life of Israel. Such a command, understood as a poignant reflection of YHWH's own way in the world (as evidenced in the exodus), clearly is intrusive in and critical of a life of self-protection, self-sufficiency, and self-indulgence. This mandate marks Israel as a community that practices an intense openness to the neighbor; it balances that openness, moreover, by a keen sense of self-criticism about sociopolitical-economic advantage. That is, the function of these commandments is not to protect acquired advantage, but to call that advantage into question when it does not benefit the community.

The command to justice is understood as marking the polity of the community of Israel. That is, justice is not charity, nor is it romantic do-goodism. It is rather a mandate to order public policy, public practice, and public institutions for the common good and in resistance to the kind of greedy initiative that damages the community. The public quality of this command is evident, on the one hand, in the primitive narrative of Achan, who withheld for private purposes the goods of the community, and so did immense damage to the community:

Israel has sinned; they have transgressed my covenant that I imposed on them. They have taken some of the devoted things; they have stolen, they have acted deceitfully, and they have put them among their own belongings. . . . And Achan answered Joshua, "It is true; I am the one who sinned against the LORD God of Israel. This is what I did: when I saw among the spoil a beautiful mantle from Shinar, and two hundred shekels of silver, and a bar of gold weighing fifty shekels, then I coveted them and took them. They now lie hidden in the ground inside my tent, with the silver underneath." (Josh 7:11, 20-21)

This same public quality of the command to justice, on the other hand, is evident in the doxological mandate to the Davidic king:

Give the king your justice, O God,
and your righteousness to a king's son.
May he judge your people with righteousness,
and your poor with justice. . . .
May he defend the cause of the poor of the people,
give deliverance to the needy,
and crush the oppressor. (Ps 72:1-2, 4)[21]

The public good requires that active social power must be mobilized to enhance the entire community and to resist personal aggrandizement of some at the expense of others.

Unambiguously, Israel believes that the violation of this mandate from YHWH, which is congruent with YHWH's own way in the world, will be inordinately destructive. The prophets observe the cost of private coveting, as, for example, by the king and the powerful around him. The same term covet (*ḥmd*) that was used in the indictment of Achan is employed by the prophet Micah:

> Alas for those who devise wickedness
> and evil deeds on their beds!
> When the morning dawns, they perform it,
> because it is in their power.
> They covet fields, and seize them;
> houses, and take them away;
> they oppress householder and house,
> people and their inheritance. (Mic 2:1-2; cf. Isa 5:8-10)[22]

In the denunciation of kingship, the kingship enjoined to justice in Psalm 72, Ezekiel sees the ruin caused when established social power enhances itself at the expense of the defenseless: "You eat the fat, you clothe yourselves with the wool, you slaughter the fatlings; but you do not feed the sheep. You have not strengthened the weak, you have not healed the sick, you have not bound up the injured, you have not brought back the strayed, you have not sought the lost, but with force and harshness you have ruled them. So they were scattered, because there was no shepherd" (Ezek 34:3-5). In this powerful tradition of obligation, Israel is understood as a community that is to be preoccupied with the well-being of the neighbor, and it is to be prepared to exercise public power for the sake of the neighbor, even when that exercise of public power works against established interests.

To be sure, many other commands are less daring, less demanding, and less noble. But if we are to identify what is most characteristic and most distinctive in the life and vocation of this partner of YHWH, it is the remarkable equation of love of God with love of neighbor, which is enacted through the exercise of distributive justice of social goods, social power, and social access to those without leverage; those without social leverage are entitled to such treatment simply by the fact of their membership in the community. While the case has sometimes been overstated, there is ample ground for the recognition that Israel, as a community under obligation, is indeed a community of social revolution in the world.[23] Israel's insistence on this command to justice, moreover, roots this concrete social insistence precisely in the character of YHWH, who loves the widow and orphan (cf. Hos 14:3).

The Invitation to See and Be Holy

A second tradition of obligation that articulates the requirement made of Israel as YHWH's partner is not so well known or so much valued in Western Protestantism. This is the tradition of seeing, which focuses on the cultic presence of YHWH, and wherein Israel is invited to gaze on a vision of YHWH's presence, holiness, and beauty.[24] This tradition has not received nearly as much attention in scholarly interpretation, and perhaps it is not as characteristic or pervasive in Israel's self-understanding. Nevertheless it occupies a good bit of textual space.

It is extraordinary that in the midst of the Sinai encounter, where Israel hears the commands and pledges loyalty to them (Exod 24:3, 7), in the same context of allegiance to command, Israel gives testimony of a very different kind of obligation, an obligation to "see God" and to be fully in the presence of YHWH. In a text commonly assigned to the Priestly tradition, it is affirmed of Moses, Aaron, Nadab, Abihu, and seventy elders that in the ascent to the mountain "they saw (ra'ah) the God of Israel . . . they beheld (ḥazah) God, and they ate and drank" (Exod 24:10, 11). It is clear that we are in a very different environment of testimony from that of the Deuteronomists who insist that, "You heard the sound of words but saw no form; there was only a voice" (Deut 4:12).

The assertion of Exod 24:9-11 does not tell us what the leadership of Israel saw. There is no doubt that this testimony means to say that one of the characteristic markings of Israel is to be in YHWH's presence, to see God, to commune with YHWH directly, face to face (Ps 63:2). This encounter at the mountain, moreover, is not instrumental, not for the sake of something else. It is a moment of wondrous abiding in the Presence.

This testimony about this singular encounter at Sinai makes clear that it is a one-time encounter, to which only the leadership is invited. It is nonetheless clear that this encounter obligates Israel not only to do justice for the neighbor, but also to be in the presence of God, to see God, to submit to the unutterable overwhelmingness that is the very character of God. It belongs to the life and character of Israel to be with and to be before this One to whom Israel is responding partner. Israelite traditions, which are rooted in the Sinai encounter, attest to the ways in which this awesome moment of presence is made continually available in Israel's cultic practice. It is clear in the development of this tradition of obligation that Israel has a keen aesthetic sensibility, suggesting that YHWH to whom Israel responds is not only righteous but also beautiful. The encounter is conducted in an environment of beauty, which makes the communion possible and which is reflective of YHWH's own character.

Beauty in the tabernacle tradition. It is clear, first, that the tabernacle tradition (Exodus 25–31; 35–40) is preoccupied with beauty. Thus the required offering for the construction of the tabernacle includes "gold, silver, and bronze, blue, purple, crimson yarns and fine linen, goats' hair, tanned rams' skins, fine leather, acacia wood, oil for the lamps, spices for the anointing and for the fragrant incense, onyx stones and gems to be set in the ephod and for the breastpiece" (Exod 25:3-7). The skilled artisans work in a variety of materials to construct an adequate and acceptable place of presence: "he has filled him with divine spirit, with skill, intelligence, and knowledge in every kind of craft, to devise artistic designs, to work in gold, silver, and bronze, in cutting stones for setting, and in carving wood, in every kind of craft . . . to do every kind of work done by an artisan or by a designer or by an embroiderer in blue, purple, and crimson yarns, and in fine linen, or by a weaver—by any sort of artisan or skilled designer" (Exod 35:31-33, 35).

The culmination of this elaborate preparation is the coming of "the glory of the Lord," which takes up residence in the tabernacle (Exod 40:34-38). The tabernacle is made into a suitable and appropriate place for YHWH's visible presence by the practice of a beauty commensurate with YHWH's character. It is possible to host the holiness of YHWH, and in this tradition the purpose of life is communion with YHWH, a genuine, real, and palpable presence.[25] Such hosting, moreover, is done only with great care, costly investment, and scrupulous attention to detail.

Aesthetic dimensions of the temple tradition. The tabernacle traditions are either an anticipation or reflection of the temple traditions.[26] The tradition of Solomon's temple reflects royal self-indulgence, which replicates other, non-Israelite royal self-indulgence. Nonetheless, the temple of Solomon is presented in Israel's testimony as a thing of beauty (Ps 48:2) befitting of YHWH, which becomes a place for YHWH's appropriate habitat in the midst of Israel. First Kings 6:14-38 makes clear that nothing is spared in order to create for YHWH a place of beauty. In due course, the glory of YHWH is seen and known to be present in the temple (1 Kgs 8:11).[27]

In the reconstruction of the temple after the exile, it is evident that similar care was taken for proportion and symmetry (Ezek 40:1—42:20).[28] The tradition of Ezekiel is more interested in symmetry and proportion than in the extravagance of the furnishings, but it is unmistakable that an aesthetic sensibility is at work, by which it is again possible for the glory of YHWH to be in the midst of Israel (cf. Ezek 43:5). The temple tradition, concerning both Solomon's temple and the Second Temple, assures that YHWH's presence is palpably available to Israel.

There is no doubt, moreover, that the liturgical experience in the temple has a powerful aesthetic dimension, for the God of Israel is known to be present in an environment of physical, visible loveliness. Thus Israel is summoned to worship YHWH in a holy place of unspeakable splendor (Pss 29:2; 96:9; 1 Chr 16:29; 2 Chr 20:21). The old, familiar translation of the recurring phrase in these texts is "the beauty of holiness." The NRSV prefers to render "holy splendor," thus accenting awe, which precludes any easy or artistic coziness. What interests us in this recurring formula, rendered either way, is that the visibly powerful sense of presence in the shrine has a mark of holiness to it, which variously reflects symmetry, proportion, order, extravagance, awe, and overwhelmingness. This is a sense of the surplus of YHWH, situated at the center of Israel's life, which is experienced as visual and which from its central and dominant position resituates and recharacterizes everything in Israel's mundane world in relation to this center of occupying holiness.

Beauty and holiness. We can make a connection between beauty and holiness, which draws us closer to the obligation at the root of this tradition of presence. We have already seen that YHWH is holy, and we have seen that YHWH is "the Holy One in Israel."[29] This marking of YHWH bespeaks YHWH's transcendence, separateness, distance, awe, and sovereignty. But what interests us now is that Israel in obedience is commensurate with YHWH. Israel is also to be holy as YHWH is holy. That is, Israel's holiness is derivative from, responsive to, and commensurate with the holiness of YHWH (Lev 11:44-45; 19:2; 20:26).

The tradition of obligation, as understood in the Priestly tradition, like the justice tradition in Deuteronomy, is rich and diverse. It cannot be easily summarized. The specific texts that explicitly enjoin holiness in Israel warn against defilement (tm') through eating (Lev 11:44-45), and against mixing the clean (thr) and the unclean (tm') (20:25).[30] The most extensive reference is in Lev 19:2-4: "Speak to all the congregation of the people of Israel and say to them: You shall be holy, for I the LORD your God am holy. You shall each revere your mother and father, and you shall keep my sabbaths: I am the LORD your God. Do not turn to idols or make cast images for yourselves: I am the LORD your God." This invitation to holiness concerns the commands to honor (yr') mother and father, to keep

Sabbath, and to shun idols and images. One may suggest that reference to three of the commands of the Decalogue permits an extrapolation to the entire ten. That is, to be holy as YHWH is holy means to devote every aspect of life to the will and purpose of YHWH. More specifically, however, with reference to the context of the Holiness Code (the name scholars have given to this section of Leviticus), Israel's obligation to holiness means to practice the disciplines of purity and cleanness of a cultic kind, which makes admission to the presence of YHWH possible.[31] That is, Israel is to order its life so that it is qualified for communion with YHWH, even as it is to practice justice for the sake of the community. In this tradition of obligation, the purpose of Israel's life is to host the holiness of YHWH. We have already seen that YHWH's holiness is indeed demanding, and there is no frivolous or careless access to that holiness.

If we understand holiness as the practice of disciplines that make entry into the presence of the Holy God possible, then we are not surprised to recognize that in a few texts, the goal and fruition of life is to see God as did the elders at Mount Sinai. In three texts, individuals in Israel give testimony about the visual experience of YHWH:

> For the LORD is righteous;
> he loves righteous deeds;
> the upright shall behold (*ḥzh*) his face. (Ps 11:7)

> As for me, I shall behold (*ḥzh*) your face in righteousness;
> when I awake I shall be satisfied,
> beholding your likeness. (Ps 17:15)

> So I have looked (*ḥzh*) upon you in the sanctuary,
> beholding (*r'h*) your power and glory. (Ps 63:2)

In all three texts, the same verb is used as in Exod 24:11. And in the first two texts, the condition of such access to YHWH is righteousness.

It does not surprise us that in these texts, as in Exod 24:11, the tradition that celebrates "seeing God" refuses to say in any way what this seeing entails, or what was seen. This profound reticence is yet another way in which Israel guards against any iconic temptation. We do not know if the rhetoric of seeing is to be taken as a metaphor for a nonvisual communion.[32] What we do know is that the practice of worship in the sanctuary and the disciplines of holiness make possible this enunciation of the fullness of the life of faith concerning communion with YHWH.

Tension between Hearing and Seeing

It is clear that hearing the commands of justice and seeing the "face" of YHWH live in profound tension with each other. This tension is no doubt deep in Israel, as bespeak the powerful advocacies of the Deuteronomic and Priestly traditions. One may imagine vigorous debate among the witnesses, of the same kind that characteristically occurs in the ecclesial communities of this text. It is clear that the two accents of these twin traditions of obligation cannot be harmonized. Nor finally are we permitted to say that one is more decisive or more ultimate than the other. It is important that the canonical form of Israel's unsolicited testimony refuses to choose between the two. In different contexts and in different circumstances, one or the other of these traditions may become crucial. It is likely a good rule of thumb, in the ecclesial communities of the text, to attend always to the tradition that is more problematic and demanding. The two traditions together are complementary of the twin affirmations we have seen earlier: that the sovereign faithfulness of YHWH is for the world (thus justice), but that YHWH's faithful sovereignty concerns YHWH's own life (thus holiness).

The obedience of Israel as YHWH's partner concerns the demanding practice of neighborliness and the rigorous discipline of presence with God. It is not possible to bring these two accents any closer together, but we may reference the notion of integrity (*tam*) as a way of linking these modes of obligation. This term means to be whole, complete, coherent, innocent, unimpaired, sound. It may be adequate to speak, in terms of this word, as "willing one thing"—that is, to live a life that is undivided, to be altogether unified in loyalty and intention.[33] Without minimizing the distinctions or tensions between the two traditions of obedience, I suggest that the Israelite with integrity is the one who fully practices neighborliness and who lives with passion the disciplines of holiness. It is the key command to Abraham in Gen 17:1.

The term integrity (*tam*) is at the center of the theological-ethical argument in the book of Job (Job 1:8; 2:3, 9; 27:5; 31:6). Indeed, the drama of the book of Job turns on Job's integrity, which Job will not renounce: "Far be it from me to say that you are right; until I die I will not put away my integrity (*tam*) from me" (Job 27:5). The well-known self-defense of Job in chapter 31, moreover, provides particulars for the life of integrity that the model Israelite lives. It is evident that the tradition of justice provides the primary content of this catalog of integrity.[34] It is equally clear, however, that the tradition of holiness is on the horizon, as in vv. 26-27, which concern false worship. Thus Job is offered as the model for faith and life, a faith that is without qualification committed in every aspect of life to obedience to YHWH.

This same preoccupation and possibility is elsewhere attested in Israelite piety. In two psalms of complaint, the ground for an appeal to YHWH is precisely the claim of *tam*:

> May integrity (*tm*) and uprightness (*yshr*) preserve me,
> for I wait for you. (Ps 25:21)

> Vindicate me, O LORD,
> for I have walked in my integrity (*tam*),
> and I have trusted (*bth*) in the Lord without wavering. . . .
> But as for me, I walk in my integrity (*tam*);
> redeem me, and be gracious to me.
> My foot stands on level ground;
> in the great congregation I will bless the LORD. (Ps 26:1, 11-12)

The work of Israel is indeed to "trust" (*bth*) in YHWH "without wavering." Israel affirms that in its role as YHWH's partner, every aspect of life, personal and public, cultic and economic, is a sphere in which complete devotion to YHWH is proper to Israel's existence in the world.

Israel's Role in the World

Beyond this twofold tradition of obedience as justice and holiness, we may notice that in some traditions, Israel's obligation to YHWH reaches well beyond justice in the community and holiness in the sanctuary. Indeed, Israel is said to have as part of its vocation and destiny a role in the well-being of the world. Three text traditions attest to this larger responsibility of Israel, a responsibility that pushes Israel beyond its own confessional recital to the larger vista of creation. That is, Israel has theological significance for the proper ordering and for the well-being of all of creation.

First, in the précis to the Sinai encounter, YHWH asserts through Moses to Israel: "Indeed, the whole earth is mine, but you shall be for me a priestly kingdom and a holy nation" (Exod 19:5-6). Thus an astonishing vocation is assigned to Israel. It is even more astonishing in the context of Sinai, fresh from Egypt, and in a tradition that is preoccupied with Israel, and without the nations even on the horizon of the text. Israel is to be a "priestly kingdom" (or "kingdom of priests") and a holy nation.[35] This peculiar phrasing is exposited nowhere in Israel's testimony. But if Israel is to be a priestly kingdom (or a kingdom of priests), we may wonder, priestly for whom or to whom? On the one hand, the answer is to YHWH, offering up sacrifices to YHWH.

But on the other hand, perhaps this nation is offered as priest for other nations, as mediator and intercessor for the well-being of the other nations of the world. The other nations also inhabit YHWH's territory, for "the whole earth is mine." The phrasing is only a tease that is left unexplored. But even in this tradition in which Israel thinks mostly about itself, we see on the horizon that Israel has an agenda other than its own well-being: the life of the world. The priestly function is to make well-being and healing in the world possible.[36] Finally, it is to make communion between YHWH and the world possible.

This remarkable role of Israel is only hinted at in the meeting of Sinai. It is made much more explicit, second, in the ancestral traditions of Genesis, which have a quite different horizon. The Abraham-Sarah tale begins abruptly, after the quick account of the way in which creation has become a world of trouble, vexation, and curse (Genesis 3–11). Through the tales of Genesis 3–11, YHWH has no effective antidote for the recalcitrance of the world; the world refuses to be YHWH's faithful creation. As the text is now arranged, Hans Walter Wolff has suggested, the call to the family of Abraham and Sarah is positioned as a response of YHWH to the recalcitrance of the world.[37] While the summons of YHWH to Abraham includes assurances and blessings that become definitional for the life of Israel, it is remarkable that the nations of Genesis 1–11 are very much on the horizon of the text: "In you all the families of the earth shall be blessed" (12:3).

The call of Israel is juxtaposed to the crisis of the world, a crisis that arises because the nations have not accepted their role in a world where YHWH is sovereign. One reason for Israel's existence is that creation is under curse for disobedience, and YHWH insistently wills that the world should be brought to blessing. Israel's life is for the well-being of the world.[38]

Hans Walter Wolff has shown how this theme of "blessing to the nations" runs as a leitmotif throughout the ancestral narrative (cf. Gen 18:18; 22:18; 26:4; 28:14).[39] The way in which Israel's life and faith evoke the well-being of the nations is not made explicit, though Wolff suggests a variety of inferences permitted by the text. It is noteworthy that the formula of 12:3 is not reiterated in the Joseph narrative. Concerning that silence in the Joseph narrative, it can be suggested that Joseph, the son of the ancestors, works a mighty blessing for Egypt (41:25-36). But the blessing for Egypt is commensurate with the reduction of Israel to bondage (cf. 47:13-26).

Two texts are especially poignant in relation to the theme of Israel as a blessing-bearer for the nations. The narrative culminates so that the old man Jacob, carrier of the blessing, at long last is ushered into the regal presence of the pharaoh, who is here emblematic of "the nations." It is clear that Jacob is the suppliant and pharaoh the one with resources to dispense. Nonetheless, the narrative deftly and laconically inverts their relationship, so that Jacob blesses pharaoh: "Then Joseph brought in his father Jacob, and presented him before Pharaoh, and Jacob blessed Pharaoh. . . . Then Jacob blessed Pharaoh, and went out from the presence of Pharaoh" (Gen 47:7, 10). Pharaoh is the recipient of the generative power of life that Israel possesses, a power for life uttered by Jacob and enacted by Joseph.

This dramatic inversion of roles is made even more extreme in Exod 12:29-32, Moses' last meeting with Pharaoh. In this midnight episode, it is clear that conventional power arrangements between master and slave have been completely subverted and no longer pertain. Even Pharaoh now knows this. Pharaoh, who has defied, dismissed, and attempted to dupe Moses, is now without resource and must petition Moses for a blessing. Pharaoh, still lord of his realm, issues a series of frantic imperatives: "Rise up, go away from my people, both you and the Israelites! Go, worship the Lord, as you said. Take your flocks and your herds, as you said, and be gone" (Exod 12:31-32). Finally, desperately, at the last moment, Pharaoh adds to Moses: "And bring a blessing on me too!" (Exod 12:32). The blessing actually given in response to the petition is not reported as it was in Genesis 47; perhaps no blessing is given. Nonetheless, the well-being of Pharaoh and of mighty Egypt is now at the behest of Israel, who carries, even as a slave community, the power of blessing on which the superpower depends.

Isaiah 40–55 provides a third cluster of texts in which Israel's obligation to YHWH is presented as a responsibility for the nations. In Isaiah of the exile, the horizon of Israel's testimony is expansive and takes in the whole human world as the scope of YHWH's sovereignty and concern. More specifically, two texts situate Israel among the nations:

> I have given you as a covenant to the people,
> a light to the nations,
> to open the eyes that are blind,
> to bring out the prisoner from the dungeon,
> from the prison those who sit in darkness. (Isa 42:6)

> It is too light a thing that you should be my servant
> to raise up the tribes of Jacob

and to restore the survivors of Israel;

I will give you as a light to the nations,

that my salvation may reach to the end of the earth. (Isa 49:6)

The two phrases, "covenant to the people" (42:6) and "light to the nations" (42:6; 49:6), have most often been taken to mean that Israel has a mandate to bring the news of YHWH's rule to the Gentile world of nations, so that the Gentile world may also be rescued and saved. On this reading, the well-being of the non-Jewish nations is entrusted to the life and work of Israel (cf. Luke 2:32).

Harry Orlinsky and Norman Snaith have issued a powerful dissent to this rather common view.[40] It is their judgment that the mission here spoken of is to Jews scattered in the known world, who are to be gathered from exile and brought home. On this reading, the poetic phrasing has a horizon no more inclusive than all members of the Jewish community. It is Orlinsky and Snaith's judgment that the notion that Jews have a mission to Gentiles is not in the purview of the text.

Perhaps Orlinsky and Snaith are right, and therefore too much emphasis should not be placed on this phrasing when considering the obligation of Israel to the nations. I mention these texts here for two reasons, with full recognition of the force of the argument of these two scholars. First, Isa 49:6 is notoriously difficult, even for their dissenting interpretation. Indeed, Orlinsky concedes that such a reading as he rejects is possible in v. 6 if it is taken without v. 7.[41] He believes that v. 7 vitiates such a reading. It needs to be recognized, however, that while v. 6 is indeed problematic on a conventional reading, it is also difficult on the dissenting reading. Second, the conventional reading is a powerful and attractive one that continues to exercise great power. It may well be, as Orlinsky suggests, that such a reading is a Christian imposition on the text, but it is not necessarily so. I conclude that these texts in Isaiah of the exile, and their seemingly expansive phrasing, need to be noted in the context of Exod 19:6 and Gen 12:3. Israel does not understand itself, in light of YHWH's governance of the world, as living in a vacuum or in isolation. Its obligation to YHWH is to take seriously all that YHWH has given it, in its context of the nations. YHWH has summoned Israel in love to be YHWH's peculiar partner. And Israel is under intense obligation to respond in obedience to YHWH's sovereign love, an obligation to be holy as YHWH is holy (Lev 19:2-4), to love the stranger as YHWH loves the stranger (Deut 10:19). Response to YHWH's sovereign goodness is Israel's proper life in the world.

Israel Recalcitrant and Scattered

The third facet of Israel's life with YHWH is that Israel did not respond to YHWH's goodness adequately or to YHWH's command faithfully; Israel thereby jeopardized its existence in the world. Israel came into existence by the sovereign freedom of YHWH, and by that same sovereign freedom Israel would perish. Thus the third dimension (or "season") of Israel's life with YHWH is as a recalcitrant partner who stands under judgment and threat for its very life.

The indictment of Israel is principally given in two modes of testimony. First, the studied narrative account of Israel's "history" in Joshua-Judges-Samuel-Kings portrays Israel as a community that has failed in its obligation to YHWH, a failure that is pervasive in the entire account.[42] This indictment of Israel culminates in 2 Kgs 17:7-41 and is echoed in Psalm 106, a recital of Israel's life with YHWH thematized as one of sin and rebellion. Second, the prophets of the monarchal period characteristically address Israel (and Judah) with a lawsuit speech form that evidences disobedience and that anticipates harsh punishment for Israel from the hand of YHWH.[43]

YHWH's majestic governance over this recalcitrant partner, which had at the outset been marked by generosity, now comes as judgment. The judgment is in fact the complete nullification of Israel, so that Israel ceases to be. The historical mode of nullification is exile. Israel is "scattered" (*puṣ*), a new term in Israel's Yahwistic vocabulary, of which YHWH is characteristically the active subject. Israel is scattered to the winds, away from its promised place, and away from its resources for identity. Exile is indeed the defeat, loss, and forfeiture of life with YHWH. The exile is to be understood as an actual geopolitical event in the life of this community. There were indeed displaced persons and refugee communities.[44] It is possible to give a geopolitical explanation for the exile: the displacement of the Jews from their homeland was an effect of Babylonian expansionism under Nebuchadnezzar.

But the exile is not exhausted in its geopolitical dimension. In the end, the exile is a theological datum concerning Israel's life with YHWH.[45] While one may quibble about how extensive the deportation was and what percentage of Israelites were removed from the land, such issues do not matter with exile as a theological datum. In its relation to YHWH, Israel is nullified, and the displacement seemed destined to last in perpetuity. In sovereign righteousness, YHWH acts in self-regard and is capable of sloughing off this partner who refuses partnership. Thus it belongs to the fundamental marking of Israel that as a people summoned in love by YHWH and addressed by YHWH's command, Israel is a community scattered by none other than YHWH, the God of sovereign fidelity and faithful sovereignty, to the null point.[46] Israel can imagine YHWH's complete negation of Israel. Israel has no guarantee of life in the world beyond the inclination of YHWH, and that inclination has now been exhausted. Israel must, in perpetuity, ponder its scatteredness, out beyond the well-being intended by YHWH.

In that situation of nullity, Israel is compelled to new ways in its practice and life of faith. We may mention five new practices that are active acknowledgments of nullification at the hands of YHWH.

Practice of Faith in Exile

Israel must intentionally and honestly face its true situation, refuse denial, and resist pretense. Exile is and will be a reality. This is now Israel's place to be, and Israel must learn to practice its life of faith in exile: "Build houses and live in them; plant gardens and eat what they produce. Take wives and have sons and daughters; take wives for your sons, and give your daughters in marriage, that they may bear sons and daughters; multiply there, and do not decrease. But seek the welfare of the city where I have sent you into exile, and pray to the LORD on its behalf, for in its welfare you will find your welfare" (Jer 29:5-7).

Repentance

Israel now undertakes repentance.[47] The tradition of Deuteronomy urges that even in exile, Israel is required and permitted to forgo its self-serving autonomy and remember its life with YHWH: "When your people Israel, having sinned against you, are defeated before an enemy but turn again to you, confess your name, pray and plead with you in this house, then hear in heaven, forgive the sin of your people Israel, and bring them again to the land that you gave to their ancestors" (1 Kgs 8:33-34).

This theology of repentance is an extraordinary development in Israel's self-discernment. One might have concluded, after Jeremiah and Ezekiel, that Israel had reached a point of no return with YHWH. But now Israel is permitted a chance: "From there [from exile] you will seek the LORD your God, and you will find him if you search after him with all your heart and soul. In your distress, when all these things [sufferings of displacement] have happened to you in time to come, you will return to the LORD your God and heed him" (Deut 4:29-30).[48] Thus repentance in itself is an act of hope. A return to YHWH, and to land and to well-being, is possible. Any such return, however, will be on the terms of the sovereign God who waits to be merciful (Deut 4:31). The repentance entails the very issues that were the causes of Israel's condemnation: remembrance, holiness, and justice.

The Practice of Grief

In the meantime, Israel is not to grow silent about its deserved plight. Israel in exile is a community that grieves and protests. Indeed, in exile the ancient social practice of lament and complaint becomes a crucial theological activity for Israel.[49] The practice of grief is an exercise in truth-telling. It is, as evidenced in Psalm 137 and Lamentations, an exercise in massive sadness that acknowledges, with no denial or deception, where and how Israel is. But this voiced grief is not resignation, for in the end faithful Israel is incapable of resignation. Resignation would be to give up finally on YHWH and on YHWH's commitment to Israel. This Israel will not do, even if YHWH gives hints of such abandonment.[50] This grief of Israel in exile spills over into protest against YHWH. For all of its acknowledgment of its own failure, Israel is not willing to let YHWH off the hook. As a result, in some of its exilic utterances Israel moves stridently past its own failure to focus on YHWH, to protest YHWH's abandoning propensity and to invoke YHWH's new attentiveness to Israel.[51]

Thus in Psalm 74, which expresses grief for the loss of the temple, Israel begins in protest and accusation:

> O God, why do you cast us off forever?
> Why does your anger smoke against the sheep of your pasture? (v. 1)

Then Israel issues a series of insistent demands to YHWH, who let all this destruction happen:

> Remember your congregation,
> which you acquired long ago,
> which you redeemed to be the tribe of your heritage.
> Remember Mount Zion, where you came to dwell.
> Direct your steps to the perpetual ruins. . . .
> Remember this, O LORD, how the enemy scoffs,
> and an impious people reviles your name. . . .
> Rise up, O God, plead your cause;
> remember how the impious scoff at you all day long.
> Do not forget the clamor of your foes,

the uproar of your adversaries

that goes up continually. (vv. 2-3, 18, 22-23)

Israel's plight is related to YHWH's own honor and reputation.

Even in the unrelieved sadness of Lamentations, the final phrasing of the poetry begins in a doxology that reminds YHWH of YHWH's proper sovereignty (5:19), asks an accusatory question (5:20), makes a strong petition (5:21), and ends in a wistful wonderment: ". . . unless you have utterly rejected us, and are angry with us beyond measure" (5:22).[52] Clearly the next move in Israel's life with YHWH is up to YHWH.

In this utterance of protest and grief that acknowledges present trouble, Israel refuses to accept present trouble as final destiny. Even in this circumstance, Israel assumes YHWH's sovereignty, YHWH's capacity to override exile. Israel makes appeal to YHWH's fidelity, which now, in exile, moves to pathos. Israel believes that the sovereign God can be evoked and moved by petition. Thus, while Israel's judgment is a function of YHWH's sovereignty, Israel's grief and protest are a complement to YHWH's faithfulness and pathos. The grief and protest permit YHWH to move beyond sovereign anger and rage to rehabilitation and restoration. It is evident, moreover, in the ongoing life of the exile of Israel, that grief as candor and protest as hopeful insistence are effective. YHWH is indeed moved toward Israel in new, caring ways.

Presence in Absence

In the meantime, with Israel in exile, far from home and from Jerusalem and temple, we may imagine that along with a theology of repentance (which was essentially a demanding imperative in Deuteronomic texts), there was a priestly theology of presence that was affirmative and indicative. The priestly disciplines and liturgies, testimonies that received normative form in exile, were strategies designed to help order an acutely disordered community and to assure Israel a mode of YHWH's presence in a venue of acute absence.[53] While the tabernacle may be in anticipation of the temple, it is also a movable temple, a mode of presence not only imagined prior to the temple of Solomon, but available after the temple of Solomon. It is a mark of the inventiveness and courage of Israel in exile that it refused to settle for flat, angry, one-dimensional absence, and continued to address itself in the direction of YHWH in YHWH's hiddenness. Thus in exile Israel is a people celebrating and practicing presence in absence.

Resilient Hope for Regathering

What most strikes one about Israel in its scatteredness is its resilient refusal to accept the exile as the culmination of its destiny. Thus the great promissory oracles of Israel in exile, in Jeremiah, Ezekiel, and Isaiah, are surely oracles addressed to the exiles.[54] But they are also oracles and articulations of hope that arise out of exile. Thus one of the characteristics of Israel in its scatteredness is the insistent hope for a gathering. The oracles in exile, heard in the mouth of YHWH, insist that the scattered may soon be gathered:

> Hear the word of the LORD, O nations,
> and declare it in the coastland far away;
> say, "He who scattered Israel will gather him,
> and will keep him as a shepherd a flock." (Jer 31:10)

> For you shall go out in joy,
> and be led back in peace;
> the mountains and the hills before you
> shall burst into song,
> and all the trees of the field shall clap their hands.
> Instead of the thorn shall come up the cypress;
> and it shall be to the LORD for a memorial,
> for an everlasting sign that shall not be cut off. (Isa 55:12-13)

> "I am going to open your graves, and bring you up from your graves, O my people; and I will bring you back to the land of Israel. And you shall know that I am the LORD, when I open your graves, and bring you up from your graves, O my people. I will put my spirit within you, and you shall live, and I will place you on your own soil; then you shall know that I, the LORD, have spoken and will act," says the LORD. (Ezek 37:12-14)

Hope belongs characteristically to Israel, and its most acute practice occurs in exile. If we fully credit the articulations of judgment in the texts contemplating exile, we may believe that YHWH's intention is to end things with Israel, who is like a pot that "can never be mended" (Jer 19:11). It is not credible, in my opinion, that the sovereign judgment of YHWH was a strategic ploy to be followed predictably by pathos-filled love. The judgment is not for instruction or chastening or improvement. It is simply judgment of a sovereign who will not be mocked.

If this assessment of YHWH's decisive negativity toward Israel is correct, then one may draw a startling conclusion about Israel in exile. As a scattered community, terminated by YHWH, Israel refused to accept the scattering as its final destiny. Israel believed and insisted, in sadness and in protest but also in anticipation, that the God who scattered would also gather. If this is correct, then we may say that Israel hoped beyond the hope or intention even of YHWH, who had no such hope or intention for Israel. That is, Israel's courage and shrillness, its defiance of its present circumstances, talked YHWH into something YHWH had not yet entertained or imagined or intended. In its argument with YHWH, Israel moved YHWH to a new place of gracious intentionality toward Israel. Israel did so partly by appealing to its own need, partly by appealing to YHWH's sovereign fidelity, and partly by shaming YHWH as Moses had done long ago. In its earlier history, YHWH had taken all the initiatives with and for Israel in creating, covenanting, and judging. But now Israel in exile, in its abandonment and desperation, takes the initiative and evokes a turn in YHWH, creating a future for Israel where none had seemed possible.

The book of Job, as difficult as it is, provides a clue to the strange emergence in the case of Israel. If the book of Job is taken as belated countertestimony of Israel, then we may imagine that in 42:7-17 we are given hints of how faith is practiced in extremis. Job in protest speaks what is "right" (42:7-8). In response, YHWH restores everything (except Job's children). YHWH "restored the fortunes" (42:10).[55] Job is not Israel, to be sure; but the script of Job lives out of the imagination of Israel. Job 42:7-17, a small postscript to the drama of the poem, holds the future of regathered Israel. That, I suggest, is how scattered Israel is in exile. What comes after, in the Old Testament, is a small postscript. But that postscript is the future of gathered Israel, the rootage of Judaism. The gathering takes place by the active engagement of YHWH's sovereign fidelity. But that awesome sovereign fidelity is surely triggered, in this paradigmatic case, by Israel who repents, who practices exilic presence, and who also grieves in honesty, protests in vigor, and hopes in insistence.

YHWH's Fresh Turn toward Israel

Israel's consignment to exile (and death and termination?) by YHWH is a principal theological datum in articulating Israel's theological self-articulation. Given the assertion that such judgment stems from YHWH's uncompromising covenantal expectation, Israel offers a variety of proximate explanations of this disastrous turn in its life: its own guilt, the inordinate fury of YHWH that is incommensurate with the affront of Israel, and the hubristic self-assertion of Babylon as a rival of YHWH. In the end, Israel's more-or-less settled verdict on the matter of exile is a complex articulation of all of these factors. In any case, the drastic rejection of Israel by YHWH is a decisive and irreversible reality in Israel's self-discernment. What Israel has been given by YHWH is now matched by what Israel has suffered at the hands of YHWH.

Our theme now, however, is YHWH's reach toward Israel beyond the scattering. It is an equally certain theological datum in Israel's self-understanding that at the depth of the exile, at the bottom of YHWH's rage toward and rejection of Israel, YHWH does an about-face and reconstitutes a viable relationship with Israel, restoring Israel to full and valued partnership. The turn in YHWH's inclination toward Israel is an extraordinary claim in Israel's faith. In this turn Israel ponders the central mystery of its own existence, and its core wonderment and amazement about YHWH.

As we have seen, Israel does not have a single, clear understanding of what produced the harsh judgment of YHWH. In like manner, Israel does not know what produced this decisive, positive turn in YHWH toward Israel. It is a hidden moment in YHWH's life. In Israel's testimony it is variously suggested that Israel has repented, that Israel's vigorous protest has moved YHWH back to fidelity, that the nations punishing Israel at YHWH's behest have overstepped their mandate, thus evoking YHWH's counteraction of rescue. On this question, special attention should be paid to Isa 40:2, which affirms of Israel "that her penalty is paid." There has been a severe and appropriate punishment of Israel (exile), but it is not a limitless punishment. The debt to YHWH has been satisfied, so that YHWH can now move positively toward Israel. Or it may be that the hurt of exile reached deep into YHWH's pathos, touching and mobilizing unrecognized measures of love and unknown, unacknowledged depths of compassion that heretofore have been completely unavailable to Israel, and perhaps to YHWH. What is clear is that Israel's life after exile, and Israel's status as YHWH's partner after rejection, are made possible only by YHWH's inexplicable turn toward Israel. Israel imagines that the new relationship it is to have as YHWH's partner is in full continuity with the past relationship; yet it is completely different, now rooted in YHWH's self-investment in Israel in quite fresh ways. That is, whatever turn has occurred is a turn on the part of YHWH.[56]

Israel is dazzled by this decisive turn in YHWH, and treasures it much more than it understands it—perhaps treasures it more than it can speak adequately about it. The three great exilic prophets make an effort to speak about this dramatic reversal, on which everything for Israel's future depends. Jeremiah employs the image of terminal illness as a way to speak about terminal judgment:

> For thus says the LORD:
> Your hurt is incurable,
> your wound is grievous.
> There is no one to uphold your cause,
> no medicine for your wound,
> no healing for you. (Jer 30:12-13)

Then, abruptly, without comment, YHWH reverses course in mid-poem:

> Therefore all who devour you shall be devoured,
> and all your foes, everyone of them, shall go into captivity;
> those who plunder you shall be plundered,
> and all who prey on you I will make a prey.
> For I will restore health to you,
> and your wounds I will heal, says the LORD,
> because they have called you an outcast:
> "It is Zion; no one cares for her!" (vv. 16-17)[57]

In Ezekiel, YHWH speaks of harsh judgment under the image of sexual infidelity, which must be punished: "You must bear the penalty of your lewdness and your abominations, says the LORD. Yes, thus says the Lord GOD: I will deal with you as you have done, you who have despised the oath, breaking the covenant . . ." (Ezek 16:58-59). But then Ezekiel moves abruptly and without explanation or justification to "yet": ". . . yet I will remember my covenant with you in the days of your youth, and I will establish with you an everlasting covenant" (v. 60).

And in Isaiah of the exile, YHWH continues the metaphor of affronted marital love, but without the pornographic propensity of Ezekiel:

> For a brief moment I abandoned you. . . .
> In overflowing wrath for a moment
> I hid my face from you. . . . (Isa 54:7a, 8a)

In both of these verses, however, the rejection is promptly countered by reembrace:

. . . but with great compassion I will gather you. . . .
but with everlasting love I will have compassion on you. (Isa 54:7b, 8b)[58]

In Isa 54:7-8, as in Jeremiah 30 and Ezekiel 16, the abrupt rhetorical turn most often is explained away by a kind of criticism that fragments the poems and so nullifies the artistic tension of the utterance. If, however, we refuse to dissolve the poems in order to make them credible to our reason or to our theology, we are left in each case with an amazing utterance, the propulsion of which is kept hidden in YHWH's own life. In each case there is a condemning utterance of YHWH. But in each case that judgment is directly countered by an utterance of reversal that generates a new possibility for Israel in history, a possibility solely dependent on the utterance and the utterer.

Israel's sense about its own life with YHWH is completely based in these utterances. It may be the case that the "return from exile" is also experienced as a historical-political inversion of fortunes, as Persian hegemony displaced Babylonian expansionism.[59] As a theological datum, however, everything depends on the generation of a future of well-being that is rooted in nothing other than in YHWH's inexplicable good intention and recommitment to Israel.

Israel Regathered in Obedience

The new, anticipated possibility for Israel as a community given new life as YHWH's partner is rooted only in YHWH's inclination toward Israel. As in every other aspect of its life with YHWH, Israel must use a variety of terms to express its new lease on life granted by YHWH. We may mention four such usages, each of which bespeaks renewed Israel as the object of YHWH's powerful verbs.

Gather. The most prominent is the verb "gather" (*qbṣ*):

See, I am going to bring them from the land of the north, and gather them from the farthest parts of the earth, among them the blind and the lame, those with child and those in labor, together; a great company, they shall return here. (Jer 31:8)

I will take you from the nations, and gather you from all the countries, and bring you into your own land. (Ezek 36:24)

Do not fear, for I am with you; I will bring your offspring from the east, and from the west I will gather you; I will say to the north, "Give them up,"

and to the south, "Do not withhold; bring my sons from far away and my
daughters from the end of the earth. . . ." (Isa 43:5-6; cf. Isa 54:7; Jer 23:3;
29:14; 31:10; Ezek 37:21; Zeph 3:20)

The term is the antithesis of scatter (*puṣ*) and appeals to a positive metaphor. The
image is of the flock of the good shepherd that had been scattered in vulnerability,
now to be gathered by the attentive shepherd into well-being.

Love. YHWH's rehabilitation of Israel is an act of "love" (*'ahab*), thus echoing
the claims placed early in the tradition by Deuteronomy:

I have loved you with an everlasting love;
therefore I have continued my faithfulness to you. (Jer 31:3)

Assemble, all of you, and hear!
Who among them has declared these things?
The Lord loves him;
he will perform his purpose on Babylon,
and his arm shall be against the Chaldeans. (Isa 48:14)

Heal. A third verb is heal, thus echoing Exod 15:26, in which YHWH promises to heal Israel of the "diseases of Egypt": "For I will restore health to you, and
your wounds I will heal, says the Lord" (Jer 30:17).

Forgive. YHWH finally overcomes the judgment of Israel by an act of free
forgiveness:

I will forgive their iniquity,
and remember their sin no more. (Jer 31:34)

Let the wicked forsake their way,
and the unrighteous their thoughts;
let them return to the Lord, that he may have mercy on them,
and to our God, for he will abundantly pardon. (Isa 55:7; cf. Jer 33:8; 36:3;
    and Ezek 16:63, though here with a different verb, *kpr*)

All of these verbs, and YHWH's actions to which they testify, mean that
Israel is freed from all that had failed. Israel is now completely unburdened by its
past, including the past of the exile (cf. Isa 40:2). This God, as the old tradition of
Exod 34:6-7a had asserted, is one who "keep[s] steadfast love for the thousandth
generation, forgiving iniquity and transgression and sin" (v. 7a). This is the God

known in Israel as the one who forgives, heals, redeems, crowns, and satisfies (Ps 103:3-5):

> He will not always accuse,
> nor will he keep his anger forever.
> He does not deal with us according to our sins,
> nor repay us according to our iniquities.
> For as the heavens are high above the earth,
> so great is his steadfast love
> toward those who fear him;
> as far as the east is from the west,
> so far he removes our transgressions from us.
> As a father has compassion for his children,
> so the LORD has compassion for those who fear him.
> For he knows how we were made;
> he remembers that we are dust. (Ps 103:9-14)

Reshaping Life in Obedience and Hope

It remained for Israel to map out and reconstruct its new life granted by YHWH in forgiveness. This remapping and reconstruction becomes the ongoing work of Judaism. It is clear that the work of Judaism is always postexile and is always in the horizon of YHWH's gathering, healing, forgiving, loving propensity. How Israel is to shape its life in response to that miracle of a future is a matter always yet to be renegotiated in light of all the negotiations already enacted.

Otto Plöger and Paul Hanson have surely been correct, from a critical perspective, in recognizing and thematizing the recurring tensions in Israel's self-articulation.[60] Plöger has done so under the rubric of "theocracy and eschatology," and Hanson has utilized the terms "visionary" and "pragmatist." In utilizing such critical constructs for theological purposes, we may make use of their work, and yet move beyond such thematization in two ways. First, such labels as those employed in a critical way are inherently reductionist, for the theological self-presentation of Judaism set out to be neither pragmatic nor visionary, but to be YHWH's partner in a real world. Second, while there are surely tensions of the kind that can be identified critically, Israel in its theological self-articulation insisted always on taking seriously both sides of the tension, and finally refused to opt for either side as a full and faithful resolution of its way with YHWH. This is evident in the canonizing process, which in the end is an accommodation of accents in tension

in the community of faith.[61] Our constructs of Israel as the rehabilitated partner
of YHWH are informed by these critical judgments, but must be articulated in a
very different way.

It is clear that emerging Judaism is enormously variegated.[62] Here we will
consider Israel's postexilic self-discernment under the rubrics of obedience and
hope.[63] No doubt Israel, in its new circumstance as a marginated political community, understood itself to be primarily a community of obedience.[64] Like all
such obedience, it is likely that the obedience here urged and practiced contained
a prudential element: if disobedience caused exile, "let's not do it again." Granting
that, as theological testimony we are bound to conclude that Israel's fresh resolve
to obedience is a serious one, undertaken in good faith. Israel now is living only by
forgiveness, living "on borrowed time," and so is markedly moved toward YHWH
by gratitude.

Israel then is a community of Torah piety.[65] We may particularly appeal to
two sources for this characterization of restored Judaism. First, the great psalms
of Torah (Psalms 1, 19, 119) surely reflect a community whose horizon is indeed
defined by the Torah, which here presumably means the whole tradition and memory that gave identity to Israel and that shaped and specified obedience. Israel as a
community of obedience resolved to "meditate day and night" on YHWH's Torah
(Ps 1:2). One may take that as an obsession of exhibitionist legalism, as is often
the case in Christian caricatures of Judaism. Or one may understand this commitment to Torah as an acceptance of the reality of YHWH as the horizon, limit, and
center of communal imagination. What is clear is that this piety, an intentional
life with YHWH, was driven neither by guilt nor by fear and coercion.

This acceptance of YHWH as the horizon of life is a matter of joy, com-
fort, and well-being (Ps 119:1-2, 50, 52, 97). Such an orientation of life sounds
outrageous and endlessly self-deceptive if measured by the norms of modernist
autonomy. But of course modern autonomy is no adequate norm for what Israel is
doing and what Israel is becoming. Israel in the postexilic period is now a vulnerable, outsider community, endlessly at risk, without serious social power. Therefore
commitment to this relationship with YHWH and to the norms of that relationship provided a source of reassuring constancy.

The second source of comment on Israel as a community of obedience is the
reform instituted by Ezra and Nehemiah.[66] Commonly regarded as the moment of
the reconstitution of postexilic Judaism, the reform led by Ezra is one of great rigor
and vigor, whereby Israel publicly pledged, as at Sinai, to be a people of the Torah
(Neh 8:9). The accent of the reordering of Israel's life is on the distinctiveness of

Israel, which entailed a "separation" (*bdl*) of Israel from the other peoples, and a fresh resolve about tithes, sabbaths, and marriage (Nehemiah 10–13). It also involved a fresh resolve about justice in the community (Nehemiah 5).

In a Christian discernment of the Old Testament and of emerging Judaism, what most needs to be resisted is the conventional Christian stereotype of legalism. In any serious commitment to obedience, to be sure, zeal may spill over into legalism. But in any attempt to set as antithesis "Christian grace" and "Jewish law," Israel's sense of itself will be distorted and caricatured. Israel, in these interpretive maneuvers and acts of self-discernment led by Ezra, is with considerable daring seeking to order its life in a way that is commensurate with the God who creates, saves, and commands.

The second mark of reconstituted Israel is that Israel is a community of hope. In its reconstituted form, Israel continued to believe that YHWH had futures yet to enact, futures of which the Israelite community would be a primary beneficiary. Thus it is telling and poignant that in Psalm 119, the quintessential psalm of Torah obedience, Israel can speak passionately of its hope along with its resolve to obey: "I hope for your salvation, O LORD, and I fulfill your commandments" (v. 166; cf. vv. 43, 49, 74, 81, 114, 147).

Three dimensions of hope. The hope of Israel is in three dimensions. First, there continued to be alive in Israel hope for a politically serious, Davidic (messianic) recovery, of which Zech 9:9-10 is a well-known witness. Second, Israel's vigorous hope moved beyond political realism in a transcendent direction, issuing in apocalyptic-visionary expectation of world scope. The most comprehensive of these hopes may be the enigmatic "Ancient of Days" in Dan 7:9. Third, in a less differentiated way, Israel continued to hope that, in YHWH's own time and way, the world would be brought right by YHWH (cf. Isa 65:17-25). This latter sort of hope is not messianic (= Davidic), but neither is it apocalyptic.

It is possible to comment on and arrange these several promises in a variety of patterns and grids, as scholars have done. For our purposes, it is enough to see that for reconstituted Israel it is a sure datum that the future is not in hock to the present and will not be extrapolated from it. The future, moreover, is not to be determined by Israel's obedience; the future, as it has been since Israel's most daring core testimony, is in the hands of the One who is sovereignly faithful and faithfully sovereign.[67]

It is enormously important for fully receiving Israel's self-construal that the profound resolve to obedience and the energetic articulation of hope in YHWH's future possibilities are kept side by side in Israel's self-presentation. This dual accent is surely definitional to Israel's self-discernment, rooted in the confession of the God who saves and commands. The God who commands continues to command, and Israel must obey in the present. And the God who saves is resolved to save in the largest scale of all creation. The obedience of Israel makes possible, on the ground, a community of holiness in a creation tempted to contaminate, and a community of justice in a creation tempted to brutality. Obedience gives sharpness and urgency to Israel's existence. But it is the promises of YHWH, in which Israel hopes, which keep this community from turning in on itself, either in despair or in self-congratulation. Israel as a holy people refuses to give up on the commandments of YHWH as the anchor of its significance in the world. Israel as a holy people refuses to doubt the promises, which assert that the future is dependent on nothing in this world, not even on Israel's obedience, but only upon YHWH's good intention, which is more reliable than the world itself.

Israel's Narrative Life in Four Texts

These themes thus form one coherent construal of Israel's unsolicited testimony about its life as YHWH's primary partner: (a) loved to existence, (b) commanded to obedience, (c) scattered to exile, (d) recipients of YHWH's hidden turn, and (e) gathered to obedience and hope.

To some extent, this sequence of themes is an articulation of Israel's normative, historical-canonical recital. Indeed, Israel cannot "tell itself" except through this normative sequence. We must be clear that while Israel's theological self-articulation is never remote from its "historical" memory, we are here concerned with these themes as theological data. Thus we see the themes not only in sequence. We also see them whole, as an interrelated network of self-discernment in which Israel is linked to YHWH's characteristic propensities. These themes, taken theologically, are not simply once-for-all occurrences. They are how it characteristically is with YHWH, and therefore how it characteristically is with Israel. At the center of this testimony is this disastrous fissure in Israel's life, matched by a profound turn in YHWH, upon which everything depends.

The construal of Israel as YHWH's partner that we offer here is pieced together from many utterances of Israel; these utterances could be pieced together somewhat differently. Having recognized that possibility, we may also notice some larger renditions of Israel's way with YHWH that follow more or less this network of assertions, albeit with important variations.

We may mention four such renditions:

(1) Deut 32:1-43[68]

vv. 1-6	introduction
vv. 7-14	appeal to the mighty acts of YHWH
vv. 15-18	indictment
vv. 19-29	sentence
vv. 30-38	assurance
vv. 39-42	confirmation of the poet's words of hope
v. 43	praise

(2) Hos 2:2-23[69]

vv. 2-13	indictment and sentence
vv. 14-15	invitation
vv. 16-20	renewed covenant
vv. 21-23	restored creation

(3) Ezek 16:1-63

vv. 1-14	YHWH's initiatory goodness
vv. 15-52	indictment and sentence
vv. 53-63	forgiveness and restoration

(4) Ps 106:1-48

vv. 1-5	introduction
vv. 6-12	rebellion and rescue
vv. 13-39	rebellion
vv. 40-43	judgment
vv. 44-46	rescue
v. 47	petition
v. 48	doxology

These four extended narratives of Israel, drawn from quite different traditions, evidence the same general pattern of sovereignty and fidelity, disobedience and judgment, rescue and rehabilitation. What may interest us is that the climactic point in these several narratives varies a great deal and on the whole is uncertain. Indeed, the climactic point must be uncertain when Israel speaks in its own unresolved circumstance. It is evident, in each of these model cases, that Israel testifies to assert that its entire life is in relation to YHWH. No other factor pertains to Israel in this theological self-discernment. This is a "God-toward" people, a fact that issues in its most determined certainty and in its most unsettling risk.

Israel and, Belatedly, the Church

As an addendum to our discussion of Israel's unsolicited testimony about itself, we may pause briefly once again to reflect on the relation of the church to Israel in making its communal, ecclesial claim as the people of God. Here we consider only one reference in the New Testament, in which Paul clearly makes a supersessionist claim by referring to the church as "the Israel of God." "For neither circumcision nor uncircumcision is anything; but a new creation is everything! As for those who will follow this rule—peace be upon them, and mercy, and upon the Israel of God" (Gal 6:15-16).

In this text, Paul completes his argument against legalism. He takes up the contrast between pragmatic concerns (circumcision) and visionary concerns (new creation). Here he opts for the visionary as the mark of "the Israel of God." Paul must argue here against those who are flatly pragmatic. Elsewhere, however, Paul can be as pragmatic in the maintenance of the community as any pragmatic framer of Judaism (cf. 1 Cor 6:12; 10:23).[70] While Paul can overstate in one direction in order to make his case against "the Judaizers," it is clear that in the long run and in the whole picture, Paul cannot escape the tensions that beset the reformation of Israel after the exile.

If Christians are to think with theological seriousness about the church as the partner of the sovereign, faithful God, then it seems clear that the same thematics pertain to that relationship as pertain to Israel as YHWH's partner: the same assurances, the same demands, the same costs, and the same surprises. It strikes me that for all the polemics that sustain supersessionism, the truth is that these two communities, because they face the same God, share the same reassuring, demanding life. It is perhaps with such realization that Franz Rosenzweig could dare to imagine that were both communities honest, they would recognize that they live parallel histories, with the same hopes to hope and the same obediences to obey.[71]

It is important, in my judgment, to add a note to this discussion that reflects my own thinking since I first published this piece in 1997. Clearly a great deal has happened at the interface of Jewish and Christian biblical interpretation since that time, of which I mention three points.

First, great attention is now being paid to the common task of Jewish and Christian biblical interpretation with honest recognition of the important differences in these two interpretive trajectories.[72] This welcome change is an outcome of a rich complexity of factors, but particular attention should be called to the work of Jon Levenson. His "wake-up call" to Christian interpreters, "Why Jews Are Not Interested in Biblical Theology," exposed the uncritical supersessionism practiced by many Christian interpreters.[73] While the matter is not at rest, clearly Christian interpreters—including this one—have paid heed and worked with greater self-critical awareness. One happy outcome of Levenson's insistence is that Levenson himself has now become a major voice in biblical theology. His series of books, most recently on resurrection faith, are indispensable instruction for Christian as for Jewish readers.[74]

Second, the issuance of "Dabru Emet," a Jewish manifesto inviting a reconsideration of the interpretive interface between Jews and Christians, is a matter of enormous importance.[75] The statement calls for—and also recognizes—a fresh possibility for genuine dialogic engagement between Jews and Christians that in the recent past has not been undertaken. Of course there is a long history of alienation and Christian oppressiveness in interpretation, so that the way forward in engagement is not an easy one. But a self-conscious resolve among both Jews and Christians is a welcome one.[76]

Third, a new Christian engagement with Judaism is as urgent as it is welcome. Such a fresh engagement concerns not only "substantive theological claims," but also modes of interpretation.[77] It is clear that Jewish interpretation does not press toward closure in the same way that Christian interpretation does, for Jewish readers can recognize and entertain the polyvalent character of the textual traditions more readily. That fresh engagement with theological claims and with the interpretive practices of Judaism, however, is a matter very different from a relationship with political Zionism in the state of Israel. There is of course an important overlap of Judaism and political Zionism, but they are not identical or coterminous, and perhaps the latter subject has no place in a statement concerning Old Testament theology. Except that a biblical interpreter cannot avoid an awareness

that it is the land promises to the Genesis ancestors that has become the ideological base of political Zionism.[78] In my judgment, then, it is important to consider
the ways in which divine promise has been taken up as political claim to generate
policies and practices that live in deep tension with the promissory traditions.
No one knows how to sort out these issues, but it is important for a Christian
interpreter to acknowledge the complex overlay of Judaism and political Zionism
that makes the topic of "Israel as YHWH's partner" so demanding. Of course no
Christian interpreter in the West can have any ease about this complexity, because
Western Christianity has a long history of political-military aggressiveness that is
regularly couched in an ideological form of divine mandate. For a Western Christian to appreciate the ideological claim as "God's chosen people," we need only
reflect on U.S. aggression under the banner of being God's "most recently chosen
people."[79] I do not suggest that this latter has the theological depth or significance
of the former and distinctions must be made. Nevertheless a critical reflection on
U.S. ideology as "chosen" is instructive for the ways in which confidence in God's
providential fidelity can tilt over into an uncritical "innocence" about one's role
in history.[80]

The Human Person
as YHWH's Partner

3

The Old Testament yields a peculiar and important notion of humanness. Scholarship, moreover, has used great energy in articulating what used to be called "an Old Testament understanding of man."[1] Furthermore, in contrast to the several ideologies of modernity, much that the Old Testament has to say about human personhood is strikingly odd. There is a reason for the oddness of Israel's testimony about humanness, a reason that has not been noticed and appreciated often enough. The oddity, I suggest, stems from the fact that *the Old Testament has no interest in articulating an autonomous or universal notion of humanness.* Indeed, such a notion is, for the most part, not even on the horizon of Old Testament witnesses.

The Old Testament has no interest in such a notion, because its articulation of what it means to be human is characteristically situated in its own Yahwistic, covenantal, interactionist mode of reality, so that humanness is always Yahwistic humanness or, we may say, Jewish humanness. The Old Testament, for the most part, is unable and unwilling—as well as uninterested—to think outside the categories and boundaries of its own sense of YHWH and YHWH's partner. As a consequence, the primary categories of Israel's faith—sovereignty, fidelity, covenant, and obedience—pertain for this topic as well. Israel makes this claim for all human persons, including those well beyond its own community. Thus Emmanuel Levinas is correct when he writes in his own mystical, lyrical way of the human person:

> But his soul, which Genesis 2:7 calls divine breath, remains near the Throne of God, around which are gathered all the souls of Israel, i.e., (we must accept this terminology!) all the souls of the authentically human humanity, which is conceived in Haim of Volozhen as being subsumed beneath the category of Israel. . . . Hence, there is a privileged relationship between the human soul, the soul of Israel, and God. There is a connaturality between man and the manifold entirety of the creature on the one hand, and a special intimacy between man and Elohim on the other.[2]

Levinas goes on to speak of "man's" commitment to the Torah as decisive for the well-being of the world.[3]

Such an odd linkage between the human and Israel does not mean that the Old Testament yields nothing beyond Jewishness. Nor does it mean that Jewish persons are superior human beings. It means, rather, that in the Old Testament all human persons are understood as situated in the same transactional processes with the holiness of YHWH as is Israel, so that in a general way the character and destiny of human persons replicates and reiterates the character and destiny of Israel. This transactional process causes a biblical understanding of human persons to stand at a critical distance and as a critical protest against all modern notions of humanness that move in the direction of autonomy.[4] This means that when the Old Testament speaks of the human person, its primary and inescapable tendency is to think first of the Israelite human person, from which all others are extrapolated.

Covenantal Notions of Personhood

Given this general linkage of the "human soul" and the "soul of Israel" (to use the terms of Levinas), we may at the outset articulate two observations in order to focus on the covenantal-transactional character of human persons that is so crucial for Israel's testimony. I intend to put my exposition completely on the side of a relational, dynamic notion of personhood, and thus to reject all essentialist notions of human personhood, even though the latter have dominated much of theological discussion.

First, a great deal of scholarly energy has gone into expositing the Old Testament phrase "image of God."[5] Five primary emphases concerning this notion should be on our horizon:

1. The human person in the image of God is characteristically "male and female" (Gen 1:27), so that the communal, intersexual character of human personhood is affirmed.[6]
2. The human person in the image of God appears to be royal, that is, the human person is charged with "dominion" over the earth (Gen 1:28).
3. The human person in the image of God, like the image of a sovereign on a coin, is a regent who represents the sovereign in the midst of all other subjects where the sovereign is not directly and personally present. Thus the human person is entrusted with "dominion" (Gen 1:28; Ps 8:5-8).
4. The human person as image is an alternative to all other images of God in this aniconic tradition, so that the human person most fully provides clues to the character of God as "person" and "personal." This claim has important positive force as well as negative, aniconic intention.
5. Reference to the image of God in Gen 5:1 and 9:6 affirms that the "primal sin" of the first couple ("the fall") does not deny to all subsequent humanity the character of the image of God.

No doubt these are all crucial theological ingredients in a responsible articulation of humanness, and they have rightly played a major role in much theological articulation. Having said that, it is easy to observe that *the notion of humanity in "the image of God" plays no primary role in Old Testament articulations of humanity;* it does not constitute a major theological datum for Israel's reflection on the topic. I do not mean that a student of Old Testament theology should not be informed by this ongoing discussion, but that the discussion is evoked by subsequent theological categories, especially Pauline, and is largely imposed on the Old Testament. As with Christian interpretation, so rabbinic interpretation as well has taken up the theme. For that reason I have concluded that the theme falls beyond the scope of Israel's intention concerning the subject.

My second observation concerns the physiology assumed in the Old Testament. Great scholarly energy has been given to Old Testament evidence about the physiology of human personhood, which revolves characteristically around the categories of *spirit* (*ruaḥ*), *flesh* (*basar*), *living being* (*nephesh*), and *heart* (*leb*). Again, we have good discussions of this subject, and a student of Old Testament

theology must attend to these matters. This matter of physiology has yielded four
important insights that have occupied the center of continued study:

1. The human person is formed of earth and is breathed upon by God, in
order to become a "living being" (*nephesh*) (Gen 2:7; cf. Ps 103:14). This means
that the human person is, at origin and endlessly, dependent on the attentive giving of YHWH in order to have life (cf. Ps 104:29-30). This dependence raises the
acute problematic of mortality, which is not in itself related to sin.[7]

2. The human person has vitality as a living, empowered agent and creature
only in relation to the God who faithfully gives breath. Thus the human person is
to be understood in relational and not essentialist ways.

3. The articulation of "breathed on dust" in order to become a "living being"
precludes any dualism. It is unfortunate that "living being" (*nephesh*) is commonly
rendered "soul," which in classical thought has made a contrast to the "body,"
a distinction precluded in Israel's way of speaking. Thus the human person is a
dependent, vitality-given unity, for which the term *psychosomatic entity* might be
appropriate, if that phrasing did not itself reflect a legacy of dualism.

4. Derivative from this physiology, though no direct part of it, is the sense that
human persons are not isolated individuals, but are members of a community of
those authorized by the life-giving breath of YHWH, and so have humanity only
in that membership.

Again, it is evident that this physiology, in the service of Israel's interactionist model of reality, stands in important tension with various modern notions of
humanness. This physiology becomes important in the Christian tradition when
consideration of incarnation and resurrection is undertaken. But because I am here
concerned with human beings as partners of YHWH, I shall insist that this physiology, which largely participates in the standard articulation of its ancient social
environment, is to be understood as a way of speaking about the human person
in order to say *theologically* what was important for Israel to say. That is, we must
know about how Israel speaks in terms of breath, flesh, soul, and heart; but it is not
this in itself that is pivotal for Israel's theological self-understanding.

I have no itch to dismiss either the notion of image or the ancient physiology
reflected in the text. But I do not want to be sidetracked from what seems to me
the central concern of Israel regarding humanity: namely, that the human person
is *a person in relation to YHWH,* who lives in an intense mutuality with YHWH.
This *mutuality* invites a "matchup" between the character of YHWH and the
character of human personhood; that matchup, however, does not compromise
the decisive *incommensurability* between YHWH and human persons. All of

that—concerning relationship, mutuality, matchup, and incommensurability—is articulated in the supple notion of *covenant,* for it is affirmed in Gen 9:8-17 that there is an "everlasting covenant" between God and "every living creature" (*nephesh hayyah*) of "all flesh" (*basar*) in the earth.[8] Among those with whom YHWH has an everlasting covenant are human persons, whose covenant with YHWH is evidently different from that of other, nonhuman creatures, though that point is not accented here.[9] Thus human persons are covenant partners with YHWH. This is not the same as YHWH's covenant with Israel but, as we shall see, Israel does permit its sense of its own covenant with YHWH to spill over in a generalizing way to this more inclusive relationship of interaction and mutuality.

Human Persons Commensurate to YHWH's Sovereignty and Mercy

We may first of all articulate the character of human-person-in-relation by focusing on three aspects of humanness that are matchups to three central claims made for YHWH.

Sovereignty and Obedience

First, YHWH as Creator of humankind and of each human person is sovereign in that relationship. Human persons are creatures who are dependent on YHWH and created for obedience to YHWH.[10] Even before any concrete content is applied to the commands of YHWH and the obedience of human persons, the category of sovereignty and obedience is a crucial and definitional mark of humans. The One who makes human life possible is holy, glorious, and jealous. Consequently, the force, possibility, and significance of human life are not lodged in an autonomous agent who has been either given full freedom or abandoned, but are lodged in and with the One who makes human life possible by the constant, reliable giving of breath. The human person is not, and cannot be, sufficient to self, but lives by coming to terms with the will and purpose of the One who gives and commands life.[11]

When we ask about the content of that sovereignty to which the appropriate response is obedience, the Old Testament is not especially forthcoming. We may reference the "commands of creation" in Gen 1:26 that authorize "dominion" and the command and prohibition of 2:15-17.[12] Along with these texts, moreover, it is customary to cite the prohibition of murder and the protection of human life in

9:1-6. To focus on these several commands, however, is to give, in my judgment, undue emphasis to the early chapters in Genesis.

It is more characteristic in Israel to imagine that human persons are in a rough way held accountable for the claims and expectations of the Torah, even though it is not assumed that all human persons or human communities were present at Sinai. Levinas demonstrates the way in which Israel may situate the human person under the commands of the Torah: "Man, by acts in agreement with the Torah, *nourishes* the association of God with the world; or, by his transgression, he exhausts the powers of that divine association. The growth of the holiness, the elevation and the being of the worlds depend on man, as does their return to nothingness. . . . it is man . . . which ensures being, elevation and holiness . . . depending upon whether man is or is not in accordance with the will of God as written in the Torah."[13] Israel is imprecise about the ways in which this responsibility for creation is to be understood, and Israel does not reflect critically on the matter of "natural revelation."[14] It is simply affirmed and assumed that the Torah and its commands pertain to all of creation and thus to human persons.

We may cite three texts in support of this notion that all human persons are summoned to obedience to YHWH's commands. In two psalms that celebrate creation, Psalms 104 and 145, the rhetoric has in purview all of creation and all human persons, with no reference to covenant or to Torah. And yet both psalms end with a sober warning:

Let sinners be consumed from the earth,
and let the wicked be no more. (Ps 104:35)

The LORD watches over all who love him,
but all the wicked he will destroy. (Ps 145:20)

No content is given in either case to "the wicked," but it is clear that the wicked are those who live their lives in resistance to the will and purposes of the Creator, and who damage creation.

In Job 31, moreover, we are provided with a concrete ethical inventory, surely reflective of Israel's best Torah thinking.[15] Here speaks no Israelite, but a human person who is accountable and obedient. There is no doubt that in such articulations as these, Israel's testimony trades upon the substance of Torah commandments. There is also no doubt that all human creatures are held accountable for the maintenance of healthy life in the world. Human persons are commanded, by virtue of their very creatureliness, to live lives for the sake of the well-being of the world.[16] There can be no pre-commandment or non-commandment human person. Being birthed into YHWH's creation brings the human person under the rule of the Sovereign who creates.

Human Freedom in the World

Second, YHWH's sovereignty is in tension with YHWH's fidelity, which is intense and deep, which issues in pathos, and which on occasion profoundly qualifies what appears to be YHWH's determined sovereignty. As the human person is matched to YHWH and as human *obedience* matches YHWH's *sovereignty*, so the human person is authorized to come to terms with YHWH's fidelity, which runs to pathos.

The assurance given to all human persons is that,

As long as the earth endures,
seedtime and harvest, cold and heat,
summer and winter, day and night,
shall not cease. (Gen 8:22)

There is a generous reliability to the order of the world, on which human beings can count. The world is ordered by YHWH so that it provides what all human creatures must have to live (cf. Pss 104:27-28; 145:15-16). Thus human creatures live in a world that leaves them elementally free of anxiety, because of the goodness, reliability, and generosity of YHWH.[17] But more than this, YHWH is

good to all,
and his compassion is over all that he has made. . . .
The Lord is faithful in all his words,
and gracious in all his deeds. (Ps 145:9, 13b)

YHWH is not hostile toward humankind and does not work in enmity, but is positively inclined to sustain, heal, and forgive. Human persons are, by the very inclination of YHWH, provided a safe life-space in which to exercise freedom, power, responsibility, and authority, in order to use, enjoy, and govern all of creation.

What are human beings that you are mindful of them,
mortals that you care for them?
Yet you have made them a little lower than God,
and crowned them with glory and honor.

You have given them dominion over the works of your hands;
you have put all things under their feet,
all sheep and oxen,
and also the beasts of the field,
the birds of the air, and the fish of the sea,
whatever passes along the paths of the seas. (Ps 8:4-8)

YHWH's profound commitment to fidelity and compassion generates life-space for wondrous human freedom in the world, freedom to eat and drink and exult in a world of goodness.[18]

But the fidelity of YHWH inclined toward pathos gives far more than this to human creatures. Because YHWH is genuinely interactive, on occasion human persons are emboldened to take the initiative with YHWH, to insist on their right over against YHWH, to address YHWH in a voice of advocacy and insistence. For this claim, Job is the supreme model. Job represents all of humanity gathered and mobilized before YHWH, insistent on rights and entitlements that belong to responsible human creatures who have full membership in YHWH's creation.

It is characteristically Jewish to go even further than this in the exaltation of human creatures, not only in the presence of God, but over against God. Again, I defer to Emmanuel Levinas. In his discussion of God's kenosis, Levinas offers two points. First, "everything depends upon man": "Man is answerable for the universe! Man is answerable for others. His faithfulness or unfaithfulness to the Torah is not just a way of winning or losing his salvation; the being, elevation and light of the worlds are dependent upon it. Only indirectly, by virtue of the salvation or downfall of the worlds does his own identity depend on it. As if through that responsibility, which constitutes man's very identity, one of us were similar to *Elohim*."[19]

The dominion of human beings over creation, expressed in Genesis 1–2 and especially in Psalm 8, yields to human creatures great power and freedom. That same permit means that human persons have standing ground over against God. As a consequence human agents can claim something like final answerability for the world (but not autonomy), and can plead to YHWH's face (like Job) for a better outcome of that defining relationship.

Levinas goes one step further in his second topic, "God Needs Man's Prayer."[20] Levinas is able to imagine that the relationship between YHWH and human beings is one of genuine mutuality. Whereas YHWH in sovereignty holds the initiative over human beings, so in pathos (Levinas's "kenosis") YHWH acknowledges the initiative of human beings and awaits the agency of human initiative. In the psalms of complaint Israel at prayer is able to cajole, threaten, and coerce YHWH in ways that assume human initiative.[21] Levinas cites Prov 15:8 as a prize example of prayer that is a need of God: "The sacrifice of the wicked is an abomination to the LORD, but the prayer of the upright is his delight."[22] The human person, in this tradition, is assigned an extraordinary role of authority and entitlement, not only in the service of God, but even over against God. There is indeed a second dimension to the covenantal, transactional quality of this relationship, which tilts the God-human encounter toward human initiative.

Dialectic of Assertion and Abandonment

Third, it will be evident that I have set up in dialectical fashion a profound tension in this relationship, a tension that is, I believe, reflective of the text and derivative from Israel's own disputatious relationship with YHWH. As humankind deals with YHWH's *sovereignty, obedience* is the proper order of the day. As humankind deals with YHWH's *fidelity moving toward pathos,* humankind is authorized to *freedom and initiative.*

There is a profound tension in this relationship, for dealing with YHWH's sovereignty and fidelity does not permit compartmentalization. In practice we incline to compartmentalization, being excessively scrupulous in some areas of command (such as money or sexuality) and completely autonomous in other spheres of life (such as money or sexuality).[23] In this relationship, however, as in any serious, demanding, intimate relationship, matters are more troubled and complex than such a sorting out might indicate. The human person, like Israel, is invited, expected, and insistently urged to engage in a genuine interaction that is variously self-asserting and self-abandoning, yielding and initiative-taking. As this tradition of testimony does not envision human persons who are arrogantly autonomous, so it does not envision human beings who are endlessly and fearfully deferential to YHWH.

It will be noticed that Emmanuel Levinas and Abraham Heschel, to whom I have made an important appeal, work out of a Jewish ethical and mystical tradition and do not cite many biblical texts for their perspective, because their argument is more broadly traditional and theological than it is textual. I have cited them, nevertheless, because this particular Jewish tradition of interpretation voices a theme that is counter to the predominant Christian inclination to accent in a singular way the tradition of sovereignty and deferential obedience. It may well be that the tradition of sovereignty and obedience is the predominant one in the biblical text; it is not, however, the only one. By itself, the accent on sovereignty and obedience is not the reason that the biblical tradition has continued to be compelling, authoritative, and endlessly pertinent to ongoing reflection about the character of humanity.

Since YHWH's self-disclosure in Exod 34:6-7, it has been clear YHWH has at YHWH's core an unsettled interiority of *fidelity and sovereignty*.[24] With reference to humankind as with reference to Israel, this unsettled interiority in YHWH has as its counterpoint in the partner an unsettled practice of *deference and autonomy,* each of which is endlessly qualified and corrected by the other. What full humanness requires and expects in this tradition, moreover, is the *courage to assert* and the *confidence to yield.* Either posture by itself betrays both the tradition and the One with whom human beings are summoned to partner. Moreover, either propensity by itself distorts the partnership and makes a caricature of the character of YHWH, who in incommensurability will be obeyed, but who in mutuality invites challenge. The high classical tradition of Christian interpretation has not paid sufficient attention to this latter aspect of YHWH's fidelity that issues in divine vulnerability toward the human partner. Consequently and inevitably, that classical Christian tradition has not reflected sufficiently on the ways in which humankind is invited to assertion in the face of YHWH. As a result of that neglect, the dominant Christian tradition has not fully appreciated the way in which *the dialectic of assertion and abandonment in the human person is a counterpart to the unsettled interiority of YHWH's sovereignty and fidelity.* It seems to me that the classical Christian tradition must relearn this aspect of the interaction of God and human persons from its Jewish counterpart. This is an enduring imperative of ecumenism, to recover from others what one's own interpretive focus has rendered unavailable.

Characteristic Markings of Covenantal Humanness

Thus far we have suggested in broad outline that the human person, as presented in Israel's unsolicited testimony, is commensurate with YHWH:

- YHWH is *sovereign*; the human person is summoned to *obedience and deference.*
- YHWH is *faithful;* the human person is invited to *freedom and initiative.*
- YHWH is covenantal in the enactment of sovereignty that claims and fidelity that authorizes; the human person is understood as *YHWH's transactional partner* who is endlessly engaged in *obedience and freedom*, in

glad yielding to YHWH's sovereignty and in venturesome freedom from YHWH's fidelity.

We now consider in more detail *the specificities of this covenantal-transactional creature* who yields in obedience and who asserts in freedom. The Old Testament provides few texts that explicitly and intentionally address the questions we are considering. Rather the evidence is provided on the run and in an ad hoc fashion. The text sketches out human persons in the actual practice of their humanness before YHWH. Methodologically I am informed by the work of Alfons Deissler, who provides a sketch of human practice through the text of Psalm 22.[25] Deissler does not derive any essentialist attributes of humanness from the text, but observes the subject of the psalm doing humanness in a concrete situation. We shall pay attention to the accent points in Deissler's exposition of Psalm 22, but shall add to it other aspects of transactional humanness that fall beyond the scope of the psalm he studied. I shall summarize the practice of covenantal humanness vis-à-vis YHWH in eight topics, organized into three groups.

Three Disciplines of Humanness

In this first group of topics, I will consider the human person as one who *listens (obeys), discerns,* and *trusts.* These three disciplines of humanness together provide a foundation for a life of buoyant freedom, free of fear and cynicism, a life rooted in complete commitment to YHWH, full adherence to YHWH's sovereignty, and full confidence in YHWH's reliable ordering of reality.

Listening (obeying). The human person, as YHWH's creature, is one who *listens* as YHWH addresses in sovereignty.[26] As YHWH speaks sovereign command, a key element of humanness is obedience, responding to the address of command that is heard. We have already noted that the command of YHWH concerns both *the practice of justice* in imitation of YHWH (Deut 10:17-19) and the *practice of holiness* in imitation of YHWH (Lev 19:2-4). This notion of humanness is parallel to and derived from the notion of Israel as YHWH's covenant partner. That is, all human persons do, after Israel, what Israel does as YHWH's partner. We may notice the parallel by comparing two texts:

- Concerning Israel: "So now, O Israel, what does the Lord your God require of you?" (Deut 10:12)
- Concerning human persons: "He has told you, O mortal (*'adam*), what is good; and what does the Lord require of you?" (Mic 6:8)

The question is put first to Israel and then to "mortals." It belongs to the character of the human creature, according to Israel's testimony, that humanness means to hear and obey the elemental, world-defining, world-sustaining, world-ordering will of YHWH for justice and holiness.

The practice of holiness concerns the disciplined awareness that life is to be ordered with the profound acknowledgment that the core of reality lies outside self and is not given over to human control. Thus the priestly instruction elaborately hedges the mystery of holiness away from human control.

The practice of justice, in concrete ways, is the enactment of YHWH's (*sedaqah*) whereby the cosmos (and the neighborhood) can be ordered for life, and whereby the human community can be kept viable and generative.[27] In the doing of justice, the role of humanness is not simply the keeping of rules, but consists in the venturesome enactment of positive good, whereby human solidarity is maintained and enhanced. The exercise of obedience is the wise use of responsible social power as given in the key warrants of the creation texts (cf. Gen 1:18, 2:15; Ps 8:6-8).

Human persons are authorized to "have dominion" over all of creation, but that dominion, given the verbs of Gen 2:15, is to "till" (*'bd*) and "keep" (*shmr*) the earth. The verbs suggest not exploitative, self-aggrandizing use of the earth, but gentle care for and enhancement of the earth and all its creatures. In this regard the mandate of obedience issues in stewardship, the wise care for the world and its creatures, who are entrusted to human administration.[28]

Old Testament testimony, however, does not linger over such theological generalities, but always gets down to cases. When the Old Testament witness gets down to cases, the practice of justice, which is a core human vocation, concerns not nonhuman creatures primarily, but the enhancement of the human community by mobilizing social power, especially the power and resources of the strong for the well-being of the whole community. While many texts might be cited, I shall select four.

First, the mandate for power for justice is voiced negatively in Ezek 34:3-4, which has as its positive counterpoint vv. 14-16:

> You eat the fat, you clothe yourselves with the wool, you slaughter the fatlings; but you do not feed the sheep. You have not strengthened the weak, you have not healed the sick, you have not bound up the injured, you have not brought back the strayed, you have not sought the lost. . . . I will feed them with good pasture, and the mountain heights of Israel shall be their pasture; there they shall lie down in good grazing land, and they shall feed

on rich pasture on the mountains of Israel. I myself will be the shepherd of
my sheep, and I will make them lie down, says the Lord God. I will seek the
lost, and I will bring back the strayed, and I will bind up the injured, and I
will strengthen the weak, but the fat and the strong I will destroy. I will feed
them with justice.

In this text, echoed in Matt 25:31-46, YHWH undertakes the rehabilitative work
that properly belongs to obedience among the powerful.

Second, in a dispute over proper obedience, the practice of rehabilitative justice is championed, as over against the pseudo-practice of holiness:

Is not this the fast that I choose:
to loose the bonds of injustice,
to undo the thongs of the yoke,
to let the oppressed go free,
and to break every yoke?
Is it not to share your bread with the hungry,
and to bring the homeless poor into your house;
when you see the naked, to cover them,
and not to hide yourself from your own kin? (Isa 58:6-7)

The true desire of YHWH is for neighborliness of a radical kind. That desire of
YHWH certainly applies to Israelites; but surely that desire can be extrapolated, so
that it is a demand made of every human person, in the interest of a viable human
community.

Third, Job 31 offers a rich and comprehensive inventory of human
obligation:

If I have walked with falsehood,
and my foot has hurried to deceit—
let me be weighed in a just balance,
and let God know my integrity!—
if my step has turned aside from the way,
and my heart has followed my eyes,
and if any spot has clung to my hands; . . .
If my heart has been enticed by a woman,
and I have lain in wait at my neighbor's door; . . .
If I have rejected the cause of my male or female slaves,
when they brought a complaint against me; . . .

If I have withheld anything that the poor desired,
or have caused the eyes of the widow to fail,
or have eaten my morsel alone,
and the orphan has not eaten from it—
for from my youth I reared the orphan like a father,
and from my mother's womb I guided the widow—
if I have seen anyone perish for lack of clothing,
or a poor person without covering,
whose loins have not blessed me,
and who was not warmed with the fleece of my sheep;
if I have raised my hand against the orphan,
because I saw I had supporters at the gate; . . .
If I have made gold my trust,
or called fine gold my confidence;
if I have rejoiced because my wealth was great,
or because my hand had gotten much;
if I have looked at the sun when it shone,
or the moon moving in splendor,
and my heart has been secretly enticed,
and my mouth has kissed my hand; . . .
If I have rejoiced at the ruin of those who hated me,
or have exulted when evil overtook them—
I have not let my mouth sin
by asking for their lives with a curse—
if those of my tent ever said,
"O that we might be sated with his flesh!"—
the stranger has not lodged in the street;
I have opened my doors to the traveler—
if I have concealed my transgressions as others do,
by hiding my iniquity in my bosom, . . .
If my land has cried out against me,
and its furrows have wept together;
if I have eaten its yield without payment,
and caused the death of its owners. . . .
(Job 31:5-7, 9, 13, 16-21, 24-27, 29-33, 38-39)

I have here quoted only the "if-clauses," which are followed in each case by a curse,
thus negatively asserting innocence.

What interests us, however, is not the dramatic structure of the chapter nor the function of its assertion in the mouth of Job, but the substance of responsibility and obligation articulated in the process of Job's acquittal. It is clear that obedience and responsibility touch every sphere and zone of human existence: sexuality, economics, religion, and personal integrity. In the final verses, moreover, human obligation includes care of the earth. It is equally clear that the main body of this text concerns responsibility to take positive, rehabilitative action toward the weak, the poor, and the vulnerable. The resources of the strong are held in trust for the community. Job's protestations of innocence, moreover, are precisely that he has devoted his great resources to the community and has not used them only for himself. Job stands as a powerful contrast to the rejected, condemned rulers of Ezekiel 34 who used their great resources only for themselves.

Fourth, Psalm 112 offers a portrayal of "the blessed person" who delights in the commandments of YHWH. Such a one is diligent, generous, and acts in justice:

> It is well with those who deal
> generously and lend,
> who conduct their affairs with justice. . . .
> They have distributed freely,
> they have given to the poor;
> their righteousness endures forever. (Ps 112:5, 9)

The conduct of such a person matches the propensity of YHWH in the matching Psalm 111.

Thus elementally, human obedience means to care for the community, to practice rehabilitative hospitality, to engage in responsible stewardship, and quite concretely,

- to share your bread with the hungry,
- to bring the homeless poor into your house,
- to cover the naked.

In our contemporary context, it may be wondered, and even debated, whether this is the work of the private sector, or if this is thought to be societal policy. The short answer is that the Old Testament makes no distinction between personal and public responsibility. The assertion of Isaiah 58 does indeed sound like individual initiative. The same is true, at first glance, in Psalm 112 and Job 31. In both of these latter cases, however, we have the characterization of a wealthy,

powerful, influential person in a feudal society who stands at the top of the economic stratification of society; action by such a powerful person is tantamount to
public policy. And clearly Ezekiel 34 is concerned with the use of the government
apparatus to take rehabilitative initiatives toward the marginated. Human agents,
in ancient society as in contemporary society, are embedded in social institutions.
These social institutions are vehicles for obedience and for the implementation of
justice in the community, which is a human obligation to the command and will
of YHWH.

The four texts that I have cited (to which many others could be added) make
clear that the large claims of obedience to YHWH come down concretely to
neighborly initiatives of a daily kind. The disciplines of hearing and responding
in obedience constitute a powerful rejection of autonomy that predictably issues
in destructive coveting, and that sets individual gain over against the community
and its needs. The obedient human agent is a creature deeply embedded in and
with and for the community.

Wisdom and discernment. Because obedience issues in the responsible use
of power for the sake of community in the service of YHWH's will for justice,
being human entails being "wise and discerning" (*ḥakam wenabon*). It is, to be
sure, a considerable leap from obedience to wisdom. On closer reflection, however,
it is clear that true wisdom is to adhere to the commands (Prov 10:8), and that the
keeping of commands entails *the practice of wisdom* (Deut 1:13-15; 4:6). Viewed
theologically, rhetoric about commands and about wisdom are intimately linked
in the Old Testament.[29] Both concern attentiveness to the mysterious, God-given
coherence of reality that is not simply at the disposal of human aggressiveness. In
the idyllic presentation at the beginning of his reign, Solomon asks for a "hearing
heart" (1 Kgs 3:9) and is given a "wise and discerning" (*ḥakam wenabon*) heart (v.
12). In the end, the wise are to celebrate YHWH's fidelity, justice, and righteousness (Jer 9:23-24).

An Old Testament articulation of humanness does not flinch from celebrating shrewdness and insight of a tough-minded kind.[30] But the discernment to
which human persons are enjoined is not simply technical knowledge. It is, rather,
a sense of how things are put together and how things work in God's inscrutable
deployment of creation. It is the delicate recognition that reality is an intricate
network of limits and possibilities, of givens and choices that must be respected,
well-managed, and carefully guarded, in order to enhance the well-being willed
by and granted by YHWH for the whole earth. In addition to Solomon, who is
presented as a model of one who can enhance his realm,[31] we may cite as a model

figure Joseph, who like Solomon is said to be "discerning and wise" (Gen 41:33). As a consequence of this special gift from God, Joseph is able to mobilize the resources of the earth and the power of the Egyptian empire for the sake of "bread for the world."[32]

Leaders in Israel are regularly expected to be "wise and understanding." In Deut 4:6, however, the matter is widened and democratized in order to make such discerning wisdom an attribute of all Israel. Insofar as this quality of discernment is sapiential, one may even extrapolate more generally beyond Israel. Such discernment is a God-given capacity of human creatures. Thus Israel's wise leaders embody this general human quality, perhaps in special measure.

This accent on discernment is not commonly made in Old Testament theology when speaking of human personhood, for in recent time focus has been on commandments and obedience. I include this emphasis and place it immediately after obedience for two reasons. First, a recovery of the wisdom-creation traditions of the Old Testament makes clear that human persons vis-à-vis YHWH are to be understood, not simply in terms of the Moses traditions that are so intensely Israelite, but also in terms of the creation traditions that proceed from a larger horizon. It is well known that the wisdom testimony of Proverbs, for example, sketches out a picture of responsible, Yahwistic humanness without any intense appeal to the commandments.[33] Humanness in this tradition means to pay attention to the generous mystery that drives reality, and to know how, in respectful and constructive ways, to channel that generous mystery toward the well-being of the earth and of the human community.

The second reason I cite this facet of humanness immediately after obedience is that I believe it is a ground from which to resist two acute distortions of humanness in contemporary society. On the one hand, the wisdom traditions make clear that obedience is not simply slavish, fearful conformity to rules and laws. Thus wisdom is a guard against *legalism*. Obedience, according to the traditions of wisdom, entails the imaginative capacity to take positive initiatives for the enhancement of creation. "Fear of YHWH is the beginning of wisdom." With that beginning as the reference point, wisdom is also the practice of vast learning and insight. On the other hand, wisdom and discernment are an antidote to *unbridled technical knowledge* in a can-do society that seems bent on damaging the earth for immediate private gain. Wisdom, the ability and willingness to see reality whole as God's generous, fragile gift, is a check on technical capacity and technical reason that refuse every restraint of value. Wisdom is an invitation to be present in the world in ways that resist both abdicating obedience and unrestrained technical freedom, by putting the inscrutable insistences and generosities of YHWH at the core of the decision-making process.[34]

Primal trust. The juxtaposition of obedience and discernment, which together give a warrant for accountability and venturesome initiative, leads to a third element, *trust*.[35] This notion of trust is very close to a phrase made popular by Erik Erikson, "basic trust."[36] By this phrase, Erikson refers to the most elemental confidence that a baby begins to have in its mother—trusting that the mother is reliably concerned and attentive even when not visibly present. From such a concrete confidence in the mother, says Erikson, the baby begins to accept a basic confidence toward the reliability of the world and all creatures. This trust is the primal alternative to a profound anxiety, which regards the world as untrustworthy, like a neglectful mother.

To be fully human, so Israel testifies, is to have a profound, unshakable, elemental trust in YHWH as reliable, present, strong, concerned, engaged for; and, like Erikson's child, to live and act on the basis of that confidence, even when YHWH is not visible and circumstance attests to the contrary. One way of speaking of this basic trust is the term *'emet* (and its variant, *'amen*), which Gerhard von Rad has nicely explicated as a full reliability on YHWH in adverse circumstance (especially when under assault in war).[37] Thus Abraham is to "believe" (*'amen*) the promise of YHWH against the data (Gen 15:6), and Judah is to "stand firm in faith" when under threat (Isa 7:9). This term, however, is most often related to the practice of Israel vis-à-vis YHWH; that is, it is intensely focused on the communal practice of Israel.

We may also consider the notion of humanness as marked by confidence of a broader kind. Thus we look to a second term that is not so focally concerned with Israel: *bṭḥ*, to trust and have confidence in YHWH and in YHWH's good governance of the world. This term for undoubting human confidence in YHWH is no less Yahwistic in substance. It is used, however, in contexts other than in the community of Israel per se. It is found especially in individual songs of complaint. In such songs, the speaker is characteristically in very difficult circumstance. Even in such circumstance, however, the speaker expresses complete confidence in YHWH, confidence that not only sustains the speaker, but also intends to motivate YHWH to act in positive ways, so as not to disappoint the trust of the speaker. That is, YHWH must act so that such confidence is not, in the end, misplaced or betrayed. Thus:

> O my God, in you I put my *trust;*
> do not let me be put to shame;

do not let my enemies exult over me.
Do not let those who wait for you be put to shame;
let them be ashamed who are wantonly treacherous. (Ps 25:2-3)

Vindicate me, O Lord,
for I have walked in my integrity,
and I have *trusted* in the Lord
without wavering.
Prove me, O Lord, and try me;
test my heart and mind.
For your steadfast love is before my eyes,
and I walk in *faithfulness* to you. (Ps 26:1-3)[38]

The Lord is my strength and my shield;
in him my heart *trusts;*
so I am helped, and my heart exults,
and with my song I give thanks to him. (Ps 28:7)

Many are the torments of the wicked,
but steadfast love surrounds those who *trust* in the Lord.
(Ps 32:10; cf. 31:14; 55:23; 56:4, 11)

It is noteworthy that trust, in many of these cases, is the alternative to fear, which
we might render as elemental anxiety:

In God, whose word I praise,
in God I *trust;* I am not afraid;
what can flesh do to me? . . .
in God I *trust;* I am not afraid.
What can a mere mortal do to me? (Ps 56:4, 11)

Surely God is my salvation;
I will *trust,* and will not be afraid,
for the Lord God is my strength and my might;
he has become my salvation. (Isa 12:2)

Human persons, as Erikson saw, are finally confronted with the options of *trust or
fear.* The celebrated human person, in Israel's horizon, is embedded deeply in trust.
This trust is not vague and amorphous; it focuses on YHWH as an active agent
who sustains and intervenes.[39] From that personal and intimate focus, however,

Israel is able to generalize, so that one may come to trust the world over which YHWH presides as a safe and reliable place in which to live.

Thus the same term, as a noun, may be rendered "security," referring to the milieu of safety available where YHWH's rule is willingly accepted and where YHWH's blessings are consequently offered and received. In such contexts, there is no cause for anxiety:

> I will give you your rains in their season, and the land shall yield its produce, and the trees of the fields shall yield their fruit. Your threshing shall overtake the vintage, and the vintage shall overtake the sowing; you shall eat your bread to the full, and live *securely* in your land. (Lev 26:4-5)

> I will make with them a covenant of peace and banish wild animals from the land, so that they may live in the wild and sleep in the woods *securely*. . . . They shall no more be plunder for the nations, nor shall the animals of the land devour them; they shall live in *safety*, and no one shall make them afraid. (Ezek 34:25, 28)

> But those who listen to me will be *secure* and will live at ease, without dread of disaster. (Prov 1:33)

In all three of these traditions—cultic blessing (Lev 26:4-5), prophetic promise (Ezek 34:25, 28), and sapiential assurance (Prov 1:33)—Israel knows about the prospect of finding YHWH's world to be a viable place in which to live free of anxiety. Such confidence is especially linked to the full functioning of creation. But it is also a more intimate confidence that YHWH is fully and adequately reliable, in the face of any threat, in any circumstance, including both external assault and the pressures of guilt and death.

In two other texts this practice of trust in YHWH is fully exhibited, even though the terms *'emet* and *bṭḥ* are not utilized. The first of these, Psalm 131, is an example of trust in the midst of the routinization of daily life. This is a psalm of utter and complete confidence in YHWH. The speaker is willing to dismiss any thinkable anxiety and to be completely at ease in confidence:

> O LORD, my heart is not lifted up,
> my eyes are not raised too high;
> I do not occupy myself with things
> too great and too marvelous for me.
> But I have calmed and quieted my soul,

like a weaned child with its mother;
my soul is like the weaned child that is with me. (Ps 131:1-2)

From this intimacy, moreover, Israel is able to generalize:

O Israel, hope in the LORD
from this time on and forevermore. (v. 3)

A second text, Dan 3:16-18, exhibits the same confidence in a quite different context. Shadrach, Meshach, and Abednego demonstrate confidence in the face of an immediate and fierce threat: "O Nebuchadnezzar, we have no need to present a defense to you in this matter. If our God whom we serve is able to deliver us from the furnace of blazing fire and out of your hand, O king, let him deliver us. But if not, be it known to you, O king, that we will not serve your gods and we will not worship the golden statue that you have set up." These three trusting Jews are fully confident of YHWH's rescue, but even failing that, they remain utterly confident. It is no wonder that "Nebuchadnezzar was . . . filled with rage" (v. 19), for such confidence puts these trusters in YHWH completely beyond the reach of the king's brutalizing intimidation. This confidence, which to the world is an absurdity, has made it possible for martyrs (witnesses) of faith not to yield in the face of severe testing.

These three aspects of humanness—obeying, discerning, and trusting—are of a piece, even though they are characteristically evidenced in different circles of tradition. These three habits (or disciplines or practices) of humanness articulate the sine qua non of what it means to be human in the purview of Israel's testimony. Humanness requires:

- *listening* and responding to the summons of the sovereign,
- *discernment* in wisdom in response to the hidden generosity of God in God's world,
- *trusting* completely, without reservation, in the reliability of YHWH and YHWH's world.

These practices provide positive linkage to YHWH, from whom life comes, and permit buoyancy for an effective life in the world. These three markings portray humanness at peace, in equilibrium, fully authorized for and entrusted with the fullness of life. These characteristic practices of humanness are commensurate with Israel's core testimony about YHWH. They are appropriate disciplines when the sovereignty and fidelity of YHWH can be credibly asserted and gladly accepted.

Life in Crisis

A second grouping of markings of humanness, in which I follow Deissler, concerns life with YHWH when human existence is troubled, disturbed, and at risk, when obedience, discernment, and trust have either failed or are shown to be inadequate. In such a time of dismay, the human person vis-à-vis YHWH must take initiatives to right the trouble, which is not the proper condition of humanness in YHWH's world.

This second grouping of practices and disciplines emerges when the human person is left in "the Pit" (cf. Pss 28:1; 30:3; 40:2; 88:6). A common image in the life of human prayer, "the Pit" refers to any diminishment or impairment of human well-being. Thus it may refer to sickness, imprisonment, social isolation and rejection, or, in extremity, physical death. It comprehends the whole gamut of troubles that beset human beings. In its realism, Israel knows that the disciplines of equilibrium—obedience, discernment, and trust—are not first of all appropriate to such human crises. Thus the human person, according to Israelite testimony, undertakes raw and insistent disciplines in the Pit, practices that are constitutive of humanness and commensurate with Israel's countertestimony concerning YHWH. These activities correspond to the evidence and conviction of YHWH's hiddenness, unreliability, and negativity.

Complaint. First, the human person in great trouble is a *"complaining* person."[40] The complaining person is one who treats his or her troubles as serious and legitimate and not to be accepted as normal. The complaining person refuses silence and resignation, but rather issues a vigorous and shrill protest grounded in the covenantal right to be granted well-being and to be taken seriously. Here we may refer to any of the complaint psalms, for which Psalm 13 is a convenient model.[41] The complaint psalm is expressed variously in a mood of vexation, insistence, anger, rage, indignation, doubt, and hope, but never indifference or resignation.[42]

The complaint is sometimes focused directly on YHWH, who has been absent, silent, indifferent, and neglectful, and who is therefore indirectly responsible for the present plight of the speaker. In such contexts it is assumed that a third party (the enemy) has been the perpetrator of the trouble, but has been able to do so only by YHWH's default. Thus Fredrik Lindström has written about the void created by YHWH's inattentiveness, which permits the power of death to seize the initiative and to cause trouble.[43] On occasion, however, YHWH is said in these prayers to be not only negligent and guilty by default, but more directly and aggressively involved as the perpetrator of the trouble.

What is important about this feature of humanness is that Israel understands, in its courageous disputatiousness, that the human agent has rights, and that these rights require voiced protest and insistence; thus the faithful person shuns every temptation of docile, deferential silence. Israel is clear, moreover, that such angry and insistent protests addressed to YHWH are not acts of unfaith, as they are often thought to be in quietistic Christian piety, but are a vigorous act of freedom and responsibility.[44] The human person must insist on his or her own well-being, even with shrillness; therefore, when appropriate, the person must call YHWH to accountability. Human persons in trouble are mandated by the character of YHWH to take the initiative toward YHWH. The purpose of the complaint is to summon YHWH to the trouble, to motivate YHWH to accept the responsibility that is properly the burden of YHWH in this relationship of fidelity and mutuality, and so to effect decisive change in circumstance.

Petition. The voicing of shrill protest and insistence is not merely catharsis. It issues in *petition*, in imperatives addressed to YHWH with urgency.[45] Petition follows complaint closely and regularly; in petition the needy person addresses YHWH in an imperative. The imperative is not trivial or routine. It consists in a command to YHWH about life-and-death issues:

> Consider and answer me, O LORD my God!
> Give light to my eyes. (Ps 13:3)

> Do not be far from me,
> for trouble is near
> and there is no one to help. . . .
> But you, O LORD, do not be far away!
> O my help, come quickly to my aid!
> Deliver my soul from the sword,
> my life from the power of the dog!
> Save me from the mouth of the lion! (Ps 22:11, 19-20)

> To you, O LORD, I call;
> my rock, do not refuse to hear me,
> for if you are silent to me,
> I shall be like those who go down to the Pit.
> Hear the voice of my supplication,
> as I cry to you for help,
> as I lift up my hands
> toward your most holy sanctuary. (Ps 28:1-2)

The speaker of imperatives addressed to YHWH, authorized by deep trouble, must find voice to express pain in speech. Everything depends on this maneuver. This is an act of profound self-assertion and self-regard, which is the key act of initiative in getting something done to assuage the trouble. This act of imperative is not done in a mood of resignation or of deference; it is an act of insistent hope. The speaker knows in profound ways that the present trouble is not how life is supposed to be, is not as YHWH intends it. Moreover, the speaker proceeds on the sure conviction that circumstance can be transformed and will be righted . . . if YHWH can be mobilized.

Everything depends on mobilizing the undoubted power of YHWH, and so the petition is regularly attended by motivations aimed at urging YHWH to a much-needed action.[46] The imperative addressed to YHWH is characteristically followed and reinforced by motivational clauses that give God reason to act. Thus the imperative is not a command, but it is an act of persuasion, "to make a persuasive case to God that divine help is the thing to do."[47]

This act of self-insistence, which is enacted in hope, assumes and articulates a right ordering of the human person vis-à-vis YHWH. The human agent legitimately takes initiative and makes an assertion, an urgent and insistent request that YHWH do for the speaker what the speaker cannot do for himself/herself. That is, YHWH retains the power in the relationship, the power to act in transformative ways. But that transformative power, of which YHWH is indisputably capable, depends on the triggering power of the human agent, for none but the needful human person can make the utterance that will move YHWH.[48] From Israel's perspective, this utterance of petition, which characteristically (but not always) results in YHWH's rescuing activity, indicates in a compelling way that life is indeed relational and transactional. Israel's understanding of complaint and petition rules out any resignation. It also rules out the notion that this action by the troubled person is simply cathartic or, as Gerald Sheppard opines, is a political stratagem to be overheard by powerful people.[49] It may be that, but it is not merely that. Israel's unsolicited testimony about human persons is that they are indeed partnered to YHWH, who is able to transform, but who must be moved to such action in concrete ways.

Thanksgiving. According to Israel, the utterance of complaint and petition issues characteristically in rehabilitative action on YHWH's part.[50] On the enactment of YHWH's transformation, the complaint and petition of the human person issues in *thanksgiving*, which we have seen is a cultic act of sacrifice, and which on occasion may take the form of generous activity toward the community.[51] It belongs to humanness to give thanks, to receive and acknowledge YHWH's rehabilitative action, and to give visible, public expression of that acknowledgment in the congregation.[52] The completion of the process of coming "out of the Pit" is the glad, visible recognition that the trouble has been overcome by YHWH; connection has been reestablished, in which the human person is properly the *recipient* of YHWH's goodness and not the primary *agent*. By this culmination of complaint and petition in thanksgiving, the human agent is restored and resituated to life in the midst of YHWH's generous equilibrium.

This sequence of complaint-petition-thanksgiving, which is the characteristic plot line of Israel's complaint psalms, is a primary datum for Israel's discernment of human personhood. It should be noted that both the courage to speak petition and the buoyancy of thanksgiving are linked to assertions of confidence and trust in YHWH. Israel has grounds in memory as well as in hope to participate in this drama with YHWH, fully prepared, even in complaint, to count heavily and finally on YHWH. As is characteristic in Israel, this central plot line of humanness was not worked out in theory, but emerged concretely in practice in response to the sort of contradictions that beset human existence. At the same time, that plot line is intensely Yahwistic and interrelational. This drama of restoration is not a thought process of an autonomous human individual; it is a genuine transaction in which this vigorous Other is indeed present and available to the process.[53]

Parallels in contemporary psychology. Contemporary psychology in its central modes—rooted in Freud and evolving into a variety of transactional theories and practices—is parallel to this plot line and (I believe) derivative. To be sure, in a secularized form, personality theories do not retain YHWH at the center of the process, but characteristically have substituted the human therapist for the role of YHWH. Because Freud lived in a positivistic climate and early psychoanalytic theory was determined to be scientific, the theological dimension of the process was mostly lost. It is welcome and surely important that with the general exhaustion of such positivism, a rapprochement with religion is under way among those who practice therapy of an interpersonal kind.[54] Indeed, I suggest that in the derivatives from object relations theory, the cruciality of an initial sense of omnipotence is precisely the sense given, claimed, and voiced in this process of complaint, petition, and thanksgiving.

Moreover, the loss of this standard practice of complaint and petition from theological perspective, which has entailed the loss of self-assertion over against YHWH and the forfeiture of countertestimony about YHWH, is precisely what has produced false selves, both in an excessively pietistic church that champions

deference and in an excessively moralistic, brutalizing society that prizes conformity and the stifling of rage. Quietistic piety and conformity moralism together
have encouraged docility and deference that generate phoniness at the most elemental levels of human existence. Israel's sense of healthy humanness is profoundly
transactional, with the two parties in turn exercising initiative. Israel, moreover,
understood that the drama of rehabilitation, including the sequence of complaint,
petition, and thanks, requires the Holy One, over against whom the human person in extremis must take shrill and vigorous initiative.

Praise and Hope

In tracing the practices and disciplines of humanness according to Israel's testimony, we may finally refer to two practices that properly are placed, understood,
and enacted at the culmination of the drama of rehabilitation: praise and hope.
Of course, the entire drama of rehabilitation is shot through with praise and hope.
The entire drama is rooted in hope, or it would never be undertaken in the first
place.[55] Praise occurs throughout the drama as motivation for YHWH. Nonetheless, praise and hope in their full utterance belong to a life that is fully and well
restored by the action of YHWH, who has been moved to action by the shrill
voicing of need.

Lyrical affirmation of YHWH. We have already seen that the drama of
rehabilitation culminates in thanks, and from thanks we are able to say that *praise*
belongs definitionally to human personhood. That is, healthy humanness requires
a lyrical ceding of self to the holiness of God.[56] As Claus Westermann has suggested, whereas thanks is particular and concrete, praise is that generalizing affirmation of YHWH that moves beyond services rendered and gifts received, to a
lyrical expression of amazement, astonishment, and gratitude toward the Holy
One who lies beyond everything the human person can generate.[57]

Thus the drama of restoration has a marking of praise to it:

In God, whose word I praise,
in the LORD, whose word I praise,
in God I trust; I am not afraid.
What can a mere mortal do to me? (Ps 56:10-11)

Awake, my soul!
Awake, O harp and lyre!
I will awake the dawn.
I will give thanks to you, O LORD,

among the peoples;
I will sing praise to you among the nations.
For your steadfast love is as high as the heavens;
your faithfulness extends to the clouds. (Ps 57:8-10)

But I will sing of your might;
I will sing aloud of your steadfast love in the morning.
For you have been a fortress for me,
and a refuge in the day of my distress. (Ps 59:16-17)

These doxologies break out in exuberance at the end of the process of trouble resolved. The speaker sings in hyperbolic language, because the impossible has happened and well-being has been restored by the sovereign fidelity of YHWH, even where circumstance seemed to dictate that well-being was impossible. To the person in the Pit, the trouble seems to last in perpetuity. But when YHWH is mobilized, all things become possible.

Praise in Israel's presentation of humanness is not limited to resolutions at the end of complaint. The texts of praise take on a life of their own, providing for Israel a corpus of hymnody marked by exuberance, hyperbole, and lack of restraint. Indeed, the lack of restraint in praise matches the lack of restraint evident in the complaints. Both modes of speech addressed to YHWH are in extremes of need and of joy:

Make a joyful noise to the LORD,
all the earth.
Worship the LORD with gladness;
come into his presence with singing. (Ps 100:1-2)

Praise the LORD, all you nations!
Extol him, all you peoples!
For great is his steadfast love toward us,
and the faithfulness of the LORD endures forever.
Praise the LORD! (Psalm 117)

Praise the LORD!
Praise the LORD, O my soul!
I will praise the LORD as long as I live;
I will sing praises to my God all my life long. (Ps 146:1-2)

Praise the LORD!

Praise God in his sanctuary;

praise him in his mighty firmament!

Praise him for his mighty deeds;

praise him according to his surpassing greatness!

Praise him with trumpet sound; praise him with lute and harp!

Praise him with tambourine and dance;

praise him with strings and pipe!

Praise him with clanging cymbals;

praise him with loud clashing cymbals!

Let everything that breathes praise the LORD!

Praise the LORD! (Psalm 150)

Praise is a key marking of Israel's discernment of humanness.[58] To be human means to be willing and able to praise. We have seen that the drama of rehabilitation consists in complaint, petition, and then thanks, as an act of shrill self-assertion. Now we see the countermove in Israel: praise as a glad act of self-abandonment, the active gesture of accepting that life is ceded beyond self, that well-being is rooted in an Other, and that without any claim for self, the human agent is glad to defer to and rely fully on YHWH, who can only be expressed in lyrical language. Such self-abandoning praise consists in the glad relinquishment that is an unembarrassed cultic act, but the relinquishment is not simply one of a cultic moment. We may believe that Israel's practice of praise included relinquishment of all resistant emotions and of all acquisitive self-securing propensities; in this practice of praise the human person lives best and well and most freely when all of the self and all of the claims of the self are given over in full, unreserved surrender to YHWH.[59]

We must note well that such an act of self-abandonment to YHWH is dialectically related to an act of self-assertion against YHWH. Because these two markings, expressed as complaint and as hymn, are genuinely dialectical, one may not give priority to either. In trying to understand how this peculiar Yahwistic dialectic actually functions, however, I suggest that practically and provisionally, priority in the dialectic belongs to the complaining activity of self-regard. I make this suggestion because (a) in object relations theory this primal experience of omnipotence is pivotal for a self that is adequate to practice covenant; (b) one must have a self in order to yield a self;[60] and (c) Western Christian piety has given this facet of Yahwistic humanness short shrift. I suggest this as a practical matter, but do not want to detract from the more important recognition that, seen as a whole, the two maneuvers of Yahwistic humanness are indeed genuinely dialectical.

Four dimensions of hope. The final markings of humanness to which we point is that the human person is one who *hopes*.[61] It is logical to place this discipline of humanness at the end of the rehabilitative drama along with praise. But Jürgen Moltmann has taught our generation that hope is not something that belongs only at the far edge of biblical faith, but in fact it pervades it.[62] Thus hope, in its effect, is close to what I have called "trust" (*bṭḥ*), a complete and pervasive confidence in YHWH in every phase of life. Moreover, Erhard Gerstenberger has made clear that the entire process of complaint and petition is only undertaken in Israel because the speaker in the Pit has complete confidence that YHWH presides over every trouble and fully intends a good resolve, and has the power and will to enact that good resolve.[63] Thus, functionally, humanness is pervasively hope-filled, not in the sense of a buoyant, unreflective optimism, but in the conviction that individual human destiny is powerfully presided over by this One who wills good and who works that good:

> Lead me in your truth, and teach me,
> for you are the God of my salvation;
> for you I wait all day long. . . .
> May integrity and uprightness preserve me,
> for I *wait* for you. (Ps 25:5, 21)

> And now, O LORD, what do I *wait* for?
> My *hope* is in you. (Ps 39:7)

> For you, O LORD, are my *hope*,
> my trust, O LORD, from my youth. (Ps 71:5; cf. 69:3, 6; 130:5; 146:5)

It is important that in these utterances, which characteristically come in the midst of complaints, Israel does not hope for something, but hopes in God. That is, YHWH is not *instrumental* to the hope of Israel, but YHWH is in fact the very *substance* of that hope. We may therefore conclude that Israel hopes, in trouble as in well-being, that YHWH shall be all in all. The act of hope is focused on restoration and rehabilitation; but beyond that, this hope is lacking in specificity. We may imagine that because Israel's life is intensely covenantal, human hope finally concerns communion and well-being with YHWH. But because Israel's faith is intensely material in its intent, human hope is also for the material gifts of life, enough to make life peaceable, safe, joyous, and fruitful.

We may identify four dimensions of hope in Israel's purview of the human person:

1. The future of the hoping human person is largely unspecified in Israel's testimony and enormously open. One prospect of the hoping human person is that such a person may come to full "knowledge of YHWH." The large royal vision of Isa 11:1-9 is focused, first of all, on the coming king of righteousness and justice. But from that image, the poem offers a vision of restored creation that culminates in this way:

> They will not hurt or destroy
> on all my holy mountain;
> for all the earth will be full of the knowledge of the LORD
> as the waters cover the sea. (v. 9)

"Knowledge of YHWH" is given peculiarly to Israel, but here it is anticipated that all creatures shall come to such knowledge. Indeed, the wisdom materials in the book of Proverbs variously speak of "the fear of the LORD" as "the beginning of knowledge" (1:7), "fear of the LORD and . . . the knowledge of God" (2:5). The usages suggest that these phrases are synonymous. It is anticipated that human persons may come to "know YHWH."

The phrase itself is not transparent in its meaning. It may refer to political-theological sovereignty of YHWH, expressed as obedience.[64] It may in some contexts mean cognitive knowledge of Israel's historical traditions.[65] But it may also mean personal engagement and intimacy with YHWH; not knowledge about, but engagement with. In the wisdom traditions, the phrase clearly refers to an awed, discerning sense of responsible, liberated, caring life in YHWH's world. In any case, the phrase is a promise and expectation that the hoping human person may be, in the end, fully immersed in the wondrous mystery that is YHWH—the overcoming of every distance between YHWH and YHWH's cared-for human creature.

2. In the tradition of presence, that is, the Priestly tradition, it is anticipated that human persons may come to live in the very presence of YHWH, so that the hoped-for goal of human existence is indeed communion with God, or in Martin Buber's terms, "meeting."[66] To be sure, the cultic apparatus is distinctly Israelite, and access to communion, as mediated in worship in these traditions, is for highly disciplined Israelites. But because the overlap of Israelite and human person is crucial to our exposition, the hope is that the absence, abrasion, and distance that occur between God and human persons are provisionally overcome in cultic worship, and are finally overcome in the full restoration of creation, wherein the human person may appear in the presence of YHWH naked, defenseless, unashamed, and

unafraid. The hope is that the fractured quality of that relationship narrated in Genesis 3 may be overcome, as hinted at in Isa 55:13 and 65:23.

We may also pay attention to the drama of the text of Psalm 73.[67] This psalm moves according to the three dimensions of the human tale we have suggested, from well-being (v. 1) through alienation (vv. 2-16), to refocus on YHWH (v. 17), and finally to new life (vv. 18-28). Our interest here is in the affirmation of v. 25: "Whom have I in heaven but you? And there is nothing on earth that I desire other than you." YHWH is the "delight" (*ḥpṣ*) of this life—YHWH alone, not the gifts of YHWH.

It may be that this poem pertains singularly to Israelites. A great deal turns on the reading of v. 1.[68] The Hebrew text has "God is good to Israel." But a variant reading in the Greek (which is much preferred) suggests "to the upright," that is, to any responsible person, such as the kind of person envisioned in the book of Proverbs. If such a reading is entertained, then YHWH is the "true desire" of all human persons who hope Yahwistically.

This accent on communion is of enormous importance, not only because of the large attention given to "hosting the holy" in the Priestly tradition, and not only because of the powerful sacramental commitments of the ecclesial community. The promise of presence and of communion is important because it tells powerfully against the commoditization of contemporary culture, as expressed in market ideology and as it invades the ecclesial community as well. If the promise concerns only God's gifts, then God becomes only instrumental to human hope, and the hoper lives in a world of commodities, which in the end give neither joy nor safety. Thus it is affirmed that YHWH is the true heart's desire of human persons, the true joy of human life,[69] and the sure possibility of life lived in hope. This hope is voiced in the familiar conclusion of Psalm 23:

> Surely goodness and mercy shall follow me
> all the days of my life,
> and I shall dwell in the house of the Lord
> my whole life long. (v. 6)

3. Having said that, Old Testament hope for the human person never flies off into spiritualizing fantasy. Alongside the promise of *presence and communion* in the Priestly traditions (and in much of the Psalter), and alongside the promise of *knowledge of God* in the sapiential and prophetic traditions, the Deuteronomic-prophetic traditions, on the whole, affirm that the promise to humanity is *a material world* in which justice will prevail, there will be bread for all, and the human

community will "dwell securely." This theological tradition of hope concerns the restoration of fertility, the yielding of the produce of the earth, so that there is enough for all (cf. Amos 9:13-15; Hos 2:21-23; Isa 11:6-9; 65:17-25).

Psalm 85:10-11, in a lyrical act of imagination, anticipates the time when heaven and earth will be in full harmony:

Steadfast love and faithfulness will meet;
righteousness and peace will kiss each other.
Faithfulness will spring up from the ground,
and righteousness will look down from the sky.

The use of the familiar covenantal vocabulary of steadfast love, faithfulness, righteousness, and peace, however, does not remain focused simply on the relationship, but turns promptly to matters of produce, blessing, and fertility:

The LORD will give what is good,
and our land will yield its increase. (v. 12)

The practice of justice bespeaks the full restoration of the generosity of creation.

In the Christian tradition, this materiality of human hope is familiarly expressed in the Lord's Prayer. The prayer is one of reconciliation. But the reconciliation among neighbors is in the context of bread enough for the day:

Give us this day our daily bread.
And forgive us our debts,
as we also have forgiven our debtors. (Matt 6:11-12)

Human hope that awaits God's generosity and extravagance is an act of expectation that flies in the face of every ideology of scarcity. Much human conflict is rooted in the conviction, born of greed and enacted in acquisitiveness, that there is not enough and one must seize what one can. Israel's sense of human hope is grounded in YHWH's faithful intention of abundance, which liberates humans from the driving grip of scarcity in order that they begin to act, in hope, out of a conviction of abundance.[70] This material *abundance* as an alternative to *scarcity* is a parallel to *communion* as an alternative to *commodity*. In both anticipations of communion and abundance, Israel's sense of the human future is derived from and legitimated by YHWH, who is accessible and generous, with self and with the blessings of creation.

4. The core narrative of human life and human destiny is "into the Pit" of trouble and "out of the Pit" by the power of YHWH. This "in-out" model of humanness is no doubt informed by Israel's own narrative of "out of bondage" and "into the land of promise," as articulated in Israel's most elemental recitals of faith. It is a model that permeates Israel's sense of life and Israel's articulation of YHWH and is evidenced in the structure and drama of the complaint psalms.

Only at the edge of the Old Testament, however, is this model of "out of the Pit" related to human destiny beyond the span of lived historical, physical existence. Only late and rarely does Israel extend its lyric of hope beyond death to life resumed after death. It is beyond doubt that the materials for this affirmation are long available in Israel's sense of the drama of human life. On the one hand, all Israel's speech about "the Pit" is already imagistically aimed at the extremity of death.[71] On the other hand, Israel's own historical experience of exile prepares for this extreme affirmation (cf. Ezek 37:1-14). Nonetheless, it is only late, apparently, that Israel has either the courage or the need to push its horizon yet further, to speak about life that endures death; or, more properly, life that resumes in the midst of the reality of death.

While Jon Levenson has shown that resurrection faith pervades the Old Testament, it is more commonly agreed by interpreters of the Old Testament that only twice does the Old Testament explicitly refer to resurrection:[72]

Your dead shall live, their corpses shall rise.
O dwellers in the dust,
awake and sing for joy!
For your dew is a radiant dew,
and the earth will give birth to those long dead. (Isa 26:19)

Many of those who sleep in the dust of the earth shall awake, some to everlasting life, and some to shame and everlasting contempt. (Dan 12:2)

The first of these verses, Isa 26:19, concerns the faithful who are in distress with grief. The verse, through the imagery of birth, refers to the resumption of the processes of fruitfulness, the recovery of the function and future of creation.[73] The reference in Dan 12:2 is from a context of persecution. Here resurrection is for all, not only the just, in order that YHWH's ethical distinctions in the earth will not be lost or defeated, but can be implemented and sustained, even if their triumph is beyond the scope of lived experience. That is, the future of life in the face of death is due to the uncompromising moral agenda of YHWH.

In these texts Israel's testimony explicitly breaks the boundary of death, in order to extend the aegis of YHWH's sovereignty and fidelity to all imaginable reality. The rhetoric does indeed move into new scope. The theological claim made here, however, is not a new one for Israel; Israel had long asserted YHWH's full sovereignty. Now, however, the extent of that fullness is made exhaustive. No realm of life, not even that which seems to limit YHWH (that is, death), can limit the claims of the God of Israel.

Too much should not be made of these two texts, nor should too much be made of the absence of more texts like them. The affirmation that YHWH will bring human life right is so deep and so wide in Israelite conviction that the lack of resurrection texts, in my judgment, does not evidence a lack of intellectual or theological courage to make a claim of this sort. Rather Israel's full trust in YHWH's will and power to right the world is such that an explicit statement is not particularly required in this faith. In its canonical testimony, Israel seldom engages in speculation about such matters. But Israel is unflinching in its theological assertion about the good destiny of human creatures who fight through the drama of rehabilitation and rest themselves in the new life YHWH gives.

In the end, the future of humanity—which we have variously addressed under the topics of *full knowledge* of YHWH, *full communion* with YHWH, and *full enjoyment* of an abundant earth—now comes to *full confidence* in YHWH at death. This confidence is only inchoately imagined in much of Israel's testimony. Much about the human future is hidden, unknown, and full of risk for Israel, and therefore unarticulated by Israel. That future, for hoping human creatures, however, is not one of threat but of peaceable confidence. That peaceable confidence is not grounded in evidence about the future, whether philosophical and logical or empirical and technological, but in the faithful sovereignty of YHWH already known in Israel's core testimony. How that faithful sovereignty will be fully enacted in ages to come is not known, and Israel manifests no great speculative curiosity on the subject. The One who has been *fully obeyed* is the One who can be *fully trusted* with whatever shape the future holds.

The several seasons of this drama of human life with YHWH—*gift* (obedience, discernment, trust), *loss* (complaint, petition, thanks), and *renewal* (praise, hope)—provide no clear scheme. I propose only to piece together provisionally the fragmentary evidence in this particular way. I do not want to reduce the elusive evidence too tightly. Enough emerges of a pattern in such an undertaking, however, to suggest what life in relation to the sovereign, faithful One can mean, in terms of *glad obedience*, *trustful freedom*, and *venturesome relatedness*. Every aspect

of this portrayal of humanness depends on seeing the human creature in relation to this God, a relationship that is a strange, resilient offer of mutuality and
incommensurability.

Covenantal Existence as Alternative Humanness

Because the struggle for humanness is crucial in the world of late capitalism, and
because much theological conflict is now extrapolated into conflicts over humanness, we may pause to consider the ways in which this construct of human personhood, which eschews all essentialism and which stakes humanness on relatedness,
contrasts with the predominant temptations of our self-destructive culture. I will
not exposit these contrasting features, but suggest an outline that evidences the
resources available in the Old Testament for an alternative, subverting notion of
humanness.

1. The human person in well-being and equilibrium:

    (a) obedience   vs.   *autonomy* that denies accountable relatedness

    (b) discernment   vs.   *technique* that denies a fabric of order

    (c) human trust   vs.   *anxiety*

2. The human person in extremis:

    (d) complaint   vs.   *docility*

    (e) petition   vs.   *resignation*

    (f) thanksgiving   vs.   *self-sufficiency*

3. The human person delivered from the Pit and living on borrowed time:

    (g) praise   vs.   *satiation*

    (h) hope   vs.   *despair*

I understand that such contrasts are much too simplistic; they run the risk of creating easy opponents for Israel's advocacy. My concern, however, is not for competing theories of personality, but for actual human practices in a commodity-driven
society that is fundamentally alienated through an ideology of consumer individualism. The point of this exercise in contrasts is to insist that in Israel's testimony,
(1) there is indeed a serious alternative to common practice in our society, (2) but

this alternative depends on active reference and engagement with YHWH, (3) in an incommensurate but mutual interaction that costs much and requires great risks, costs and risks commensurate with a possible reliving of human life.

Given the practices of contemporary society, especially in its religious activity, this sketch of the human person as a partner to YHWH yields important resources for pastoral care. It is no secret that the so-called pastoral care movement could make little use of scholastic theology or its subjective-liberal alternative early in this century. As a consequence, there was an eager and mostly uncritical embrace of psychological categories in the emergence of self-conscious pastoral care.[74] It is to be celebrated that present thinking and practice in pastoral care are reengaging with theological categories, not to reject psychological learnings, but to treat such learnings with a greater critical alertness, informed by a theological grounding.

The model of humanness that I have sketched here, which I take to be faithful to Israel's testimony, provides a model of human health and wholeness that is a stunning alternative to the notions of humanness offered in what I now term *commodity militarism*. When the contrasting models are made clear, it is evident that pastoral care, which I have elsewhere called a work of transformation,[75] is indeed the work of conversion, in order to embed one's self in this alternative relationship and in the testimony that sustains this alternative relationship.

The work of conversion is slow, gentle, detailed, and ad hoc. But the model gives clarity for the work of day-to-day summons, nurture, and authorization. It is the claim of Israel's testimony that this Yahwistic relationship is indispensable for full humanness. This testimony asserts that no other humanness can finally be full and joyous, because it is not able to tell the truth of humanness, truth focused in YHWH and in relation to YHWH.

Covenantal Humanness in Two Texts

We may conclude our reflection on human personhood by considering in some detail two texts that peculiarly illuminate our theme.

Psalm 103

The speakers in this great hymn are Israelite, and its assumptions of humanness are Israelite. And yet the addressees of Psalm 103, the ones invited to join the praise, are not particularly identified as Israelites. On the one hand, the address is intimate and personal, "my soul" (vv. 1-2, 22b). On the other hand, the addressees include all of YHWH's creatures in heaven and on earth:

Bless the LORD, O you his angels,
you mighty ones who do his bidding,
obedient to his spoken word.
Bless the LORD, all his hosts,
his ministers that do his will.
Bless the LORD, all his works,
in all places of his dominion. (vv. 20-22a)

Thus the psalm is cosmic and universal in scope, but comes down to the particular realities of the individual person who speaks. The speaker is portrayed as, and summoned to be, a human being engaged in praise. But in neither the universal nor the intimate address is an appeal made to concrete Israel.

What interests us in this psalm is that after the hymn enumerates YHWH's characteristic actions toward humanity that serve well-being (vv. 3-5), the psalm takes up the two major predicaments that place all human persons in extremis, namely *guilt and mortality*. I take up this psalm because, writ large, guilt and mortality constitute the defining fissures in human life, the place wherein the old equilibriums fail, where the human agent is required to take venturesome action in order to engage YHWH in a drama of rehabilitation. Indeed, in that moment of the fissure, so Israel suggests, everything about the future depends on the readiness of human agents to take venturesome action toward YHWH.

Concerning the reality of guilt, Psalm 103 asserts:

He will not always accuse,
nor will he keep his anger forever.
He does not deal with us according to our sins,
nor repay us according to our iniquities.
For as the heavens are high above the earth,
so great is his steadfast love
toward those who fear him;
as far as the east is from the west,
so far he removes our transgressions from us.
As a father has compassion for his children,
so the LORD has compassion for those who fear him.
For he knows how we were made;
he remembers that we are dust. (vv. 9-14)

The speaker does not wallow in a guilty conscience and does not appeal to anything like original sin. The speaker simply knows that sin is a reality that disrupts life, so that the human agent is alienated from the Holy One and is help-less in the face of that alienation. Having introduced the topic of guilt for trans-gression, the psalm speaks no more of the reality of the human creature, except as recipient of YHWH's actions. The reality of human sin requires Israel to bear witness to YHWH. YHWH is here said to have real anger at sin (v. 9), but an anger that has limits. The overriding reality of YHWH, as concerns human guilt, is that YHWH is marked by steadfast love (vv. 8, 11) and compassion (vv. 8, 13). YHWH overrides the power and significance of sin and, with the gentleness of a father, embraces the fragility of human life (vv. 13-14). To be sure, the object of this inclination on YHWH's part is not just any human agent, but one who actively and seriously embraces YHWH as partner—that is, who "fears him" (vv. 11, 13). The human extremity of guilt is overridden by a God who in mutuality has compassion, but who is completely incommensurate in overriding and vetoing this human reality.

The second great human crisis, mortality, is treated in parallel fashion in the psalm:

> As for mortals, their days are like grass;
> they flourish like a flower of the field;
> for the wind passes over it, and it is gone,
> and its place knows it no more.
> But the steadfast love of the LORD is from
> everlasting to everlasting
> on those who fear him,
> and his righteousness to children's children,
> to those who keep his covenant
> and remember to do his commandments. (vv. 15-18)

At the center of these verses is yet another affirmation of YHWH's *ḥesed* (v. 17). Again, to be sure, that offer of fidelity is given to the ones who fear, obey, and keep covenant.

In both cases, which mark all human persons, the theological datum that counts is not anything about human persons, but a statement about the partner to human persons who overcomes the risk and the danger of both guilt and mortal-ity. Notice that in this articulation, there is almost no explanation or speculation about why this reality of YHWH is the way it is. Everything depends on this relation to the One who is utterly reliable. This utterly reliable One is the primary truth about human personhood.

The Book of Job

The second text we mention in our concluding comment on human personhood is the book of Job. While the book of Job is certainly, in its canonical presentation, an Israelite document that pertains to Israelite faith, it intends clearly to ponder the human predicament. Many scholars now agree that the three parts of the book, the prose introduction (chapters 1–2), the poetry in the center (3:1—42:6), and the prose conclusion (42:7-17), are to be seen as a dramatic, artistic whole.[76] This may be the fullest, most self-conscious reflection on humanness in the Old Testament.

The three parts of the book, in canonical form, may provide a grid for the drama of human life with YHWH, a drama that begins in blessed equilibrium (chapters 1–2), moves into and through a disputatious encounter (3:1—42:6), and then culminates in restoration and affirmation (42:7-17). This sequence nicely reflects the sequence of orientation/disorientation/new orientation that I suggested for the Psalms some time ago, a sequence that focuses on the middle term of disorientation.[77] I may also suggest that the whole drama of the book of Job correlates roughly with the grid of humanness I have suggested above:

- blessed equilibrium: obedience, discernment, trust
- disruption: complaint, petition, thanksgiving
- restoration: praise, hope

I suggest three matters of interest for our topic:

Open drama with YHWH as key character. Neither the more explicitly Yahwistic prose at the beginning and end, nor the implicitly Yahwistic poetic center, is permitted to override the other element. It is traditional in popular thought to let the patient Job silence the impatient one, whereas in critical scholarship the protesting Job is valued at the expense of the deferential one. But in this full drama of humanness, each element is in place properly and crucial to the whole. If we move beyond literary and form-critical distinctions, we may say that theologically Job moves to a "second naiveté," in which he denies nothing, but in the acknowledgment of his trouble, he continues in a transaction with YHWH that is not fully resolved or free of pain but is the crucial condition of his life.[78] This human life, as modeled by Job, never arrives at a stasis; it is a dramatic process that stays always open. The open, dramatic process of human life fully credits YHWH as a key character, in presence and in absence, who is the overriding and shaping reality of Job's existence. Full and faithful human life requires continuing engagement in this open drama with this character, YHWH.[79]

The marginal Satan. The role of Satan is marginal to the drama of the book, but Satan is there, as the serpent is in Genesis 3. Not a great deal is made of Satan in the book of Job. I suggest, however, that the character of Satan constitutes (at least in Israel's testimony) the statement that the issues of human life are both more inscrutable and more ominous than simple moralism, either covenantal or sapiential, will allow. There is something large and external at work in the world that is antagonistic to human life.[80]

What matters for the practice of humanness here is that YHWH governs and finally overrules and dispenses with this ominous force. Whatever it is that militates against viable human life is, so the text allows, subject to the will and purpose of YHWH. Job therefore not only has no knowledge about Satan, he also has no occasion to spend his energy on this character. He need deal only with YHWH, with whom his destiny is deeply embedded.

Job as counterpoint to Abraham. We may finally consider Job as counterpoint to Israel's model person of faith, Abraham. It would be possible, with Ernst Bloch, to juxtapose Job and Moses;[81] or, as Ezek 14:14 and 20 do, to situate Job with Noah and Daniel. I take Abraham as his counterpart, however, because Abraham is the supreme person of faith, who lives completely inside Israel's narrative construal of reality.[82] Abraham evidences in Genesis 22 his unqualified faith in YHWH, and in 17:1 is summoned to integrity ("blameless," *tamim*). Like Abraham, Job is "blameless," a man of unqualified faith (Job 1:2). The two are alike. And yet they are very different, for Job is a mature man who will not submit blindly. Indeed, Job is such a model human that we are not fully at ease in situating him in Israel's covenantal narrative of faith. Thus he stands a little distance from the simple picture of Abraham. And yet, as Jon Levenson has seen, following the rabbis, Abraham in Genesis 18 also turns out to be seen standing over against YHWH and willing to carry on a risky dispute with YHWH, precisely as a man of faith.[83]

Thus the disputatious Job is a man of faith; and Abraham, the man of faith, is capable of intense dispute with YHWH. I submit that popular interpretation has cast both figures too simplistically and one-dimensionally. A closer study evidences that both characters as practitioners of faith are able to submit in obedience. And both, on occasion and when appropriate, enact faith as counterinsistence in the face of YHWH. Abraham, it turns out, is not only a good Israelite but a profoundly human person. Job, it is clear, is in the end not only a man but a man of faith. Both live fully toward YHWH. But without any awkwardness, both know what to do in extremis.

There is no doubt that YHWH relates to human creatures as free and sovereign. They are created out of YHWH's great generosity, and perhaps out of YHWH's yearning. They are situated in the midst of YHWH's sovereignty and commanded to live on YHWH's terms. When those terms are violated, trouble comes. The world of human persons in their life with YHWH is a fairly tight moral system. The amazing alert offered in these texts is that in the midst of the sanctions that YHWH pronounces, in the face of guilt and in the face of mortality, in the face of both situations in which the human person is helpless, YHWH is attentive. Full of steadfast love and compassion, YHWH is like a father who pities, like a mother who attends. YHWH is indeed for human persons, for them while they are in the Pit, willing and powering them to newness. It is the central conviction of Israel that human persons in the Pit may turn to this One who is powerfully sovereign and may find that sovereign One passionately attentive. That is the hope of humanity and in the end its true joy. ▬

The Nations as
YHWH's Partner

4

T here is no doubt that in Israel's testimony, Israel itself is presented as YHWH's preferred and privileged partner. Israel is endlessly fascinated and perplexed by its own life vis-à-vis YHWH's sovereignty and fidelity. We have seen, moreover, that as a second partner to YHWH, the human person is characterized in this testimony only by derivation and extrapolation from the character of Israel, so that human persons are and do, by reiteration and replication, what Israel is and does. Like Israel, human persons are formed in love and summoned to obedience. Like Israel, human persons face judgment as a result of disobedience, come to trouble, and must take initiatives out of that trouble. Like Israel, human persons are beyond trouble opened for a new life of obedience, praise, and hope. The second partner lives always in reflection from the first partner, Israel.

When we come to a third partner who is linked to YHWH by YHWH's freedom and passion and who stands as the direct object in YHWH's characteristic sentences with transformative verbs, the same linkage to Israel pertains. Israel did not live its life or practice its faith in a sociopolitical vacuum. From beginning to end, Israel lived among the nations who, in varying ways, decisively impinge upon

Israel's life. On the one hand, Israel had to work out its relation to the nations, which was not obvious in light of Israel's peculiar theological identity. On the other hand, Israel had to articulate how the nations were related to YHWH, a relation that in part was mediated through Israel but in part stood independent of Israel. The tension between "through Israel" and "independent of Israel," as we shall see, is a complicated matter, and one that admitted of no obvious or simple articulation. It is true that the Old Testament is pervasively preoccupied with Israel; for that reason it comes as a surprise to notice the richness of the material in which this testimony is willing and able to open its horizon beyond Israel, to the larger scope of YHWH's freedom and passion.

The Large Horizon of YHWH's Governance

We may begin our study of this third partner of YHWH by reflecting on a pivotal and characteristic affirmation of the Jerusalem liturgy, a liturgy in which Israel bears witness to the nations concerning YHWH: "Say among the nations, 'The LORD is king!'" (Ps 96:10). The purpose of the liturgy, reflected in Psalm 96, is *to assert and to enact YHWH's legitimate governance* over the nations and the peoples of the world (v. 10), and over the "gods of the peoples" (v. 5). This liturgical exclamation asserts the primary claim of this testimony: YHWH holds sovereign authority over all the nations and all the nations must come to accept that rule, which is characterized by equity (v. 10), righteousness, and truth (v. 13). Negatively, this assertion constitutes a rejection of any loyalty other nations may give to any other gods and a rejection of any imagined autonomy on the part of any political power. Positively, the assertion promptly brings the nations under the demands, promises, and sanctions of YHWH's will for justice.

The rhetoric of Ps 96:10 is so familiar to us that we may miss its remarkable character. In a quick liturgical utterance, the temple-dynastic establishment in Jerusalem sweeps away all other claims to legitimacy and subsumes all other worldly powers under this theological governance.

This assertion is situated in the Jerusalem temple, which means that the Yahwistic claim is shadowed by the interest of the Davidic-Solomonic establishment. That is, the Yahwistic claim, surely theological in intent, is never completely free of socio-economic-political-military interest. Israel, as a witness, is not above giving testimony that serves its own interest and reputation. Thus our theme of "nations" never completely escapes this ideological dimension, although, as we shall see, the testimony includes significant, self-conscious critical moves against that ideological interest.

Recognition of the ideological element in the assertion of Ps 96:10 in itself does not dispose of nor delegitimate the theological claim that is here made. Simply because we recognize such an interest does not mean that the claim of YHWH's sovereignty is reduced to and equated with Israelite interest, for this is, nonetheless, a God who is committed to justice and holiness that are certainly not coterminous with Israel's political interest. In the process of working out this quandary, moreover, Israel makes important interpretive moves beyond its own self-interest.

The nations are subjects of YHWH's sovereignty, to whom YHWH relates in freedom and passion. The liturgic declaration of Ps 96:10, said in v. 2 to be "gospel" (*bsr*), receives a fuller narrative articulation in Gen 9:8—11:30. This text, which pieces together narrative and genealogy from different sorts of materials in different traditions, bears witness to the claim of YHWH's postflood governance of the nations. The genealogies of the nations are contemplations of the juxtaposition of universalism (or, better stated, internationalism) and particularism of Israel that pervades this material.[1] We may, in this horizon-giving material, identify the following motifs.

Motifs in Genesis Genealogies

First, YHWH makes an "everlasting covenant" with Noah and Noah's descendants, with "every animal of the earth," with the whole of creation. YHWH's sovereignty over creation is cast in the language of fidelity and promise (Gen 9:8-17). The entire world of creation is in covenant with YHWH.[2]

Second, Noah and his sons are the progenitors of all creation, so that the Noachic covenant applies to all of the nations. This assertion begins in the reiteration of the promise spoken over creation (1:28), now reasserted to the family of Noah (9:1, 7). The human community is placed under the power of YHWH's generous blessing.[3] It is intended that all descendant nations shall be fruitful and productive beneficiaries of YHWH's will for life, as evidenced in the blessing-laden character of creation.

Third, all of humanity is derived from this family. Thus the horizon is focused on Noah and his sons (9:1, 18-28). The sons are transformed, in the next extrapolation, to nations (10:1-32). Of these, the family of Shem becomes the focal point, so that the family of humanity is drawn inexorably toward Israel (11:10-29). By this route, all nations are bound together, all live under the life-giving covenant of YHWH, and all are recipients of YHWH's blessing for life.

Fourth, the nations are restless with their status as subjects of YHWH and recipients of YHWH's gifts (11:1-9). They crave autonomy (v. 4). As a consequence of their rejection of the status as covenanted, blessed, promised subjects of YHWH, the nations who were authorized by YHWH now are "scattered" (*puṣ*) and the coherence and unity of humanity irreversibly violated (v. 8).[4] The nations are made to receive "scattering," exposed displacement, just as Israel's worst negation is the scattering from which it is always being gathered.[5] In the process of this recalcitrance, the blessed state of the family of humanity has been transformed into a circumstance of vexation, alienation, and jeopardy. As the tracing of humanity in the family of Noah becomes ever more specific, the jeopardy of the human community culminates in 11:30: "Now Sarai was barren. . . ." Until this point, we do not identify Sarai and Abram as a special family of blessing. Here they are presented only as the quintessential family of failure, in which the primal promise of fruitfulness, already uttered over creation, has been nullified in barrenness.

From a critical perspective, this portrayal of humanity in Genesis 9–11 is enormously difficult. But as a theological datum, the arrangement of texts announces the major themes that concern the nations as YHWH's partner. The themes are fully resonant with the liturgical proclamation of Ps 96:10:

- YHWH is king, and so the nations are under *promise*.
- YHWH is king, and so the nations bear a *blessing*.
- YHWH is king, and so the nations live in covenant under *command*.
- YHWH is king, and so the recalcitrant nations are *scattered*.

The story of the nations, up until Gen 11:29, is in fact deeply unresolved, as indeed it is in the world. This skillful rendering of the nations affirms both the glad sovereignty of YHWH over the nations and the problematic character of the relationship that gives life to the nations, but on terms that the nations characteristically refuse. Israel's unsolicited testimony leaves for more concrete probing the questions whether the scattered nations have a future, and whether YHWH's free sovereign will, as it has for Israel, can move to a restorative passion. This overview, given at the outset of Israel's testimony, poses the questions. The answers can only be given concretely, in particular cases.

The Nations vis-à-vis Israel

The nations are a proper subject of YHWH's attention. According to the juxtaposition of Genesis 9–11 and 12:1-3, moreover, the nations are with YHWH and under YHWH's sovereignty, even before the existence of Israel. But Israel's portrayal of the matter is, in the first instance, always aimed at keeping the nations in the purview of Israel. Thus our first exploration of nations as partner of YHWH will consider *the destiny of the nations as a partner, when the nations must make their way in a testimony that is Israel-driven*, testimony that interprets everything as though its primary point of concern is Israel. That is, "nations as partner" is first of all a function of the scandal of Israel's particularity, Israel's self-preoccupation, and Israel's self-serving ideology that shows up as testimony. The nations must make their way, according to this unsolicited testimony, in a world of Israel's preferential status with YHWH.

Enthronement Psalms in Israel's Ideology

We may consider Psalm 2 as an entry point into this Israelite ideological reading of the nations.[6] We have taken Psalm 96, one of the enthronement psalms, as our starting point for our topic. These psalms of enthronement (Psalms 47, 93, 96–99) concern the kingship and governance of YHWH, and Israel is not explicitly on the horizon of Psalm 96 (but see 97:8; 99:6-7). But the enthronement psalms that exalt YHWH are, in the Psalter, a close fit to the royal psalms that are preoccupied with the royal house, and so they draw YHWH's sovereignty into the Israelite-Davidic hegemony.[7] Psalm 2, as a case in point, is placed at the outset of the Psalter, along with Psalm 1, in order to establish Davidic hegemony in the liturgical imagination of Israel, along with Torah obedience, as a pivotal theological accent in Israelite piety.[8] Psalm 2 vigorously asserts YHWH's governance and rejects the attempt of the nations to cast off YHWH's rule (as in Gen 11:1-9):

> Why do the nations conspire,
> and the peoples plot in vain?
> The kings of the earth set themselves,
> and the rulers take counsel together,
> against the Lord and his anointed, saying,
> "Let us burst their bonds asunder,
> and cast their cords from us."
> He who sits in the heavens laughs;
> the Lord has them in derision.
> Then he will speak to them in his wrath,
> and terrify them in his fury. (Ps 2:2-5)

In this lordly utterance, it is clear in v. 2 ("and his anointed") and in vv. 6-7 that YHWH's governance of the nations is in and through David and the Jerusalem monarchy. David is at the same time both an embodiment of Israelite privilege in the world and a concrete political means whereby YHWH rules in the earth. The twin themes of YHWH's governance and David's priority nicely join our topic of the nations to the claim of Israel, a claim that resists the notion that the nations are in fact a full partner of YHWH.

Violent Destruction of Nations

In this linkage of nations and Israel, there is a deep claim at the core of Israel's ideological self-understanding that YHWH intends to displace and destroy the "seven nations" in order to make room for Israel in "the land of promise."[9] Thus one aspect of "nations as partner" is a violent insistence that the nations do not count when YHWH gives gifts to Israel.[10] This way of thinking is found in the most militant assertions of Israel's preferentiality, found, not surprisingly, in the traditions of Deuteronomy:

> When the LORD your God brings you into the land that you are about to enter and occupy, and he clears away many nations before you—the Hittites, the Girgashites, the Amorites, the Canaanites, the Perizzites, the Hivites, and the Jebusites, seven nations mightier and more numerous than you— and when the LORD your God gives them over to you and you defeat them, then you must utterly destroy them. Make no covenant with them and show them no mercy. Do not intermarry with them, giving your daughters to their sons or taking their daughters for your sons, for that would turn away your children from following me, to serve other gods. (Deut 7:1-4a)

> When the LORD your God has cut off before you the nations whom you are about to enter to dispossess them, when you have dispossessed them and live in their land, take care that you are not snared into imitating them, after they have been destroyed before you; do not inquire concerning their gods, saying, "How did these nations worship their gods? I also want to do the same." (Deut 12:29-30; cf. 4:38; 7:22; 8:20; 11:23)

This is an exceedingly harsh presentation of the nations in the interest of Israel. We may term this presentation ideological, because it is likely that "the seven nations" are a theological construct without any historical base, and because in this case the sovereignty of YHWH is drawn most blatantly and directly into the service of Israel's political agenda. The "seven nations" are presented as rival claimants to the land, and so their destruction serves negatively to establish the legitimacy of Israel's claim to the land.[11]

This capacity and willingness to slot the seven nations under the rubric of extermination is linked to a larger agenda about the land; it places at the center of our topic an explicit endorsement of violence, which of necessity is finally situated in YHWH's own will and purpose. These nations are on the horizon of the narrative only because they are an impediment to Israel, an impediment of which YHWH will, so the testimony asserts, dispose. This extreme ingredient in our general topic comes to its most strident expression in the notion of *ḥerem,* the authorization to destroy the nations as "devotion" to YHWH, and in the odd, troubling fixation of the tradition on the Amalekites as the quintessential and paradigmatic enemy of Israel (cf. Exod 17:8-16; Deut 25:17-19; 1 Sam 15:18-21).[12]

Blessing to the Nations

This vigorous negation of "the seven nations" is found especially in the Moses-Joshua traditions and in the Deuteronomic materials that are aggressively exclusivistic (cf. Deut 23:2-8).[13] The remarkable countertheme to this harshness, still with Israel as the focus, is the program of the ancestral narrative of Genesis 12–36, wherein Israel is the one who blesses the cursed nations (cf. 12:3; 18:18; 22:18; 26:4; 28:13).[14] Hans Walter Wolff (and a host of scholars after him) has seen that the summons and mandate to Abraham (and Sarah) in Gen 12:1-3 is situated as the antidote to the sorry state of the nations in Genesis 3–11.[15] The nations are under curse (cf. 3:14-19; 4:11-12; 9:25), and now Israel is presented as the agent and instrument of YHWH in the world, to bring a blessing to the world of curse. This series of texts is as close as Israel comes to a theology of mission, whereby Israel has a vocation of transformation vis-à-vis the nations.[16]

The narrative of Genesis 12–36 (and by extension Genesis 37–50) still focuses on the special status of Israel. But here, in contrast to the Moses-Joshua-Deuteronomy traditions, the nations are prominently on the horizon, regarded as legitimate and treated positively. Thus the rejected brothers, Ishmael (25:9) and Esau (35:29), are allowed dignity and space within the narrative. While they compromise nothing of the specialness of Israel, the Genesis narratives stand outside the orbit of Mosaic ideology and contain nothing of aggressive exclusivism.[17] The vocation of transformation is still presented as a thoroughly Israelite reality, but now Israel's vocation is regularly in the presence of other peoples, and most often to their benefit—the nations characteristically profit from Israel's presence among them. In these narratives the linkage of Israel to the nations, unlike that of the traditions derivative from Moses, is positive, affirmative, and intentional.

Thus both of these traditions, ancestral and Mosaic-covenantal, treat the nations as incidental to the life and destiny of Israel and not for their own sake; but they do so very differently. These two clusters of texts set the outer limits of the nations vis-à-vis Israel: on the one hand as an *impediment* to be eliminated, according to YHWH's will; on the other hand to be *blessed* and enhanced, according to YHWH's mandate.

Nations Join in Praise and Obedience

Both of these traditions concerning ways in which Israel is to relate to the nations continue to be available in ongoing Israel, for either constructive ("blessing") or destructive ("blot out") use. Without for an instant minimizing the cruciality of the negative tradition of the legitimated destruction of the nations, there is also evidence that as Israel kept the nations on its horizon, Israel could imagine that the nations could share willingly in the service of YHWH, becoming a part of YHWH's community of praise and obedience. This account of the expansiveness of Israel's generosity toward non-Israelites shows it as a generosity rooted in its discernment of the expansiveness of YHWH. It must be recognized, however, that this emphasis on praise and obedience stays within the orbit and categories of Israel's own life with YHWH. There is an ideological, self-serving hint that the nations are permitted linkage to YHWH, but only on Israel's terms.

And yet, Israel's ideological self-service is not great in this emphasis, because without respect to Israel as such, praise and obedience are indeed the ways in which YHWH's sovereignty will be embraced by other peoples. In praise and obedience, the nations are to do what Israel does vis-à-vis YHWH. But they are to do it as themselves, and not as Israel nor as an adjunct to Israel.

The nations are summoned to praise YHWH in an act of lyrical self-abandonment, so that the sovereignty of YHWH is acknowledged and gladly accepted. In Ps 86:9-10 it is anticipated that the nations will join in praise of YHWH:

> All the nations you have made shall come
> and bow down before you, O LORD,
> and shall glorify your name.
> For you are great and do wondrous things;
> you alone are God.

This anticipation is in the context of an assertion of YHWH's incomparability, which all nations must recognize soon or late. The basis of that recognition is that

YHWH does "wondrous things" (*niphle'ot*) that will draw the nations, like Israel, to glad praise. In Psalm 117, the anticipation is transposed into a summons:

> Praise the LORD, all you nations!
> Extol him, all you peoples!
> For great is his steadfast love toward us,
> and the faithfulness of the LORD endures forever.
> Praise the LORD!

The nations are invited (and expected) to join Israel in praise. The ground for such praise is not unlike that of Ps 86:9-10, only now the "wondrous things" are made a bit more specific. They are actions marked by YHWH's most characteristic adjectives, "steadfast love and faithfulness." In making this summons to the nations, doxological Israel makes a bold connection. We may believe that YHWH's acts of "steadfast love and faithfulness" are characteristically and quintessentially taken as actions toward Israel. Their significance, however, reaches well beyond Israel.

In Israel's perception, however, these characteristic actions of YHWH are so compelling and so overwhelming that the nations will want to join Israel in praise, on the basis of actions done for Israel. This is made especially clear in Psalm 126, where the confession of the nations concerning YHWH (v. 2) is symmetrical to Israel's own confession of YHWH, but it is given *prior* to Israel's confession. The nations are drawn to what they see of YHWH in the life of Israel. We may allow that the actions of steadfast love and faithfulness done toward Israel are taken as paradigmatic of the same actions YHWH performs for the other nations, but that is not expressed in this summons. Indeed, if such an extrapolation is granted, then we are observing a move well beyond Israel's self-satisfied ideological claim.

In a third text of praise-by-the-nations, Psalm 67, our theme receives its fullest exposition.[18] Verse 1 contains phrasing quite parallel to the familiar blessing of Num 6:24-26, a conventional blessing pronounced over Israel. Verse 1, moreover, is dominated by the direct object "us," clearly indicating Israel. The verse invites rich blessings upon "us." But the blessings, graciousness, and presence of v. 1 are instrumental, serving only as an introduction to v. 2. The point of blessing to Israel is in order that YHWH's "way" and "saving power" (*ysh'*) will be known among the nations. Israel offers to be a case study, so that the nations may know of YHWH (v. 2) and may join in "thanks" (*ydh*, v. 3, rendered twice in NRSV as "praise"). In v. 4, the language is not unlike Psalm 96, concerning YHWH's governance of all the earth, and v. 5 reiterates v. 3. In vv. 6-7, yet another step is taken away from the specificity of Israel, now surely in the rhetoric of creation, blessing, and fruitfulness. Thus the psalm moves from Israel (v. 1), to the nations (vv. 2-5), to all creation (v. 6).

In v. 7 two readings are possible, depending on the identity of "us." If the "us" of v. 7 refers again to Israel as in v. 1, then the two lines of v. 7 again make the odd but crucial connection between Israel (line 1) and "all the ends of the earth" (line 2). It may be, however, that the "us" of v. 7 is not the same as in v. 1, but now has been expanded and redefined to refer to all of creation—"all the ends of the earth." Thus v. 7, the clue to the connections the doxology makes, either links "us" (Israel) to the praise of the earth, or it shows the "us" of Israel now completely moving beyond Israel to the larger sphere of YHWH's glad sovereignty. Either way, the psalm envisions a whole earth and all its peoples now gladly affirming YHWH's sovereignty and gratefully receiving from YHWH all the blessings of a rightly governed creation.

The obedience of the nations is not as clear as is the praise. We may, however, refer especially to Isa 2:2-5 (cf. Mic 4:1-4). In this anticipatory text, the unsolicited testimony of Israel envisions a time when all nations will come in procession to Jerusalem, there to be inducted into YHWH's way, to be judged by YHWH, and to make decisions that lead to peace. The text is a bold and daring act of imagination. On the one hand, the focus of the process is toward Jerusalem, the place of YHWH's residence. Of course the Jerusalem focus is never without some claim for the cruciality of Israel, and more specifically for the large claims of the Davidic house. To that extent, the vision is powerfully Israelite, and not without specific ideological intent.

On the other hand, it is important to note that in this oracle, nothing is made of the Davidic connection. The focus is on the Torah that is situated in Jerusalem, to which the nations come for instruction:

> Many peoples shall come and say,
> "Come, let us go up to the mountain of the LORD,
> to the house of the God of Jacob;
> that he may teach us his ways
> and that we may walk in his paths."
> For out of Zion shall go forth *instruction,*
> and the word of the LORD from Jerusalem. (Isa 2:3)

The verbs of v. 3 are *teach* (*yrh*) and *walk,* and the important nouns are *torah* (derived from the verb *yrh,* rendered as "instruction" in the NRSV), and *word of YHWH.* Jerusalem is the place where the concrete clues to well-being are given, which come as the requirements of YHWH for a viable life. The oracle operates on the claim that the nations, short of the Jerusalem Torah, do not have the knowledge about peace and justice that is necessary, and so must come here to receive necessary guidance.

Two matters are important in this vision. First, the nations come gladly, willingly, and expectantly. They are not coerced or compelled by the political force of the Davidic house, but have come in recognition that this is the only place where the way to peace and justice is available. Second, in the process of coming gladly, it is affirmed that the nations, like Israel, are subject to the Torah of YHWH. That is, the Torah is as pertinent to the nations as it is to Israel. This makes clear that the nations must deal with YHWH's sovereignty; it also makes clear that the Torah, while seated in Jerusalem, is no exclusive Israelite property. It belongs to the nations as much as to Israel.[19]

YHWH and the Superpowers

The nations, in their dealings with YHWH, are not always presented as having to deal with Israel at the same time. It is thinkable in Israel's testimony, though not often articulated, that YHWH's sovereignty extended *directly* to the nations, without mediating reference to Israel either as the vehicle of blessing to the nations or as the agent of destruction, or even as the locus of Torah. To be sure, these testimonies do not break completely out of Israelite categories, and one would not expect them to. There is, nonetheless, a marginal awareness in Israel's testimony that the relation of the nations to YHWH is, on occasion, direct and not dependent on or derivative from Israel's status and condition. This applies particularly to the oracles against the nations, a standard genre of prophetic speech that is present in most of the prophetic collections (cf. Isaiah 13–23; Jeremiah 46–51; Ezekiel 25–32; Amos 1–2; Zephaniah 2).[20]

Oracles against the Nations

These oracles occupy a distinct place in the prophetic literature and seem to be an enactment of the proclamation of Ps 96:10, that is, a way in which YHWH exercises kingship in the world. YHWH has "become king" over the nations and will exercise that sovereignty.[21]

To be sure, difficult historical questions are involved in these oracles, but theologically they are not difficult to situate in our exposition. Their assumption is that YHWH has created the nations (see the verb in Ps 86:9), has given them life, authorized them to be, and placed in their midst the possibility of life and blessing. This general assumption is everywhere the beginning point in these oracles. The oracle itself, however, characteristically takes the form of a judgment speech. In these oracles, the nations have violated the mandate and command of YHWH to which they are subject, and so they must be punished or even nullified. This characteristic presentation of the nations is an enterprise of enormous boldness and imagination. Klaus Koch uses the term *metahistory* for the claim made that YHWH can call the nations to accountability because there is in the historical process a reality that overrides historical realities.[22] Because of YHWH's massive, overriding sovereignty, these oracles assert that the nations are subject to a divine governance, a requirement, and an expectation, no matter how secure and self-sufficient they seem to be or think they are. This governance, moreover, cannot be overcome, disregarded, or evaded.

The governance of YHWH may be violated when YHWH is mocked by arrogance (Isa 37:17, 23) or when Israel is abused (Isa 47:6). What astonishes us and warrants our attention is that on occasion the affront against YHWH is not a direct mocking of YHWH or an abuse of Israel, but abuse of a third party that has nothing to do with Israel but, as it turns out, has everything to do with YHWH:[23]

> For three transgressions of the Ammonites,
> and for four, I will not revoke the punishment;
> because they ripped open pregnant women in Gilead
> in order to enlarge their territory. . . .
> For three transgressions of Moab,
> and for four, I will not revoke the punishment;
> because he burned to lime the bones of the king of Edom. (Amos 1:13; 2:1)

This rhetoric permits Israel to enunciate the claim that under the aegis of YHWH's sovereignty, there is a kind of international law or code of human standards that seems to anticipate the Helsinki Accords of 1975 in a rough way, a code that requires every nation to act in civility and humaneness toward others.[24] Any affront of this standard is taken to be an act of autonomy, arrogance, and self-sufficiency, which flies in the face of YHWH's governance.[25] YHWH is the guarantor, not only of Israel, but of the nations in their treatment of each other.

The sanctions these oracles express consist in punishment for the offending party at the hand of YHWH, most often termination. This theological claim is a remarkable one. Clearly Israel, in its intellectual milieu, did not attend to secondary causes. But we must not, in my judgment, imagine this to be a simpleminded supernaturalism.[26] The theology of these oracles is not simply an abstract defense of YHWH's sovereignty, nor is it merely an ideological protection of Israel. It is, along with a defense of YHWH and a protection of Israel, a notice that more is at work in international processes than brute power. There are limits to brute power, and the curb on such brutalizing, arrogant power is the indefatigable resolve of YHWH, which regularly defeats the greatest powers who thought they were situated for success to perpetuity. Israel had no way (and no desire) to speak about this limit on public-military power, except by reference to YHWH's sovereignty, which concerned uncompromising demand and irresistible sanction. The demand and the sanction serve, theologically, to enhance YHWH; they also serve as a non-negotiable line of defense against barbarism. Israel's testimony asserts that there is at work in the world a defense of human rights that is beyond the challenge or resistance of even the most powerful state. That is what it means to "judge the world in righteousness, equity, and truth" (cf. Pss 96:10, 13; 67:4; Isa 2:4).

The upshot of these oracles against the nations, organized around indictment (derived from command) and sanctions (which implement curse), is that the nations characteristically are under threat from YHWH because they refuse to be YHWH's obedient subjects and vassals.[27] For the most part, the oracles against the nations are simple lawsuits of indictment and sentence, beyond which there is no future for recalcitrant nations. This is the great preponderance of Israel's testimony.

While Israel's testimony has in purview the nations close at hand (as in the "seven" of Deuteronomy and those in Amos 1–2), great attention in the Old Testament is given to those nations that are the dominant superpowers: Egypt, Assyria, Babylon, and Persia.[28] Everything for Israel depends on the relation of these powers to YHWH, because Israel is almost always in the position of the client of one of the superpowers, and always in a position to be made a victim of aggressive, expansionist colonialism. For that reason we shall consider the destiny of each superpower on the horizon, in their sequence, according to the imaginative utterance of Israel.

Egypt: Abuser and Oppressor

Egypt is the first superpower Israel faces, one that endlessly occupies Israel's imagination, even as it endlessly occupied Israel's geopolitics. When the narrative of Israel's life begins, Egypt is already there, established, prosperous, enjoying a monopoly of food (Gen 12:10). Egypt is the place where Israel fled in famine and was fed (41:53 and the entire Joseph narrative), and Egypt is the land that receives the special blessing of father Jacob (47:7-10).

All of that is a backdrop that articulates the goodness and generosity of YHWH in making Egypt a place of fruitfulness and blessing but that is not the primary presentation of Egypt in Israel's unsolicited testimony. Egypt may be blessed by YHWH, but it is characteristically a place of abuse and oppression. In the end, in Israel's rhetoric of demonization, Egypt is the very embodiment of primordial evil (cf. Ps 87:4), which brings death and destruction in its wake (Exod 1:22). Egypt embodies the antithesis of YHWH's good intention for Israel and the terminal point of YHWH's attentive care for Israel.[29]

As a consequence of its role as abuser and oppressor, Egypt stands completely under the lawsuit speech of Israel, which is characteristic of the prophetic oracles against the nations. The indictment of Egypt is of course that Egypt abused Israel, but much more than that, Egypt is the recalcitrant vassal of YHWH who refuses to obey YHWH and who thereby disrupts YHWH's good creation.[30] Thus Terence Fretheim can write, "Pharaoh's anti-life measures against God's creation have unleashed chaotic powers that threaten the very creation that God intended."[31] Egypt under Pharaoh is the great disrupter of creation, whose actions evoke a punishing chaos from which all suffer.[32]

The lawsuit against Egypt, a paradigmatic complaint against a paradigmatic enemy, is given in two prominent places. In the narrative of Exodus 1–15, pharaoh refuses to obey YHWH's command, "Let my people go" (*shlh*) so that Pharaoh is visited by punishment culminating in broad-scale death (Exod 12:29-32). The second, most extensive articulation of the lawsuit against Egypt, a recalcitrant vassal of YHWH, is in Ezekiel 29–32. This indictment of Egypt is staggering, both in its sheer quantity and in its hyperbolic fierceness. This is the enemy par excellence, on whom YHWH (Israel) heaps scorn and rage. The pivotal indictment that warrants such venom is not primarily concerned with Israel, but consists in defiance of YHWH:

> I am against you,
> Pharaoh king of Egypt,
> the great dragon sprawling
> in the midst of its channels,
> saying, "My Nile is my own;
> I made it for myself." (Ezek 29:3)

It is YHWH who gave Egypt life by providing the Nile. But in the recalcitrant imagination attributed to Pharaoh, the gift of YHWH is converted into a royal property. It is, moreover, this inversion, this fundamental rejection of the truth of YHWH, that gives Pharaoh occasion to transform the gift of the Nile into a canal of death (Exod 1:22; 7:14-25; cf. Isa 19:5-10). That is the whole of the matter . . . except that in Ezek 32:31-32, at the end of the most enormous lawsuit speech against Egypt, a curious note is added. The conventional rendering of the key term is "be consoled" (*nḥm*): "When Pharaoh sees them, he will be consoled (*nḥm*) for all his hordes—Pharaoh and all his army killed by the sword, says the Lord God. For he spread terror in the land of the living; therefore he shall be laid to rest among the uncircumcised, with those who are slain by the sword—Pharaoh and all his multitude, says the Lord God."

On this reading, it is anticipated that when Pharaoh sees the death of many other enemies, he will be consoled. The calculus of such a response is problematic. Recently, however, Ellen Davis has offered a different reading of the verb: that "Pharaoh will repent" of all the devastation he has wrought.[33] On this reading (as of now a minority one), Pharaoh will at long last, at the eleventh hour, repent and become a willing vassal of YHWH. If this reading can be accepted (and I find it persuasive), the brutal, sad tale of Egypt unexpectedly portrays even Egypt coming, at the last moment, out of the fissure of devastating punishment to new life with YHWH. Such a reading is a resilient insistence in Israel that YHWH's will cannot finally be thwarted. In any case, Egypt is a cipher for massive resistance to YHWH, one of two such ciphers in the Old Testament, Babylon being the other.[34] (The final end of Egypt is here held in abeyance; we will return to Isa 19:23-25.)

Assyria: Arrogance and Autonomy

The second, utterly recalcitrant international power, a suitable twin for Egypt (cf. Hos 7:11), is Assyria.[35] Assyria occupies much of Israel's political attention and theological imagination in the monarchal period. While Assyria is politically and experientially as important as Egypt, it does not receive as full a theological exposition in the rhetoric of Israel as does Egypt. Nonetheless it occupies a parallel position, and what is said of Egypt readily applies as well to Assyria. Assyria stands under the same lawsuit of YHWH as does Egypt, and for the same reasons.

We may focus our attention on three texts concerning Assyria. Isaiah 10:5-19 provides a complete "philosophy of history" concerning Assyria and all such superpowers. The indictment and sentence of Assyria take place in a sequence of two conventional parts. First, Assyria is a usable instrument of YHWH in international politics:

> Ah, Assyria, the rod of my anger—
> the club in their hands is my fury! . . .
> Shall the ax vaunt itself over the one who wields it,
> or the saw magnify itself against the one who handles it? (Isa 10:5, 15)

YHWH is willing and able to use such a tool, and Assyria, we are led to believe, willingly accepts its role as an obedient vassal in the service of YHWH. Assyria conforms to YHWH's intention to "take spoil and seize plunder" against "a godless nation," Israel (Isa 10:6). This Assyria does willingly. We may set aside the issue of whether this is genuine obedience or simply a convenient warrant for brutal acquisitiveness. Such a distinction does not delay the poet.

Second, Assyria, in arrogant boasting and haughty pride (v. 12), oversteps the mandate of YHWH, begins to act autonomously (v. 13), and sets out to destroy this "godless nation" (v. 6). This is clearly an act of disobedience against YHWH, for YHWH does not intend the destruction of Israel, even when angry with Israel. The indictment of Assyria thus concerns its autonomy, which is not congruent with YHWH's intent.

What astonishes us is that Assyria is indicted for not limiting its destructiveness, as though Assyria is supposed to know YHWH's intention of limited assault against Judah without being told. Assyria should have known that YHWH's anger toward Israel is not unlimited and endless! This great, ruthless empire, preoccupied with its own designs, should have curbed its military capacity in recognition of YHWH's core commitment to Israel, a commitment around which ancient Near Eastern politics are said to revolve.

And so this recalcitrant vassal, who violated its mandate from YHWH, is subject to massive, destructive punishment, according to the will of YHWH:

> The glory of his forest and his fruitful land
> the Lord will destroy, both soul and body,
> and it will be as when an invalid wastes away.
> The remnant of the trees of his forest will be so few
> that a child can write them down. (Isa 10:18-19)

Assyria will be terminated; no power can stand against YHWH's will.

The second text that works the same themes with reference to Assyria is Isaiah 36–37 (2 Kings 18–19).[36] The rhetorical pattern here is somewhat more dramatic than in Isaiah 10, but the issues are much the same. In this encounter, now situated later in the life of Judah when Hezekiah, the obedient king, governs Jerusalem, Assyria is not said to be on a mission from YHWH (as in chapter 10) but is simply enacting its own territorial expansionism. Assyria here is not at all doing YHWH's will, even though the voice of Assyria in this text speaks in theological accents. Indeed, Assyria here is seen to be directly opposing the intentions of YHWH. Because the threat to Judah is cast in theological categories, the affront of Assyria is all the greater. Assyria, in its arrogance, both claims a mandate from YHWH (36:10, perhaps referring back to chapter 10) and completely misunderstands YHWH by refusing to recognize YHWH's incomparability, comparing YHWH to other, impotent gods (36:18-20). In this text, the great affront of Assyria is that it mocks YHWH: it refuses to take YHWH seriously, to acknowledge YHWH's incomparability, and to accept YHWH's sovereignty.

The judgment on Assyria, in this text, is pronounced by the prophet in 37:26-29. The rhetoric is structured as a lawsuit:

- Indictment:

   Because you have raged against me
   and your arrogance has come to my ears,

- Sentence:

   I will put my hook in your nose
   and my bit in your mouth;
   I will turn you back on the way
   by which you came. (37:29)

The great empire has been able to have military success, only by the decree of YHWH:

   Have you not heard
   that I determined it long ago?
   I planned from days of old
   what now I bring to pass,
   that you should make fortified cities
   crash into heaps of ruins,
   while their inhabitants, shorn of strength,
   are dismayed and confounded;
   they have become like plants of the field
   and like tender grass,

like grass on the housetops,
blighted before it is grown. (37:26-27)

This assertion parallels the mandate of 10:5 but makes it more extensive. Arrogance and autonomy bring to a failed end what might have been a YHWH-ordered success. There are limits to brutality and self-aggrandizement. Thus again, as in 10:5-19, Assyria is mandated, violates the mandate, and is severely and irreversibly punished.

The third text concerning Assyria, which need only be mentioned here, is the poem of Nahum against the capital city of Nineveh. Not much attention is given in the poem to an indictment of Nineveh, though the poet can voice the warrant for the destruction now celebrated:

From you one has gone out
who plots evil against the LORD,
who counsels wickedness. . . .
Because of the countless debaucheries of the prostitute,
gracefully alluring, mistress of sorcery,
who enslaves nations through her debaucheries,
and peoples through her sorcery. (Nah 1:11; 3:4)

Mostly, however, the poem of Nahum is unrestrained rage that anticipates the destruction of Nineveh at the hand of YHWH. While the substance of this poem is profoundly emotional, with severe hatred as its substance, the poem is kept within the orbit of YHWH. The Israelites profoundly resent Assyria and Nineveh. Their testimony makes the claim that their deep antipathy toward Nineveh is rooted in YHWH's own profound antipathy toward the Assyrians (on which see Ps 139:21). The rage of Israel at barbarism is the rage of an oppressed people, too long exploited.

The rhetoric, however, claims more than simple rage. It claims that emotive aversion to brutality is located in the heart of YHWH, so that political abuse becomes, in the end, theological reality. I write this during the celebration of the fiftieth anniversary of V-E day, with its accompanying ecclesial discussion of whether to pray for the forgiveness of Adolf Hitler. Assyria is like Hitler for Judah, perhaps eventually to be prayed for in Israel, but not soon, not yet in the poem of Nahum. Thus Assyrian imperialism is contained Yahwistically in the categories of mandate-violation and mandate-sanctions. The empire cannot outflank YHWH, who wills compassion in the political process.

Assyria, in the Old Testament, comes to a condemned, hopeless end . . . except for Isa 19:23-25, to which we shall return. Perhaps we may find an adumbration of the oracle of Isa 19:23-25 in the narrative of Jonah. To be sure, this narrative does not concern itself with Assyria, but this is precisely the sort of unsolicited testimony that helps us most to understand YHWH's partners. According to this narrative, Assyria (Nineveh) does repent, does submit to YHWH, and so is the recipient of YHWH's steadfast love (Jonah 3:5-10). The ground for steadfast love—even for Nineveh—is found in a quotation of the primal assertion of Exod 34:6-7a. The story line of Jonah indicates that such an outcome for the hated and feared empire is contrary to the wish-world of Israelite ideology. Where YHWH is not simply reduced to an agent of that ideology, such an outcome is possible.

Babylon and Nebuchadnezzar

The third superpower with which Israel had to deal is Babylon, regularly linked to the person of Nebuchadnezzar. The contours of the relationship between YHWH and Babylon are the ones by now familiar to us: mandate, defiant autonomy, punishment.

The positive mandate given Babylon by YHWH, on the horizon of Israel's testimony, is especially championed by the tradition of Jeremiah, refracted through the convictions of Deuteronomic circles.[37] Because those circles of political interpreters are ready to comply with Babylonian policy, it does not surprise us that the tradition of Jeremiah understands Babylon (and Nebuchadnezzar), in their onslaught against Jerusalem, to be doing YHWH's bidding (as did Assyria in Isa 10:5). Thus YHWH, in this testimony, refers to Nebuchadnezzar as "my servant" (Jer 25:9; 27:6). Nebuchadnezzar, moreover, is expected to show mercy toward Judah congruent with YHWH's own propensity:[38] "Do not be afraid to serve the Chaldeans. Stay in the land and serve the king of Babylon, and it shall go well with you. . . . Do not be afraid of the king of Babylon, as you have been; do not be afraid of him, says the Lord, for I am with you, to save you and to rescue you from his hand. I will grant you mercy, and he will have mercy on you and restore you to your native soil" (Jer 40:9; 42:11-12). As a tool of YHWH's measured punishment of Judah, Nebuchadnezzar's role against Judah, it is anticipated, will also be measured and limited. Thus YHWH and Nebuchadnezzar are allied, with an agreed-upon policy that is severe but not without limit and restraint.

The actual working out of Babylonian policy, however, reflects no such restraint, no mercy congruent with the intended mercy of YHWH (see Jer 6:22-23).

Predictably the erstwhile ally of YHWH is indicted by YHWH as a recalcitrant
vassal and an arrogant violator of YHWH's sovereign intention for Judah, as for
Babylon. Thus the book of Jeremiah, so long supportive of Babylonian policy as
reflective of YHWH's intention, culminates in a savage, extended oracle against
Babylon (chapters 50–51).[39] There is, in Judah, gleeful anticipation of Babylon's
fall:

> Declare among the nations and proclaim,
> set up a banner and proclaim,
> do not conceal it, say:
> Babylon is taken,
> Bel is put to shame,
> Merodach is dismayed.
> Her images are put to shame,
> her idols are dismayed. (50:2)

Moreover, the nation from the north (50:3) that will take Babylon will be cruel
and will show "no mercy" (50:42), just as Babylon had shown no mercy on Judah
(6:23). Superpowers like Babylon have a Yahwistic warrant in geopolitics, according to this witness, but a Yahwistic restraint applies to them, beyond which they
cannot go in brutalizing autonomy.

Thus after the mandate of YHWH to Nebuchadnezzar, the recurrent theme
in Israel's testimony concerning Babylon is indictment and sentence: the destruction of the superpower as the implementation of YHWH's sovereign will for world
history. Two texts from the tradition of Isaiah bear on this theme. In Isaiah 13–14,
Babylon is invested with primordial, Promethean power and significance, in which
Babylon stands as a bold, mythic alternative and contrast to YHWH. The ambition of autonomous Babylon is transparent:

> You said in your heart,
> "I will ascend to heaven;
> I will raise my throne
> above the stars of God;
> I will sit on the mount of assembly
> on the heights of Zaphon;
> I will ascend to the tops of the clouds,
> I will make myself like the Most High." (Isa 14:13-14)

But the one who anticipates "ascending to heaven" will in fact be brought low:

> But you are brought down to Sheol,
> to the depths of the Pit. (v. 15)

Such pretensions to power and ambition are workable in a world of raw power and unashamed might. The testimony of Israel, however, counters such a representation of reality with an insistence that raw power and unashamed might are never unchecked, but are always and everywhere subject to the will and restraint of YHWH. Because of YHWH's metahistory, the mighty must surely fall.

The tradition of Isaiah had already waxed eloquent about the exalted being humbled, the high being made low. The initial poetry on the theme concerns Israel:

> The haughtiness of people shall be humbled,
> and the pride of everyone shall be brought low;
> and the LORD alone will be exalted on that day. (Isa 2:17)

Now, however, the issues concern the superpower Babylon. YHWH will cause a reversal with the superpower, as YHWH has caused it with beloved Israel. In the tradition of Isaiah, Babylon is the quintessential embodiment of pride and autonomy that must surely fail.

This sequence of YHWH's action toward Babylon (which parallels Isa 10:5-19 concerning Assyria) is succinctly expressed in 47:6-7, 9, 11:

- Mandate from YHWH:

  > I was angry with my people,
  > I profaned my heritage;
  > I gave them into your hand, . . .

- Failure of the mandate and consequent indictment:

  > . . . you showed them no mercy;
  > on the aged you made your yoke exceedingly heavy.
  > You said, "I shall be mistress forever,"
  > so that you did not lay these things to heart
  > or remember their end.

- Sentence:

  > . . . both these things shall come upon you
  > in a moment, in one day;
  > the loss of children and widowhood

shall come upon you in full measure,

in spite of your many sorceries

and the great power of your enchantments. . .

But evil shall come upon you,

which you cannot charm away;

disaster shall fall upon you,

which you will not be able to ward off,

and ruin shall come on you suddenly,

of which you know nothing.

As in 10:6 with Assyria, Babylon did not stay within its mandate from YHWH. Babylon failed to show the mercy required (cf. Jer 40:9; 42:11-12). As a consequence, Babylon, a power willed to proximate power by YHWH, forfeits power by overstepping Yahwistic restraint. The pivotal notion is "mercy." Of course, no mention of showing mercy had been made to Babylon (as no mention had been made to Assyria in Isaiah 10). Indeed, this invading people is initially summoned for "no mercy" (Jer 6:23). But, according to Israel's testimony, Nebuchadnezzar should have known. He was, after all, dealing with YHWH and with YHWH's beloved people. YHWH was angry (*qsph*) to be sure, but anger is not YHWH's final intention. Nebuchadnezzar was not told; but he should have known. For not knowing, the "glory and grandeur" that was Babylon must end.

That much is conventional in Israel's testimony about this third superpower; but the testimony of Israel cannot finish so simply with Babylon, as it tended to do with Egypt and Assyria. In the book of Daniel, oddly enough, Nebuchadnezzar resurfaces, now surely as a dehistoricized cipher for world power in general and for the abusive belated Hellenistic rulers in particular. What is odd about this articulation of Nebuchadnezzar is that YHWH's relation to Nebuchadnezzar, as given here, is not flat and predictable, but remarkably nuanced and differentiated.

We may pay particular attention to two extended narratives. First, in Daniel 3, Israel bears testimony that the king who was nullified for his autonomy is transformed into a worshiper of YHWH. This narrative does not move through the conventional sequence of mandate–indictment–judgment; the narrative shows the rehabilitation of the king, from one crazed with self-importance into an acceptable, willing subject of YHWH. The story moves in three clear dramatic scenes:

1. At the outset, Nebuchadnezzar is a shameless, autonomous ruler: "You are commanded, O peoples, nations, and languages, that when you hear the sound of the horn, pipe, lyre, trigon, harp, drum, and entire musical ensemble, you are to fall down and worship the golden statue that King Nebuchadnezzar has set up.

Whoever does not fall down and worship shall immediately be thrown into a furnace of blazing fire" (Dan 3:4-6).

2. Nebuchadnezzar must deal with the three representative Jews, Shadrach, Meshach, and Abednego, and is foiled by them as a result of their intense faith (vv. 8-27).

3. Out of that bewildering encounter, Nebuchadnezzar is converted, and issues as a decree a doxology to their God:

> Blessed be the God of Shadrach, Meshach, and Abednego, who has sent his angel and delivered his servants who trusted in him. They disobeyed the king's command and yielded up their bodies rather than serve and worship any god except their own God. Therefore I make a decree: Any people, nation, or language that utters blasphemy against the God of Shadrach, Meshach, and Abednego shall be torn limb from limb, and their houses laid in ruins; for there is no other god who is able to deliver in this way. (vv. 28-29)

The importance and the astonishing character of this narrative is that it breaks the simple pattern of divine judgment against the nation, and allows for the reconstitution of a superpower obedient to the God of Israel. According to this testimony, YHWH is not, in principle, opposed to superpowers, but only to those that disregard the mandate of heaven and arrogate to themselves ultimate power and authority. It is deeply ironic that for this remarkable assertion of YHWH's relation to worldly power, the testimony of Israel focuses on Nebuchadnezzar, the one who presided over the pivotal dismantling of Israel.

In Daniel 4, the same sequence of transactions between YHWH and Nebuchadnezzar is narrated, this time with richer rhetorical flourish.[40] At the outset, Nebuchadnezzar sings praise to the Most High God:

> How great are his signs,
> how mighty his wonders!
> His kingdom is an everlasting kingdom,
> and his sovereignty is from generation to generation. (v. 3)

The subsequent narrative tells how this extraordinary doxological commitment has come to be on the lips of the Babylonian king. The narrative is a complicated one, featuring a dream and its interpretation (vv. 4-27), and then the implementation of the dream (vv. 28-37). The story line is, as we have seen in chapter 3:

1. Nebuchadnezzar is sure in his self-congratulations (4:29-31).
2. Nebuchadnezzar is profoundly debilitated, as the dream had anticipated (vv. 31-33).
3. His reason returns (v. 34a), issuing in doxology to "the Most High," and in the restoration and enhancement of his rule (vv. 34b-37).

The story of Nebuchadnezzar is no longer one of mandate–disobedience–punishment; now it is autonomy–demise–restoration.

In this narrative of the humiliation and exaltation of Nebuchadnezzar, we may notice two decisive utterances by Daniel who in this narrative enacts the claims of Israel's faith. First, Daniel repeatedly affirms that: "the Most High is sovereign over the kingdom of mortals; he gives it to whom he will and sets over it the lowliest of human beings" (4:17; cf. vv. 25, 32). YHWH, not Nebuchadnezzar, is sovereign and is the one who establishes proximate sovereignty in the earth. All worldly power is provisional, derivative, and penultimate, and may be given and taken away by the authority of YHWH. Indeed, YHWH is completely free in actions concerning world power, and need conform to no worldly expectation:

All the inhabitants of the earth are accounted as nothing,
and he does what he wills with the host of heaven
and the inhabitants of the earth.
There is no one who can stay his hand
or say to him, "What are you doing?" (v. 35)

The Israelite answer to this rhetorical question, from beginning to end, is:

. . . no one . . . can stay his hand
or say to him, "What are you doing?"

Second, Daniel urges the king, still in his crazed autonomy, to practice "mercy to the oppressed" (v. 27). This is the mercy that Jeremiah (40:9; 42:10-12) anticipated from Babylon, and that in Isa 47:6 is noticed as absent from Babylonian policy. It is characteristically Jewish to assert that world power is entrusted with mercy, even as YHWH's own governance is endlessly rearticulated in mercy. This counsel of Daniel is, at the end, reiterated in Nebuchadnezzar's own mouth:

Now I, Nebuchadnezzar, praise and extol and honor
the King of heaven;
for all his works are truth,
and all his ways are justice;

and he is able to bring low
those who walk in pride. (v. 37)

Nebuchadnezzar has caught on! The one who rules the nations rules in truth and in justice (cf. Ps 96:10, 13), and even the model superpower now accepts this inescapable reality. The rehabilitation of Nebuchadnezzar, in this astonishing redefinition of world power, is fully authorized by YHWH, when the king of Babylon conforms to the reality of YHWH's own nonnegotiable intention.

Persia: Positive, Responsive Partner

The fourth and final superpower with whom Israel had to deal is Persia. Persian policy and influence were profound on the shaping of Judaism. Our knowledge of this relationship is only now being seriously addressed as a major issue in Old Testament interpretation.[41] It is clear, moreover, that the rhetoric and imagination of the Old Testament are not evoked by Persia in the way that the previous superpowers had done. Thus, even though the Persian Empire is crucial for the shaping of Judaism, it does not figure so largely in matters that concern theological interpretation.

We may therefore confine ourselves to two sorts of statements concerning YHWH's relation to Persia. First, as with Assyria (Isa 10:5) and Babylon (Jer 25:6; 27:6), Persia is understood in Israelite testimony to be a world power designated by YHWH to overthrow its predecessor, in this case Babylon, and thereby to permit a Jewish homecoming from exile. In Jer 51:41-42, "a people coming from the north" surely is Persia, who is to be "cruel and without mercy" toward Babylon. Persia now is assigned the role, in Yahwistic purview, previously assigned to Babylon. The accent in Israel's testimony, however, is not on Persian treatment of Babylon, but on the role to be played by Persia as the rescuer of Israel.

The two central and most remarkable texts are in Isaiah of the exile:

Thus says the LORD, your Redeemer,
who formed you in the womb:
I am the LORD, who made all things,
who alone stretched out the heavens,
who by myself spread out the earth;
who frustrates the omens of liars,
and makes fools of diviners;
who turns back the wise,
and makes their knowledge foolish;
who confirms the word of his servant,

and fulfills the prediction of his messengers;
who says of Jerusalem, "It shall be inhabited,"
and of the cities of Judah, "They shall be rebuilt,
and I will raise up their ruins";
who says to the deep, "Be dry—
I will dry up your rivers";
who says of *Cyrus*, "He is my shepherd,
and he shall carry out all my purpose";
and who says of Jerusalem, "It shall be rebuilt,"
and of the temple, "Your foundation shall be laid." (Isa 44:24-28)

Thus says the LORD to his anointed, to *Cyrus*,
whose right hand I have grasped
to subdue nations before him
and strip kings of their robes,
to open doors before him—
and the gates shall not be closed:
I will go before you
and level the mountains,
I will break in pieces the doors of bronze
and cut through the bars of iron,
I will give you the treasures of darkness
and riches hidden in secret places,
so that you may know that it is, I, the LORD,
the God of Israel, who calls you by your name.
For the sake of my servant Jacob,
and Israel my chosen,
I call you by your name,
I surname you, though you do not know me.
I am the LORD, and there is no other;
beside me there is no god.
I arm you, though you do not know me,
so that they may know, from the rising of the sun
and from the west, that there is no one besides me;
I am the LORD, and there is no other.
I form light and create darkness,
I make weal and create woe;
I the LORD do all these things. (Isa 45:1-7)

It is necessary to consider these more extended texts because of the references to Cyrus, the first and for Israel the most decisive of the Persian kings and the one who destroyed the kingdom of Babylon. In the first of these texts, YHWH's dictum authorizing Cyrus (44:28) occurs in a sequence of sovereign utterances of YHWH that concern, most broadly, creation and, most explicitly, the rebuilding of Jerusalem. That is, the rebuilding of Jerusalem is rhetorically on a par with creation. Cyrus, moreover, is "my shepherd" (v. 28), a term regularly reserved in Israel for Davidic kings. Thus Cyrus is positioned in terms of Israel's creation theology and in line with royal theology.

The second oracle is more astonishing on two counts. First, Cyrus is "his messiah" (45:1; the Hebrew word can be rendered "anointed").[42] The rhetoric reassigns a Davidic title to Cyrus, who now becomes the carrier of Israel's most urgent hopes. Israel's theological horizon now reaches well beyond itself, into the Gentile world, in order to identify the continuing working of YHWH's saving intention. Second, this oracle is directly addressed to Cyrus by YHWH, "though you do not know me" (v. 4), "so that you may know . . ." (v. 3). The address to Cyrus may be fictive and strategic for Israel's hope in exile. Nonetheless, YHWH is willing, according to this rhetoric, to engage this foreign ruler, as with the Assyrians and Babylonians before him, to do a work that enhances Israel.

Israel employs remarkable theological rhetoric in order to define Persia (and Cyrus) as YHWH's agent in the world of international power. As we have it in the testimony, Persia effectively implements the restorative policies of YHWH. It is true, at least to some extent, that Persian imperial policy was more respectful of local traditions (including local Jewish traditions) than were the Assyrians or Babylonians.[43] It is beyond doubt, moreover, that this articulation of Persia is done through the testimony of those Jews most sympathetic to and most dependent upon Persian beneficence. In any case, this testimony portrays Persia as a patron of a recovering Jewish cult in Jerusalem, as is evident in the testimony given by Haggai and Zechariah and in the reform movement of Ezra and Nehemiah, financed by Persia (cf. Ezra 1:2-4; 6:3-5; 2 Chr 36:23).

The political-theological claim made for the Persians is telling: "So the elders of the Jews built and prospered, through the prophesying of the prophet Haggai and Zechariah son of Iddo. They finished building by command of the God of Israel and by decree of Cyrus, Darius, and King Artaxerxes of Persia" (Ezra 6:14). The cruciality of Persian support for the reconstructive work of Yahwism is indicated by the fact that in much of this literature, time is reckoned by Persian royal chronology, a concession not granted by Israel to any other superpower.

We may finally mention that Dan 6:1-28 presents testimony in which (a) Daniel is protected by God, and (b) the Persians are deferential to Daniel and to the God of Daniel. In the end, Darius issues a doxological decree:

> For he is the living God,
> enduring forever.
> His kingdom shall never be destroyed,
> and his dominion has no end.
> He delivers and rescues,
> he works signs and wonders in heaven and on earth;
> for he has saved Daniel
> from the power of the lions. (Dan 6:26-27)

Darius the Persian is able to enter fully into praise of the God of Israel. Compared to the complicated and vexed story of YHWH with the Egyptians, the Assyrians, and the Babylonians, the story of YHWH with the Persians lacks disjunctive drama. On the horizon of this testimony, the Persians are not recalcitrant vassals of YHWH, need not be broken by YHWH, and so need no Yahwistic recovery. In this modeling of nations as partners, Persia is the exemplar of a positive, responsive partner.[44]

The Possibility of Legitimate Power in the World of YHWH

We are now in a position to summarize and schematize the data concerning YHWH's relationship to these four superpowers. Our attempt to do this, of course, depends on piecing together bits of testimony that do not easily or intentionally form a pattern. Without suggesting that the articulation of these several partnerships is everywhere the same, we may roughly suggest the tendency in Israel's testimony as shown in the chart on the following page. Even if things are not perfectly symmetrical, this presentation of YHWH and YHWH's partners constitutes a remarkable sketch. We may make the following observations on these data.

YHWH's mandate. YHWH intends that there should be world powers, and that these world powers should indeed govern, but govern within the bounds of YHWH's mandate. The mandate variously consists in special consideration for Israel and occasionally the more generic practice of human civility. Thus Egyptian prosperity is verified by Jacob's blessing (Gen 47:7-10), Assyria is mandated to be a devastating power (Isa 10:5-6; 37:26-27), Babylon is given a mandate by YHWH (Jer 25:9; 27:6; Isa 47:6a) and is crowned with well-being (Dan 4:19-22). Persia is given a mandate unlike that of Assyria and Babylon, for now the purpose of the mandate from YHWH is the rehabilitation of Jerusalem. The Old Testament witness is explicit in voicing YHWH's powerful, positive interest in the public process.

Temptation to absolutize power. The seduction to autonomy, which is assigned in this testimony to the first three of these superpowers, is the temptation to absolutize power that appears to be absolute but is not. Clearly such absolutizing is impossible in a world where YHWH's sovereignty is said to be beyond challenge. The reality of YHWH, in Israel's interpretive horizon, keeps all imperial pretensions penultimate.

Taxonomy of YHWH's Relationship to Four Superpowers

	Mandate	*Autonomous Rebellion*	*Dismantling*	*Rehabilitation*
Egypt	Gen 47:7-10 (all of Exodus 5–15)	Exod 5:2	Exod 15:4-10 Isa 19:23-25[45]	Ezek 32:31?
		Ezek 29:3 (all of Ezekiel 29–32)		
Assyria	Isa 10:5-6 Isa 37:26-27	Isa 10:7-14 Isa 37:29a	Isa 10:15-19 Isa 37:29b	Isa 19:23-25
				Jonah
Babylon	Jer 25:9; 27:6 Isa 47:6a	Isa 47:6b-8	Isa 47:9, 11	
		Isa 14:13-14	Isa 14:15	
	Dan 4:19-22	Dan 3:4-6 4:29-30	Dan 3:23-27, 31-33	Dan 4:34-37
Persia	Isa 44:24-28 45:1-7			

Decisive break in power. In the case of the first three superpowers, we have considered, there is a decisive break in their power. In world history, great kingdoms rise and fall. It is noteworthy in this testimony, and not everywhere self-evident, that no explanation for the fall of great powers is credited except the governance of YHWH. YHWH's sovereignty is partly raw, unchallengeable authority, partly devotion to Israel, and partly intolerance of arrogant injustice. It is important for our purposes to recognize that this fissure in the life of a great power is parallel to the fissure of exile in the life of Israel. Where YHWH is not obeyed, a decisive break occurs in every individual life and in the life of every community or state. No power can live defiantly in the face of YHWH's sovereignty.

Hope for recovery. The notion of the recovery of lost power is characteristically an act of hope, not yet accomplished yet in reportable history. This act of hope, in the largest horizon of world history, is closely parallel to the hope of Israel that is mostly detained and not yet actualized. The hope for Egypt, based on an available reading of Ezek 32:31, is modest indeed, pending one text to which we have yet to come. The hope for Assyria, pending the same text, has broken beyond concrete history and lives in the world of Israel's imaginative rhetoric. The tale of Jonah probably has an agenda quite other than the destiny of Assyria (Nineveh) and is most often interpreted with other accents. That tale does suggest, nonetheless, that even hated Nineveh (Assyria), upon repentance (see Ezek 32:31 on Egypt), is a possible focus of YHWH's steadfast love. The references to Babylon in the book of Daniel are especially important on this score, and suggest that Nebuchadnezzar has sanity restored, and his governance as well, when he learns that "the Most High is sovereign over the kingdom of mortals, and gives it to whom he will" (Dan 4:34). This is a hard lesson for the powerful; but it must be learned, according to the witness of Israel. This tale of Nebuchadnezzar, moreover, provides a positive case in that the lesson is indeed learned, to the great advantage of the superpower. Worldly power finally need not be defiant of YHWH.

Parallels to YHWH's relation to humans. The pattern of blessing–breakpoint–restoration is quite like the sequence of ways in which YHWH relates to *Israel,* and mutatis mutandis, the ways in which YHWH relates to *human persons.*

Two Texts of Radical Hope

We come to two remarkable texts that I have deferred until now. Both concern YHWH's intention for the nations as it is given us in Israel's testimony. These texts in turn enunciate hope for Israel's "little neighbors," and then for the great superpowers.

Our first text of radical hope for the nations is in Amos 9:7:

Are you not like the Ethiopians to me,
O people of Israel? says the LORD.
Did I not bring Israel up from the land of Egypt,
and the Philistines from Caphtor
and the Arameans from Kir?[46]

This odd verse, not closely linked to its immediate context, is apparently uttered in
a context of Israel's celebrative self-preoccupation. It is addressed to an Israel that
is utterly convinced of its own peculiar role as YHWH's exclusive partner and as
the peculiar object of YHWH's transformative verbs.

The utterance of this verse in the Amos collection does nothing to undermine
or question the positive claim that YHWH is a God who saves, rescues, and liberates. What is challenged is Israel's attempt to monopolize this claim, to imagine
that as YHWH is the only subject of the transformative verbs, so Israel is the only
possible object of YHWH's transformative action. The exodus of Israel is fully
affirmed: "Did I not bring Israel up from the land of Egypt?" The clear answer
is, "Yes!"

The stunning departure from self-congratulation is that this testimony makes
the same affirmation of YHWH available for other peoples, including Israel's most
serious enemies, the Philistines and the Arameans. Indeed, if the Ethiopians are
understood as blacks, and so referenced by race, racist bias is here rejected as well
as ethnocentrism. What happens in this striking assertion is that *Israel's monopoly
on YHWH is broken*. This does not deny that Israel is the primal recipient of
YHWH's powerful, positive intervention; it does, however, deny any exclusive
claim or any notion that Israel is the singular center of YHWH's attention. That
surely is the force and intention of this utterance.

We may also notice two other claims, perhaps not so intentional, but present nonetheless. First, it is asserted that Israel's closest neighbors, most despised
and most feared, are the objects of YHWH's transformative attentiveness. The
way in which Israel is treated by YHWH in the exodus is the way in which every
people may expect to be treated by YHWH. Second, it is asserted that YHWH is
characteristically and everywhere the subject of the verb "bring up" (*'lh*). Because
this exodus God avowedly performs rescues indiscriminately, even among Israel's
enemies, all of world history is reconfigured as an arena for YHWH's great, positive, transformative actions.

Our second concluding text concerns the superpowers. Isaiah 19:23-25 is
commonly regarded as late in Israel's imagination, and it surely lives at the edge
of Israel's horizon concerning the nations. Nonetheless, it is a piece of Israel's

testimony concerning the future of the nations under the sovereignty of YHWH. The prophetic utterance has in purview the whole of the Fertile Crescent. The geopolitical arrangement of the Fertile Crescent is always Egypt in the south and Israel in the vulnerable middle. In this case, it is Assyria in the north, though over time the key player in the north changes, even if policies remain much the same. The dynamic of this "map of the world" makes clear that the two superpowers, north and south, Egypt and Assyria, are perpetual enemies, and that Israel is in the middle with two exposed frontiers.[47]

This poetic scenario of Isaiah 19 envisions, "on that day," an end to this perpetual hostility. "On that day," when YHWH's intention is fulfilled, there will be a free flow of traffic (and no doubt commerce) between these powers, without barriers, customs, tariffs, or hostility. Moreover, there will be common worship, all submitting to a God larger than their own state ideology. The ultimate promise for the nations as partners of YHWH is the complete end of hostility and the rule of a shared *shalom*.

In Isa 19:24-25, the vision grows more radical—now not only peace and traffic and trade, not only shared worship, but now a positive relationship to YHWH for all three parties:

On that day Israel will be the third with Egypt and Assyria, a blessing in the midst of the earth, whom the Lord of hosts has blessed, saying, "Blessed be Egypt my people, and Assyria the work of my hands, and Israel my heritage."

This utterance takes up three special names for Israel that are rooted in its peculiar and privileged relationship to YHWH: "my people," "the work of my hands," and "my heritage." These three names, all heretofore assigned exclusively to Israel, are now distributed across the Fertile Crescent, assigned to people who have been a great threat to Israel and a great vexation to YHWH. In this daring utterance we witness the process by which other peoples are redesignated to be YHWH's chosen peoples so that, taken paradigmatically, all peoples become YHWH's chosen peoples.

In the end, Israel retains one phrase of privilege, "my heritage" (cf. Deut 32:9; Jer 10:16). Thus Israel has lost its monopoly on two of its pet names. The loss must be like the loss when an older child begins to notice that pet names are being reused, now for a new member of the family. This redistribution of names of affection bespeaks a loss of privilege for Israel, as did the assertion of Amos 9:7. It is unmistakable that these two references in Amos 9:7 and Isa 9:24-25 constitute countertestimony, counter to the unqualified sense of privilege Israel claims for itself vis-à-vis YHWH in its core testimony. This recognition of countertestimony reminds us that countertestimony is not always negative, but may be healthy and emancipatory, whenever the core testimony becomes ideologically self-serving and self-indulgent. By this poetic act Israel is permitted to assume a normal role among the nations, without a privilege that always endangers, even as it enhances. This revisioned Near East leaves all of these states not only renamed by a Yahwistic name, but also blessed. The old acrimonies, hostilities, and defiances, in an instant of utterance, become decisively inappropriate and unnecessary. For now the entire geopolitical horizon is brought under the governance of YHWH's fruitfulness.

It is remarkable that the utterance of Isaiah 19 pertains to the two most despised and perhaps cruelest enemies of Israel. This is the real move beyond the fissure in the life of the nations, taken not in response to their repentance (though I do not discount the significance of Ezek 32:31 and Jonah for the larger drama of the nations), but as a free, unqualified, inexplicable promise of YHWH. The promise is an invitation to Israel to move beyond itself and its self-serving ideology, to reposition itself in the family of YHWH's beloved nations, and to reimagine YHWH, beyond any self-serving, privileged claim, into the largest possible horizon, as the one who intends well-being for all the nations, including the ones formerly defiant and condemned.

YHWH's Freedom with the Nations

YHWH does indeed deal with the nations according to YHWH's own freedom and passion. YHWH's *freedom* is evident in two dimensions of the grid I have sketched concerning the history and destiny of the nations. First, YHWH in freedom has the power and capacity to recruit nations for YHWH's own purposes, even if those purposes are not the intention of the nations, or even if those purposes run against the expectation of Israel. Thus nations are pressed into YHWH's service, both to punish Israel (Assyria, Babylon) and to save Israel (Persia). That is, a large divine intentionality operates in the geopolitical process that runs well beyond and perhaps counter to what the agents of the process themselves imagine. While it may have been repulsive to have Nebuchadnezzar termed "my servant" (Jer 25:9; 27:6) in the process of nullifying Judah, it was no less abhorrent to have Cyrus termed "his messiah" (Isa 45:1) in support of Judah (cf. Isa 45:9-13). YHWH's governing capacity is not derivative from or contingent on the intention of the nations or of Israel, but operates in complete and commanding freedom.

Second, YHWH's freedom is evident in YHWH's capacity, according to Israel's testimony, to terminate nations, even great superpowers. We would not have imagined, of any of the great superpowers of the time, that they would abruptly drop out of the geopolitical process. Of course, this nullification of power can be explained in a variety of geopolitical terms. But Israel's testimony resolutely intends to offer a peculiar version of reality, which serves to subvert every version of reality that relies finally on sociopolitical or military explanations. In the end, the nations figure in the testimony of Israel as functions and instruments for YHWH's work in the process of the nations. It is an act of sanity, Israel proposes, when Nebuchadnezzar finally comes to his senses and is able to reimagine and resituate his own proximate power in relation to that of YHWH:

> When that period was over, I, Nebuchadnezzar, lifted my eyes to heaven, and my reason returned to me.

> I blessed the Most High,
> and praised and honored the one who lives forever.
> For his sovereignty is an everlasting sovereignty,
> and his kingdom endures from generation to generation.
> All the inhabitants of the earth are accounted as nothing,
> and he does what he wills with the host of heaven
> and the inhabitants of the earth.
> There is no one who can stay his hand
> or say to him, "What are you doing?" (Dan 4:34-35; cf. Jer 49:19)

It is much less explicit that YHWH's governance of the nations is marked as much by *passion* as it is by freedom. Here we move in the realm of inference, but we must at least ponder the rehabilitative utterances of YHWH concerning the nations, which we have noticed in Amos 9:7, Isa 19:23-25, Isa 56:3, 6-7, and Jonah. In each of these, YHWH makes a positive move toward the nations, for which there seems to be no evident motivation. The texts do not explicitly indicate any positive passion on YHWH's part toward the nations.[48] Knowing what we know about YHWH's passion toward Israel, however, we may at least wonder if there are not inchoate hints in these texts that "God so loved the world"—the world of the nations.

Thus in Amos 9:7, we are told of multiple exoduses worked by YHWH. We are not told that the Philistines or the Arameans groaned and cried out, as did Israel in Exod 2:23; we may, however, entertain the notion that something like that happened. Indeed, the remarkable promise made to Egypt in Isa 19:23-25 is preceded by an equally remarkable assertion concerning Egypt and its cry to YHWH in vv. 20-21: "when they cry to the LORD because of oppressors, he will send them a savior, and will defend and deliver them. The LORD will make himself known to the Egyptians; and the Egyptians will know the LORD on that day, and will worship with sacrifice and burnt offering, and they will make vows to the LORD and perform them." Since Exod 11:6 and 12:23, Egypt has had to "cry out."[49] Here YHWH hears and answers. Such a usage is of course remote from the Exodus narrative. The connection, however, indicates how all of Israel's memory is available and usable in the ongoing work of testimony. But we do know that when YHWH utters such a promise over Israel, it is because YHWH is moved, either by old commitments or by present troubles.

We may wonder if the same motivations operate with the nations as with Israel. In the formula for the inclusion of foreigners in Isa 56:3-6, Herbert Donner has seen that the text directly challenges the Torah provision of Deut 23:2-8.[50] We do not know why. But the culminating assertion of Isa 56:7 suggests that YHWH has finally an inclusive propensity:

> these I will bring to my holy mountain,
> and make them joyful in my house of prayer;
> their burnt offerings and their sacrifices
> will be accepted on my altar;
> for my house shall be called a house of prayer
> for *all peoples.*

Positive assertion on the part of YHWH nullifies the old exclusion of Israel's enemies. YHWH, belatedly, appears here to accept Israel's ancient enemies as legitimate candidates for membership in the covenant. In the narrative of Jonah, moreover, a dramatic act of repentance on the part of Nineveh authorizes and evokes YHWH's positive and forgiving response (3:5-10). The protest of Jonah, however, suggests that even the repentance of Nineveh would not have been sufficient cause for forgiveness and acceptance, unless YHWH were already "a gracious God" (4:2). That is, with the most recalcitrant of nation-partners, YHWH acts in a characteristic rehabilitative way, moving beyond the harshness of rejecting sovereignty, in order to reembrace the established enemy.

In all of these cases, the move beyond judgment and nullification toward new national possibility is rooted in YHWH's freedom, freedom to restore an enemy. But more is at work in these instances than unfettered freedom. There is also a predilection toward forgiveness, restoration, and rehabilitation, propelled by an old and enduring positive concern and not undercut even by resistance and rebellion. I do not want to overstate this point, but these odd and intriguing verses are indeed present in Israel's testimony. These texts suggest that, at the edge of Israel's notice, and therefore at the edge of YHWH's propensity, free sovereignty is given a cast that has the marking of enduring, responsive generosity.

YHWH in Geopolitical Scope

It is not usual for the nations to figure so prominently in an Old Testament theology, as I have taken time and space to do here. That decision on my part warrants an explanatory comment. I judge "the nations" as partner to YHWH's sovereignty and pathos to be important for our consideration for two reasons. First, *attention to the texts corrects the easy impression that the Old Testament is singularly preoccupied with YHWH's powerful commitment to Israel.* It is true that Israel is the singular topic of YHWH's sovereignty and freedom in this testimony. To that extent, Israel's testimony is an interpretive comment about itself.

But this claim of centrality for Israel needs to be sharply qualified. Israel does not live in a sociopolitical vacuum. Israel is always in the presence of more powerful nations that impinge on Israel's life and destiny in uninvited ways. Moreover, YHWH has a rich field of engagement with the nations. Some of that engagement is conditioned by the centrality of Israel in this articulation of world history, but much of it is not. According to this testimony, YHWH's concern with the nations is not shaped or determined simply by the needs and propensities of Israel. YHWH has YHWH's own life to live, and will not be monopolized by Israel. This recognition requires something of a rearticulation both of Israel who is not alone the partner of YHWH, and of YHWH who is not exclusively committed to Israel.

The second reason I have taken so much time and energy on this topic is a contemporary interpretive concern. Over the long haul of the Enlightenment, Western Christianity has been progressively privatized in terms of individuals, families, and domestic communities. By and large, out of bewilderment and embarrassment, the ecclesial communities have forgotten how to speak about national and international matters, except in times of war to mobilize God for "the war effort." The inevitable outcome of this privatization is to relinquish geopolitics to practical, technical analysis, as in Joseph Stalin's cynical question, "How many divisions has the Pope?" That is, *if the theological dimension drops out of international purview, and with it any credible, critical moral dimension, then the world becomes one in which might makes right.* To some extent, that is what has happened among us, because Yahwistic rhetoric in this arena of life strikes any modern person as mindless supernaturalism.

Two matters suggest to me, in terms of theological intentionality, that in contemporary circumstance in the West we may courageously reconsider the forfeiture of Yahwistic rhetoric. First, the studies of Paul Kennedy, *The Rise and Fall of the Great Powers*, and (to a lesser extent) of Douglas Johnston and Cynthia Sampson, *Religion: The Missing Dimension of Statecraft*, invite such reconsideration.[51] Kennedy's book makes the remarkable argument that military power, if cut off from the realities of territory, population, and natural and economic resources, brings devastation to a nation-state. Kennedy's book is a cold, social scientific analysis, and Kennedy apparently would resist any move to introduce a moral dimension into his calculus. It occurs to me, however, that Kennedy's analysis, offered in very different categories, is not far removed from prophetic analysis. It is the characteristic urging of Israel's prophets that arrogant nations, which overreach in imagined self-sufficiency, operate autonomously at their own peril. YHWH, in this rhetoric, is a critical principle of restraint, which arrests both self-aggrandizement and brutality in the service of self-aggrandizement.

The book by Johnston and Sampson is much less satisfying, because it is concerned with what appear to me calculated dimensions of religious rhetoric that appeal to prudence more than to any more profound critical principle. Nonetheless, their consideration of the general theme suggests that any discernment of power that eliminates moral issues is inadequate. This is not simply a matter of rhetoric, but it is a substantive question about whether any restraints and sanctions are operative in the geopolitical process. Given our long-term Enlightenment silence on the question, it is at this juncture worth recognizing that Israel had no doubt on this interpretive issue.

The second reason for reconsidering the forfeiture of Yahwistic rhetoric concerns the immediate context of interpretation at the end of the twentieth century and the outset of the twenty-first century. No interpreter can fail to notice the extraordinary demise of the Soviet Union, the remarkable, relatively nonviolent end of apartheid in South Africa, and the opening of ideological intransigence in Northern Ireland. Interpretation now takes place in a context of the astounding reordering of power in the world. The issues are enormously complex, of course, and no doubt many factors, some visible and some hidden, have been at work in these turns of power. I do not propose any theological naiveté about a theo-moral dimension to these matters.

One may, nonetheless, after the manner of Israel's unsolicited testimony, entertain the thought that the resilient intention of YHWH for justice in the world is at work. That resolve for justice, which negatively limits raw power and which positively emboldens advocates of justice, can indeed be delayed by terror, intimidation, and brutality. At the outset of the new century, we may reraise the question in light of undoubted delay: Can that impetus for justice that Israel finds rooted in YHWH's own resolve be fully stopped? Perhaps one may suggest that theological rhetoric, even as it can be recruited for repressive purposes, also was, in these most recent cases, near the heart of the turn of power. That is, God-talk is not mere strategic rhetoric, though it may be that. It is also an utterance of a substantive claim that a crucial force is embedded in geopolitics that is beyond conventional manipulation.

Having said that about our contemporary circumstance of interpretation, I offer two addenda. First, surely the Holocaust places an awesome question mark over any claim of a moral dimension in world history. Continued reflection on that unutterable event continues to revolve precisely around that issue. The analysis of Zygmunt Bauman, *Modernity and Holocaust*, understands even the Holocaust as an extreme articulation of uncriticized, unchecked moral autonomy.[52]

Second, most readers of this exposition of Old Testament theology will be citizens of the United States, "the last superpower," which has survived and prospered until the very "End of History."[53] I intend that my analysis of YHWH and the nations should finally settle in the presence of the United States, which has at the moment no viable competitor for hegemony, and which is in an economic, military position to imagine, like Egypt, that it produces its own Nile.[54] The good news is that there is a residue of moral awareness in the ethos of the United States. The threat to that good news is that economic ideology and military self-justification tend easily and eagerly to override that residue of awareness. In such a situation one may wonder: Have we arrived at last at a nation-state that is finally immune to this witness of metapolitics, so that we come to a point in which Israel's witness is seen to be outmoded or self-deceived rhetoric? Or is the United States, like every superpower before it, on notice? *Liberal autonomy* is certainly the primary alternative in the modern world to this ancient insistence on *covenantalism*. Israel makes its testimony amid competing testimonies. I imagine that this ancient witness would judge liberal autonomy to be nothing new, but one often and anciently utilized in the service of self-deceiving self-sufficiency.   ▭

Creation as YHWH's Partner

5

I now consider the most expansive horizon of Israel's testimony concerning the transactional quality of YHWH's life. YHWH takes creation—the whole known, visible world—to be YHWH's partner. This is of course a commonplace of theology, because Genesis 1–2 is perhaps the most familiar biblical text in our culture. But the character of the relationship between Creator and creation is not so obvious as familiarity with the theme might suggest. The transactional quality of this relationship is what must concern us, but it has been covered over and made invisible, both by the reductionism of church theology and by the confusion of creation with the categories of natural science.[1] As we have seen with Israel's testimony about the human person as YHWH's partner and the nations as YHWH's partner, in this case as well it seems clear that Israel's own lived experience and sense of itself vis-à-vis YHWH matter greatly in determining how Israel bears witness to creation as YHWH's partner. As with the other partners, creation as YHWH's partner is read through Israel's sense of itself.

A World Blessed and Fruitful

Creation, the network of living organisms that provides a viable context and home for the human community, is an outcome of YHWH's generous, sovereign freedom.[2] No reason is given for YHWH's unutterable act of forming an earth that is viable for life. Here I focus on the outcome of that generous divine activity. With a consensus of Old Testament scholarship, it is clear in Israel's horizon that creation is not ex nihilo.[3] That is, YHWH did not create the world where there was nothing. Rather YHWH so ordered the "preexistent material substratum," which was wild, disordered, destructive, and chaotic, to make possible an ordered, reliable place of peaceableness and viability.[4] This divine act of ordering is an act of sovereignty on the largest scale, whereby YHWH's good intention for life imposes a will on destructive forces and recalcitrant energies. The outcome, according to Israel's testimony, is a place of fruitfulness, abundance, productivity, and extravagance—all terms summed up in the word *blessing*. Thus in Gen 1:28, at the center of that first great chapter, YHWH asserts, in a mood of authorization: "God blessed them, and God said to them, 'Be fruitful and multiply, and fill the earth and subdue it; and have dominion over the fish of the sea and over the birds of the air and over every living thing that moves upon the earth.'"

It is YHWH's will for this newly ordered world that it should be fruitful, invested with "the power of fertility."[5] YHWH has authorized in the world the inscrutable force of generosity, so that the earth can sustain all its members, and so that the earth has within itself the capacity for sustenance, nurture, and regeneration. This capacity for generosity is no human monopoly; it is assured that every genus and species of creation can "bring forth," according to its kind.

The evident wonder and inexplicable gift of blessing evokes in Israel awed doxology, which is the appropriate response to the miracle of creation that enacts YHWH's will for life:

> The heavens are telling the glory of God;
> and the firmament proclaims his handiwork.
> Day to day pours forth speech,
> and night to night declares knowledge.
> There is no speech, nor are there words;
> their voice is not heard;
> yet their voice goes out through all the earth,
> and their words to the ends of the world. (Ps 19:1-4)[6]

The earth is the LORD's and all that is in it,
the world, and those who live in it;
he has founded it on the seas,
and established it on the rivers. (Ps 24:1-2)

Psalm 104 provides the fullest and most extensive Israelite witness to creation, as a
dynamic operation of life-giving blessing:

You cause the grass to grow for the cattle,
and plants for people to use,
to bring forth food for the earth,
and wine to gladden the human heart,
oil to make the face shine,
and bread to strengthen the human heart.
The trees of the LORD are watered abundantly,
the cedars of Lebanon that he planted.
In them the birds build their nests;
the stork has its home in the fir trees.
The high mountains are for the wild goats;
the rocks are a refuge for the coneys.
You have made the moon to mark the seasons;
the sun knows its time for setting.
You make the darkness, and it is night,
when all the animals of the forest come creeping out.
The young lions roar for their prey,
seeking their food from God.
When the sun rises, they withdraw
and lie down in their dens.
People go out to their work
and to their labor until the evening. (Ps 104:14-23)

All creation—including human creatures but not especially human creatures—
are looked after, cared for, sustained, and protected by the generous guarantees
that the Creator has embedded in the creation. Israel is dazzled. This emphasis
on generativity is expressed in largest scope in Israel's doxologies; it is also made
intimate and concrete in Israel's horizon, because the sure sign and embodiment
of the generosity of creation is the birth of a baby, which assures well-being of
the family into the next generation. This is evident in the ancestral narratives of

Genesis 12–36, but it is made even more concrete in psalms that voice the joys of a secured home:

> Sons are indeed a heritage from the LORD,
> the fruit of the womb a reward.
> Like arrows in the hand of a warrior
> are the sons of one's youth.
> Happy is the man who has
> his quiver full of them.
> He shall not be put to shame
> when he speaks with his enemies in the gate. (Ps 127:3-5)

> Happy is everyone who fears the LORD,
> who walks in his ways.
> You shall eat the fruit of the labor of your hands;
> you shall be happy, and it shall
> go well with you.
> Your wife will be like a fruitful vine
> within your house;
> your children will be like olive shoots
> around your table.
> Thus shall the man be blessed
> who fears the LORD.
> The LORD bless you from Zion.
> May you see the prosperity of Jerusalem
> all the days of your life.
> May you see your children's children.
> Peace be upon Israel! (Psalm 128)

This latter psalm envisions in general the productivity of the world, which supplies daily needs, and then it more specifically alludes to the birth of children. The casting of these psalms is intensely patriarchal—sons are most prized in Psalm 127 (with no mention of daughters), and the role of the wife in 128:3 is to create blessedness for the man.[7]

Even the patriarchal casting, however, does not detract from the awareness that the birth of a baby, the inscrutable gift of newness into the routineness of daily human life, in a peasant hut and among the urban elite, is the most specific evidence of the wonder, generosity, and generativity of creation as intended by

YHWH. In Ps 128:5-6, moreover, this intimate gift of a child in the family is generalized into a gift of prosperity for all of Israel.

Wisdom, Righteousness, and Worship

Concerning this blessing of life that YHWH guarantees for all creatures, Israel's unsolicited testimony treats three themes that we may regard as addenda to this exuberant reception and celebration of blessing. First, creation requires of human persons, the ones given dominion, that they practice *wisdom*.[8] Claus Westermann concludes: "But the Old Testament knows a wisdom . . . that grows out of God's power to bless, and therefore, even though it is secular wisdom, has a direct relationship to God's activity and work."[9]

Wisdom is the critical, reflective, discerning reception of YHWH's gift of generosity. That gift is not for self-indulgence, exploitation, acquisitiveness, or satiation, all practices of "foolishness." Wisdom urges careful husbanding, so that resources of creation may be used for the protection, enhancement, and nurture of all creatures. Wisdom is the careful, constant, reflective attention to the shapes and interconnections that keep the world generative. Where those shapes and interconnections are honored, there the whole world prospers, and all creatures come to joy and abundance. Where those shapes and interconnections are violated or disregarded, trouble, conflict, and destructiveness are sure. There is wisdom in the very fabric of creation. Human wisdom consists in resonance with the "wisdom of things," which is already situated in creation before human agents act on it.

Second, this ordering of creation, with which human wisdom may resonate, has *an ethical dimension* to it, which H. H. Schmid terms *righteousness*.[10] The world, as YHWH's creation, is not ordered so that some may set themselves over against the creaturely community to their own advantage. The world, as YHWH's creation, requires daily, endless attention to the gifts of creation, for their abuse and exploitation can harm and impede the generosity that makes life possible. Creation, moreover, has within it sanctions to bring death on those who neglect the enhancement of generosity.[11]

Third, while creation as generosity is not an Israelite property, Israel's testimony holds that *public worship is a context within which the generosity of creation can be received and enhanced.*[12] The power of blessing is alive and loose within the world; at the same time, in such a well-known text as Num 6:24-26, the power for blessing is situated or intensified in the holy place and in the utterance of designated and professional "blessers":

The LORD bless you and keep you;
The LORD make his face to shine
upon you, and be gracious to you;
The LORD lift up his countenance
upon you, and give you peace.[13]

It may well be that this cultic articulation of the power of blessing is simply to be understood as the sociological monopoly of God-given power of blessing by the priests. Except that in Israel, this cultic concentration of blessing in legitimate utterance was found to mobilize and mediate the gifts of generosity that are present in all of creation.[14]

Creation as Counterexperience in Worship

One other peculiar practice in Israel's worship life bears on our theme. It is evident in Gen 1:1—2:4a that creation and its gift of blessing are understood to be accomplished through (a) utterance, (b) separation of day from night and the waters from the waters, and (c) in the culminating practice of Sabbath.

It is widely held that creation became a crucial claim of Israel's faith in exile, when Gen 1:1—2:4a is commonly dated. This setting for creation faith suggests that affirmation of creation as an ordered, reliable arena of generosity is a treasured alternative to the disordered experience of chaos in exile. If this critical judgment is accepted, creation then is an "enactment," done in worship, in order to resist the negation of the world of exile. As a consequence, creation is not to be understood as a theory or as an intellectual, speculative notion, but as a concrete life-or-death discipline and practice, whereby the peculiar claims of YHWH were mediated in and to Israel.

This assumption has led a series of scholars to notice that the Priestly construct of the tabernacle in Exodus 25–31 has an odd and seemingly intentional parallel to the creation liturgy of Gen 1:1—2:4a.[15] The instructions for the making of the tabernacle, given by YHWH to Moses, consist in seven speeches, matching the seven days of creation, and culminating, like Gen 2:1-4a, in the provision for the Sabbath (Exod 31:12-17).[16] Moreover, the assertion that the tabernacle is finally "finished" (Exod 39:32; 40:33) corresponds to the "finish" of creation in Gen 2:1-2.[17]

This parallelism suggests that while creation may be an experience of the world, in a context where the world is experienced as not good, orderly, or generative, Israel has recourse to the counterexperience of *creation in worship*. Such an exercise, we may suspect, permitted Israelites who gave themselves fully over to the drama and claims of the creation liturgy to live responsible, caring, secure, generative, and (above all) sane lives, even in circumstances that severely discouraged such resolved living. Thus creation, in such a context, has concrete and immediate pastoral implication.

Creation in Jeopardy

The world of blessing under the settled rule of YHWH is a major affirmation of Israel's testimony. This affirmation would suggest that trust in the world and its generosity is a settled given in Israel's faith and in Israel's experience. Any such settled theological claim in Israel is sure to be unsettled, both by experience that Israel refused to deny and by texts that testify to that experience.

So it is with Israel's sense of creation. Israel bears witness to the awareness that there is alive in the world a force that is counter to the world of YHWH, a force that seeks to negate and nullify the world as a secure place of blessing. There is no doubt that Israel took over this mythic-poetic articulation from its cultural environment and antecedents; one cannot, however, for that reason discount it. This awareness of a counter-creation force was articulated in prebiblical texts because life includes this dimension of chaotic experience. We may believe, moreover, that Israel rearticulated this claim in its own texts, not because Israel was a careless borrower of texts from its environment, but because these articulations are seen to be a faithful witness to a dimension of reality that Israel is not able or willing to deny.

Israel bears witness, as did its antecedents, to an enduring force of chaos in its life. This chaos may go by many different names—Tiamat, Leviathan, Rahab, Yam, Mot—which we may summarize under the names of Death or Nihil. In a variety of texts, this rhetoric in Israel points to a recognition that something is at work in the world seeking to make impossible the life of blessing willed by YHWH. Israel, moreover, finds itself helpless in the face of this powerful force. Israel has no resources of its own with which to cope or respond to this threat. In turn we shall consider two ways in which Israel situated this undoubted experience in its theological rhetoric.

Dualism-in-Creation

First, it is possible to conclude, with some Israelite texts, that this power of the Nihil is still loose in the world and still actively opposes YHWH. That is, in the sovereign act of creation, whereby YHWH orders chaos, YHWH provisionally defeated the power of the Nihil but did not destroy or eliminate the threat of chaos. As a result, this power of the Nihil from time to time gathers its force and conducts forays into creation to work havoc, for it has not yet come under the rule of YHWH. Thus is posed a primordial dualism in which YHWH has the upper hand but is not fully in control, and so from time to time creation is threatened.

The clearest exposition of this dualism-in-creation is in Jon Levenson's book *Creation and the Persistence of Evil.*[18] It is Levenson's formidable argument that evil does indeed continue with vitality, and therefore YHWH's sovereignty over creation is fragile and under threat.[19] Levenson opposes the scholastic claim of Yehezkel Kaufmann and asserts that "the defeated enemy" (chaos) still survives, and therefore creation rhetoric is juxtaposed to threat.[20]

The two texts that provide the core of Levenson's case are in Psalm 74 and Isaiah 51:

> Yet God my King is from of old,
> working salvation in the earth.
> You divided the sea by your might;
> you broke the heads of the
> dragons in the waters.
> You crushed the heads of Leviathan;
> you gave him as food for the
> creatures of the wilderness.
> You cut openings for springs and torrents;
> you dried up ever-flowing streams.
> Yours is the day, yours also the night;
> you established the luminaries and the sun.
> You have fixed all the foundations of the earth;
> you made summer and winter. (Ps 74:12-17)

> Awake, awake, put on strength,
> O arm of the Lord!
> Awake, as in the days of old, the generations of long ago!
> Was it not you who cut Rahab in pieces,
> who pierced the dragon?
> Was it not you who dried up the sea,
> the waters of the great deep;
> who made the depths of the sea a way
> for the redeemed to cross over? (Isa 51:9-10)

Both of these texts mention the chaos monster. In both texts, moreover, this poetic language is drawn close to Israel's lived reality. In Psalm 74 it is the reality of the destroyed temple in Jerusalem; in Isaiah 51 it is the exile. These lived realities cause Israel to recall the ancient threat of chaos, surely with the surmise that YHWH's absolute sovereignty is in jeopardy.[21]

This sort of dualism works against much settled theology of an ecclesial kind. In Levenson's case, he resists the Jewish theological claims of Kaufmann. But we should also note that in Christian theology, perhaps especially in high Calvinism with its remarkable assertions of YHWH's sovereignty, the same temptation to an absolute claim for YHWH is made. Against such a settled notion, Karl Barth says of the threat of *das Nichtige* (nothingness): "There is opposition and resistance to God's world-dominion. There is in world-occurrence an element, indeed an entire sinister system of elements which is not comprehended by God's providence in the sense thus far described. . . . This opposition and resistance, this stubborn element and alien factor, may be provisionally defined as nothingness."[22]

Levenson, in the face of the data of the texts, makes two theological claims. First, it is promised in Israel that soon or late (likely late), YHWH will prevail over the threats (see, for example, Isa 25:6-8). Second, creation requires for its durability the special act and special solicitude of God.[23] It is Israel's claim that YHWH enacts this special solicitude on a regular and reliable basis. The precariousness is that YHWH can never be at ease, for given any relaxation of YHWH's attentiveness, the power of the Nihil will immediately surge into the unattended space.

This notion of an effective, powerful adversary to YHWH the Creator pervades the mythological world of the Old Testament.[24] Some residue of this thinking is evident in the serpent in Genesis 3 and the emergence of Satan in Job 1–2 and 1 Chronicles 21.[25] It is possible, as Paul Ricoeur suggests, to see these powers of negativity as unresolved elements in the character of YHWH, which are split off as "agents." In any case, this line of thinking poses important questions for Old Testament theology. Such thinking, rooted in texts that are poetic but unambiguous, flies in the face of more settled ecclesial thinking. There is a temptation to gloss over and ignore such texts and to treat them only in terms of the history of religion, beyond which Israel's more mature faith has moved.

It is my estimate, informed as I am especially by Levenson, but also by Bernhard Anderson, Karl Barth, and Terence Fretheim, that to disregard these texts and their theological counterclaim is impossible on the basis of the texts; moreover, such disregard forfeits important theological-pastoral resources. Here I refer to two studies, one concerning public power and the other concerning personal misery.

Fretheim on Pharaoh as mythic force. Terence Fretheim has done a careful and bold rereading of Exodus 1–15 and the distinctive role played by Pharaoh in the narrative.[26] Pharaoh, in this narrative, is presented as a *historical* character. In his study of the Exodus plagues, however, Fretheim suggests that Pharaoh's oppressive policies are a deep disruption of creation. That is, the plagues are not natural acts that concern Israel; they are "hypernatural" occurrences, whereby Pharaoh is presented as a *mythic* force that disrupts the generativity of creation and draws YHWH's retaliatory punishment. On the basis of this narrative, Fretheim makes possible an awareness that historical agents do indeed take on mythic proportion in their embodiment and enactment of the Nihil. This is an important interpretive maneuver in light of contemporary world history, a period of human history visited by unthinkable devastation, wrought by human agents in their mythic capacity—for example, Auschwitz, Hiroshima, Dresden, and the Soviet Gulags. Such an interpretive stance permits one to look candidly into the face of evil, without offering any too-easy Yahwistic antidote.

Lindström on personal crises. Fredrik Lindström has done a detailed study of the psalms of complaint.[27] It is his judgment that these psalms operate with a profound dualism. That is, trouble has come upon the speaker when (and only when) YHWH is negligent, so that the power of the Nihil occupies neglected territory. These psalms, on Lindström's reading, give almost no attention to sin and guilt, but are pleas that a neglectful YHWH should again pay attention, for the power of the Nihil cannot withstand the solicitous attention of YHWH. Moreover, the psalms are cult-centered, believing that the cult is where YHWH must come to reassert a generative sovereignty over against the power of the Nihil.

It is especially important that Lindström did his study at the behest of a pastor friend dealing with people living with AIDS. It is Lindström's intent to show that the power of the Nihil is not to be reduced to or explained by human sin and guilt. Rather, the onslaught of negation is due to the power of death still on the loose in creation, which may at any time cause havoc. Lindström's analysis makes clear that this notion of dualism is not a speculative, intellectual exercise, but a serious pastoral resource. Such dualism is not, moreover, a diminishment of YHWH. To the contrary, it is an assertion of how urgently indispensable YHWH is to a viable life in the world. YHWH is the guarantor of blessing; but where that power of blessing is not concretely enacted and guaranteed, the undoing of creation takes place.

YHWH Conquers the Forces of Evil

A second way of speaking about this negation in Israel's testimony is to recognize that there is indeed such negation in the world; but instead of a primordial dualism in which negation operates independently of and against YHWH, some texts see the power of negation as a force now conquered by YHWH, in the service of YHWH, and operative only at the behest of YHWH. This view has the merit of precluding a primordial dualism, and it avoids situating some power of reality beyond the sphere of YHWH's sovereignty. But this gain is traded off for the assignment of severe negation to YHWH's own sovereign capacity, in which YHWH does evil as well as good (cf. Deut 32:39; Isa 45:7).

The hymnic tradition of Israel, surely aware of the old and pervasive mythos of primordial combat, exuberantly announces that YHWH has defeated and dispelled the forces of evil. Among the more important assertions of that singular, unchallengeable sovereignty of YHWH are statements that YHWH is indeed the Creator of all the "hosts," the powers of heaven and their work at YHWH's command:

> To whom then will you compare me,
> or who is my equal? says the Holy One.
> Lift up your eyes on high and see:
> Who created these?
> He who brings out their host and numbers them,
> calling them all by name;
> because he is great in strength,
> mighty in power,
> not one is missing. (Isa 40:25-26)

The whirlwind speeches in Job, moreover, claim control of creatures by YHWH who were erstwhile monsters, but who are now obedient, treasured creatures in whom YHWH revels (Job 40:15-24; 41:1-34). YHWH is said also to control the floodwaters of the cosmos (Job 38:8-11, 25-33). The most idyllic statement is in Ps 104:25-26, which assumes YHWH's complete mastery of threatening forces:

> Yonder is the sea, great and wide,
> creeping things innumerable are there,
> living things both small and great.
> There go the ships, and Leviathan that you formed to sport in it.[28]

In this view, which competes with dualism and likely predominates in Israel's testimony, there are no causes of the destabilization of creation except the will of YHWH, who in freedom and sovereignty can indeed destabilize the world, when YHWH's sovereignty is excessively mocked and sufficiently provoked.

Of course, the classic case of such radical destabilization of the world at the behest of YHWH is the flood narrative of Gen 6:5—7:24. There is no doubt that YHWH has caused the floodwaters, and there is no doubt that it was disobedience (corruption and violence, 6:11-13) that evoked YHWH to act: "And all flesh died that moved on the earth, birds, domestic animals, wild animals, all swarming creatures that swarm on the earth, and all human beings; everything on dry land in whose nostrils was the breath of life died. He blotted out every living thing that was on the face of the ground, human beings and animals and creeping things and birds of the air; they were blotted out from the earth" (Gen 7:21-23). This is indeed the complete undoing of creation at the behest of the Creator (cf. Isa 54:9-10).

More tersely, the narrative of the destruction of Sodom is a parallel story. In sovereign freedom YHWH undertakes the radical punishment of the city, by unleashing all the ominous forces of creation: "Then the LORD rained on Sodom and Gomorrah sulfur and fire from the LORD out of heaven; and he overthrew those cities and all the Plain, and all the inhabitants of the cities, and what grew on the ground" (Gen 19:24-25). The destruction of Sodom continues to play upon the imagination of Israel (cf. Isa 1:9-10; 3:9; Jer 23:14; 49:18; 50:40; Ezek 16:46-51; and Hos 11:8-9).

The situation, moreover, is not different in the plague narrative, in which YHWH unleashes the forces of thunder, hail, and fire against Pharaoh, a recalcitrant vassal:

> Then Moses stretched out his staff toward heaven, and the LORD sent thunder and hail, and fire came down on the earth. And the LORD rained hail on the land of Egypt; there was hail with fire flashing continually in the midst of it, such heavy hail as had never fallen in all the land of Egypt since it became a nation. The hail struck down everything that was in the open field throughout all the land of Egypt, both human and animal; the hail also struck down all the plants of the field, and shattered every tree in the field. (Exod 9:23-25)

Indeed, Fretheim observes that at the end of the plague cycle (acts of sovereignty, evoked by disobedience), YHWH's final assault on Pharaoh is a return of the earth to the "heavy darkness" of the first day:[29] "The the LORD said to Moses, 'Stretch out your hand toward heaven so that there may be darkness over the land of Egypt, a darkness that can be felt.' So Moses stretched out his hand toward heaven, and there was a dense darkness in all the land of Egypt for three days. People could not see one another and for three days they could not move from where they were" (Exod 10:21-23a; cf. 12:29-30).

The unleashing of these forces in the three paradigmatic accounts of flood, Sodom, and Egypt pertains to the powers that are believed, in the divine speeches in the book of Job, to be the gifts of creation held only by the Creator. YHWH has retained these awe-evoking powers for YHWH's own self. Thus while YHWH can unloose the forces of blessing (or fecundity) into the world, YHWH can also unloose the forces of curse and death—and will do so, in an extreme case, when YHWH's sovereignty is mocked. From my perspective, this is almost a grotesque articulation of YHWH's relationship to the world. This view of YHWH's potentially destructive capacity, however, is evidently a staple of Israel's sense of the world, for which Israel exhibits neither wonderment nor embarrassment.

Indeed, this capacity of YHWH is stylized in the standard recital of covenant curses that provide sanctions for the commandments.[30] YHWH, according to this testimony, warns Israel at the outset:

> I in turn will do this to you: I will bring terror on you; consumption and fever that waste the eyes and cause life to pine away. You shall sow your seed in vain, for your enemies shall eat it. . . . If in spite of these punishments you have not turned back to me, but continue hostile to me, then I too will continue hostile to you: I myself will strike you sevenfold for your sins. I will bring the sword against you, executing vengeance for the covenant; and if you withdraw within your cities, I will send pestilence among you, and you shall be delivered into enemy hands. . . . I in turn will punish you myself sevenfold for your sins. (Lev 26:16, 23-25, 28)

YHWH promises disease, pestilence, drought, wild animals, sword, famine, and finally desolation. The threat includes historical-military assault, but it also includes the complete disruption of the processes of food production that depend on the fruitful function of creation. Israel makes no distinction between "historical" and "natural" threats; both are of a piece, and both do damage to Israel's environment. The food-producing, life-sustaining infrastructure of creation will be terminated, because YHWH will be obeyed. When YHWH is not obeyed and when the limits of creation are not respected, all of creation is placed in profound jeopardy. There are limits to YHWH's toleration of Israel's recalcitrance in this curse recital, just as there were limits for the world (Genesis 6–7) and for Sodom (Genesis 19).

The implementation of such curses is evident in the lawsuit speeches of the prophets. Zephaniah, in a harsh articulation, imagines the termination of creation:

> I will utterly sweep away everything
> from the face of the earth, says the LORD.
> I will sweep away humans and animals;
> I will sweep away the birds of the air
> and the fish of the sea. (Zeph 1:2-3)

Jeremiah envisions a great drought that will undo the earth (Jer 14:4-6). Most especially, Amos provides a catalog of curses, in a highly stylized form that seems to echo the old curse tradition:[31]

> I gave you cleanness of teeth in all your cities,
> and lack of bread in all your places,
> yet you did not return to me, says the LORD.
> And I also withheld the rain from you
> when you were still three months to the harvest;
> I would send rain on one city,
> and send no rain on another city;
> one field would be rained upon,
> and the field on which it did not rain withered;
> so two or three towns wandered to one town
> to drink water, and were not satisfied;
> yet you did not return to me, says the LORD.
> I struck you with blight and mildew;
> I laid waste your gardens and your vineyards;
> the locust devoured your fig trees and your olive trees;
> yet you did not return to me, says the LORD.
> I sent among you a pestilence after the manner of Egypt;
> I killed your young men with the sword;
> I carried away your horses;
> and I made the stench of your camp go up into your nostrils;
> yet you did not return to me, says the LORD.
> I overthrew some of you,

as when God overthrew Sodom and Gomorrah,

and you were like a brand

snatched from the fire;

yet you did not return to me, says the LORD. (Amos 4:6-11)

It may well be that the affront to YHWH concerns only the people Israel in any one particular context, or perhaps only one of the other peoples, as in the case of Egypt. But when the punishment is administered, it is characteristically undifferentiated. It strikes at "the whole earth."

This entire sequence of texts bespeaks YHWH's terrible and ready capacity to enact curses upon the earth, which disrupt the system of blessing and fertility and make the world unlivable. Just as Israel's doxologies celebrate the world when it is under the blessing of YHWH, so the various narratives and poems of judgment witness to the capacity of YHWH to place the whole earth under the power of curse, which produces only death.

In its most stylized articulations, as in Leviticus 26 and Amos 4, the curses are the direct and enraged enactment of YHWH. But there is also a second form of curse, in which creation by itself turns deathly (without the disruptive agency of YHWH) in response to recalcitrance, abuse, disobedience, and oppression. That is, the uncompromising requirements of creation are self-actualizing in their sanctions. This is expressed, for example, in Hos 4:1-3, which we may take as paradigmatic for the awareness that creation can be nullified when the affront against YHWH's will for creation becomes intense enough:

There is no faithfulness or loyalty,

and no knowledge of God in the land.

Swearing, lying, and murder,

and stealing and adultery break out;

bloodshed follows bloodshed.

Therefore the land mourns,

and all who live in it languish;

together with the wild animals

and the birds of the air,

even the fish of the sea are perishing.[32]

To be sure, YHWH is present in the process of dismantling, but there is no direct agency from YHWH. The scope of the indictment is "the land," but as the term 'ereṣ is used in vv. 1, 2, and 3, it seems to move from the "land of Israel" to "the earth"—the whole of creation. In any case, the assertion of the poem is that as a consequence of the violations of vv. 1-2, without any stated intervention on the part of YHWH, creation is undone through drought. The disappearance of "wild animals . . . birds of the air . . . fish of the sea" bespeaks the collapse of the entire life-producing structure of the earth. Local disobedience, here disobedience to the Decalogue, will evoke YHWH's enormous power of anti-creation.

In the canonical shape of Israel's witness, all of this threat from YHWH and YHWH's capacity to turn the processes of blessing into the dead end of curse come to focus in the exile. The exile of Israel concerns not just geographical displacement, but the cessation of life possibilities, the withdrawal of fruitfulness. The fullest, most drastic articulation of YHWH's deathly judgment on Jerusalem as "the end of creation" is given in Jer 4:23-26:

> I looked on the earth, and lo,
> it was waste and void;
> and to the heavens, and they had no light.
> I looked on the mountains, and lo,
> they were quaking;
> and all the hills moved to and fro.
> I looked, and lo, there was no one at all,
> and all the birds of the air had fled.
> I looked, and lo, the fruitful land was a desert,
> and all its cities were laid in ruins
> before the LORD, before his fierce anger.

This poem, in a stylized and intentional catalog, walks through all the elements of creation. It begins in earth and heavens and culminates with "fruitful land and cities." All are gone! Everything is systematically dismantled. The nullification is complete and intentional. Reality has returned to *tohu wabohu,* the pre-creation state of Gen 1:2—that is, the disordered, formless mass of "preexistent material substratum,"[33] before YHWH had uttered a sovereign word or committed a forming action in order to turn this mass into a fruitful place of blessing and joyous life. All of this undoing and nullification has happened because of YHWH's "fierce anger." What YHWH has formed in generosity as a place of blessing can, in YHWH's indignation, revert to a place of curse. The world that YHWH created in freedom can be terminated, nullified, and abandoned in like freedom.

This massive, ruthless portrayal of the story of creation as YHWH's partner has two qualifications that Israel never finally resolves or fully integrates into its high claim for YHWH. On the one hand, the complete sovereignty of YHWH, as Levenson has shown, never completely drives out what seems to be the autonomous force of chaos. On the other hand, the freedom assigned to YHWH as Creator, in Israel's rhetoric, is never free of moral conditionality. An indication of this conditionality is voiced in the conclusions of the two great creation hymns:

> Let sinners be consumed from the earth,
> And let the wicked be no more. (Ps. 104:35a)
> The LORD watches over all who love him,
> But all the wicked he will destroy. (Ps 145:20)

These caveats that occur surprisingly at the end of wondrous doxologies indicate that there is no free lunch with creation. Thus Israel has brought negation upon itself. The negation of creation is not completely a free act of YHWH, but is at the same time an act required and mandated by covenant sanctions. YHWH's sovereign freedom, according to Israel's testimony, must endlessly contend with these two qualifications.

The World beyond Nullification

The astonishing feature of this statement of YHWH's freedom and sovereignty (though less astonishing in light of what we have seen about Israel as partner, the human person as partner, and the nations as partner) is that *Israel's witness does not leave the account of creation as YHWH's partner as a tale of termination, negation, and nullification.* It is evident that something is at work in YHWH's interior, something to which Israel boldly bears witness, that works against, disrupts, and mitigates YHWH's free exercise of wrathful sovereignty. Something moves against destructiveness, either to qualify it or to begin again postdestruction. There is, in any case, more to YHWH's relation to creation than a one-dimensional response of indignant sovereignty.

I will divide my consideration of this mitigating factor in the life of YHWH into two parts. First, I shall consider the qualification given in the texts of termination; second, I will consider three other texts that suggest not only a limit on the rage of YHWH, but a quite new intention of blessing on YHWH's part.

Qualification in Texts of Termination

Several mitigating factors in the texts of destruction evidence that YHWH is unable or unwilling to "go the whole way" with the termination of creation.

Flood. In the flood narrative of Gen 6:5—7:24, we have seen YHWH's resolve to "blot out" humanity (Gen 6:7) and the narrative report of fulfillment: "He blotted out every living thing that was on the face of the ground, human beings and animals and creeping things and birds of the air; they were blotted out from the earth" (7:23). But of course, the resolve of 6:7 is already modestly countered in the verse that follows: "But Noah found favor in the sight of the LORD" (6:8). The theme of the exception of Noah is reiterated in 7:23b: "Only Noah was left, and those that were with him in the ark." And yet a third time, Noah is a mitigating factor: "But God remembered Noah and all the wild animals and all the domestic animals that were with him in the ark. And God made a wind blow over the earth, and the waters subsided" (8:1).

Bernhard Anderson has shown that architecturally, 8:1 is the pivotal point of the narrative, after which the waters recede, the threat of the flood ends, and the earth is made safe again.[34] Noah is not said to be loved by YHWH; but it is said, "Noah found favor in the sight of the LORD." In 6:9, moreover, Noah is said to be "righteous," but the governing statement in what is usually thought to be the older text is "found favor" (*ḥnn*), thus making contact with YHWH's graciousness (same word as in Exod 34:6). The narrative asserts that, along with YHWH's indignant sovereignty, there is "favor," and YHWH "remembered Noah." The narrator does not say that YHWH remembered Noah's righteousness, but simply remembered Noah, the one who was situated in YHWH's "favor." (See the same divine remembering in Gen 19:29 and 30:22.) We are led to believe, subsequently, that it is this odd and unexplored relation to Noah, perhaps in righteousness, perhaps in graciousness, that leads to the restoration of blessing in a cursed earth (Gen 8:22) and eventually to a promise of "everlasting covenant," in which YHWH pledges: "I establish my covenant with you, that never again shall all flesh be cut off by the waters of a flood, and never again shall there be a flood to destroy the earth" (9:11). Not much is made of Noah in the subsequent testimony of Israel (cf. Ezek 14:14, 20; 2 Pet 2:5). Noah is in any case the occasion for YHWH's reversal of field, the reason whereby YHWH may relove and reembrace the world as a system of blessing.[35]

Sodom. In the Sodom story, the countertheme is even more minimal, but it is there. The story turns on the effort to save Lot (Gen 19:17) and the loss of Lot's wife (19:26). What interests us, however, is in 19:29: "God remembered Abraham, and sent Lot out of the midst of the overthrow, when he overthrew the cities in which Lot had settled." This terse statement is parallel to that of 8:1, and it performs the same function. YHWH has no compelling memory of Lot, but YHWH remembers Abraham, already identified in this story as an intimate of YHWH and as a carrier of the blessing (18:17-19). Abraham is the one on whom YHWH has staked everything positive, so that Abraham becomes the wedge whereby the power of blessing is reasserted into the creation under curse.

Plagues against Egypt. The curses (plagues) enacted against Egypt and Pharaoh are massive and uncompromising, but they are qualified by an exemption for Israel:

> Only in the land of Goshen, where the Israelites were, there was no hail. (Exod 9:26)
>   . . . but all the Israelites had light where they lived. (10:23)

> But not a dog shall growl at any of the Israelites—not at people, not at animals—so that you may know that the LORD makes a distinction between Egypt and Israel. (11:7)

Perhaps these exceptions are to be understood simply as comments on the "chosenness" of Israel, and there is that motif in the story. But read from the perspective of the future of creation, Israel, in this narrative, is the means whereby the history of blessing for the world is kept alive in a world under curse.

Chaos but not "full end." In the wholesale judgment of Jer 4:23-26, everything reverts to originary chaos. The prose comment on the poetry reinforces the devastation: "For thus says the LORD: The whole land shall be a desolation . . . " (Jer 4:27a). But then this is added: ". . . yet I will not make a full end" (4:27b). This last phrase has suffered at the hands of many commentators, who deem it a later addition. But there it is! Why? Was it added because the traditionists could not tolerate the nullification of the world in such a massive way, and so they toned it down? Perhaps. But in theological exposition, we are entitled to the thought that YHWH could not tolerate the termination of the world. YHWH has too much at stake in the creation. The "grace" (ḥn) extended to Noah, to Abraham (Lot), to Israel and Moses continues to mean something. YHWH is, perhaps at great cost, resolved to maintain creation as a system of blessing, and so will not give in, even to YHWH's own propensity to enraged destruction. Israel ponders this terrible interiority in YHWH, and Israel dares give it voice. YHWH is deeply torn about the future of the world. Dare we suggest that it is this quality of tornness in YHWH's own life that, according to Israel's unsolicited testimony, constitutes the hope of creation?

Renewed Creation out of Hopelessness

I mention three texts that articulate the way in which YHWH acts in astonishingly new ways for the sake of creation, when all seemed hopelessly to have come to an end.

Hosea 2:2-23. This text concerns Israel in the first instance, as YHWH's rejected partner, and not creation. I cite it in this context, however, because in the horizon of this poem, Israel's past and future are intimately linked to the presence and/or absence of blessing in creation. The poem is arranged in two parts, which we may treat as Israel under curse (vv. 2-13) and Israel under blessing (vv. 14-23). In the first part YHWH had given to Israel the abundance of creation:

> She did not know that it was I who gave her
> the grain, the wine, and the oil,
> and who lavished upon her silver
> and gold that they used for Baal. (v. 8)

But now, in rage, YHWH will withdraw the blessings of creation, so that Israel's life is no longer viable:

> Therefore I will take back
> my grain in its time,
> and my wine in its season;
> and I will take away my wool and my flax,
> which were to cover her nakedness. . . .
> I will lay waste her vines and her fig trees . . .
> I will make them a forest,
> and the wild animals shall devour them. (vv. 9, 12)

The guarantees and gifts of creation are in YHWH's sovereign grasp, to give and to withdraw.

In the second part of the poem YHWH is moved by passion to allure Israel back to a relationship. Among the acts of allurement is a covenant with the elements of creation, the ones lost in 2:3: "I will make for you a covenant on that day with the wild animals, the birds of the air, and the creeping things of the ground" (2:18). The result of that restoration of relationship is the resumption of the processes of fruitfulness in creation:

> On that day I will answer, says the LORD,
> I will answer the heavens

CREATION AS YHWH'S PARTNER

and they shall answer the earth;

and the earth shall answer the grain, the wine, and the oil, and they

shall answer Jezreel;

and I will sow him for myself in the land.

And I will have pity on Lo-ruhamah,

and I will say to Lo-ammi,

"You are my people";

and he shall say, "You are my God." (vv. 21-23)

In the future to be given by YHWH, it is no longer possible to keep distinct the future of Israel and the future of creation, for Israel is deeply situated in the minuses and pluses of creation.

This poem is of interest for our theme on several counts. (a) The statement of the poem, when considered as a statement about creation, concerns YHWH's capacity to nullify creation. (b) The poem has as its primary subject Israel, so that creation is not a mechanistic system, but is fully embedded with the practice of human covenanting. (c) The well-being or failure of creation depends on the practice of fidelity, not least the fidelity of YHWH. It is likely that this poem, and others like it, have been read too singularly with reference to Israel, when the poem can also be seen as concerning the way in which YHWH's unsettled interior inclination also impinges on the well-being or nullification of creation.

Isaiah 45:18-19. Isaiah of the exile intends to counteract and overcome the several nullifications of the exile. Among these is the rhetoric of Israel that links exile to the nullification of creation, as we have seen it most vividly in Jer 4:23-26. I take Jer 4:23-26 to be a hyperbolic way in which Israel speaks about its exilic situation as a crisis of world proportion. In order now to overcome that hyperbolic rhetoric, Israel must counter it in equally hyperbolic positive speech. Thus in Isa 45:18-19 the poet speaks twice of chaos (*tohu*): "he did not create it a chaos. . . . 'Seek me in chaos,'" in order to present the contrast of a well-created order over which YHWH the Creator presides. Appeal to the reality of chaos is made a foil for the positive affirmation of YHWH, now available on the far side of exile. Thus chaos language is peculiarly appropriate for Israel's exile. Speech of new creation or re-creation or restored creation functions for Israel's emergence from the nullity of exile.

Isaiah 62:3-5. In the extravagant poetry of Isaiah 60–62, the poet strains to voice the new possibility of Israel after exile. In the midst of that exaggerated rhetoric of possibility, these verses concern the restoration of the fecundity of creation:

You shall be a crown of beauty in
the hand of the LORD,
and a royal diadem in the hand of your God.
You shall no more be termed Forsaken,
and your land shall no more be termed Desolate,
but you shall be called My Delight Is in Her,
and your land Married;
for the LORD delights in you,
and your land shall be married.
For as a young man marries a young woman,
so shall your builder marry you,
and as the bridegroom rejoices over the bride,
so shall your God rejoice over you. (62:3-5)

The specific language of fertility interests us because of the power of its contrasts. Thus the "forsaken" and "desolate" one is now "My Delight Is in Her" and
"Married." The last term is explicated in vv. 4b-5, appealing to the joy of the newly
married. It is crucial that the term *married* (*be'ulah*) appeals to the oldest traditions known to Israel concerning fertility. This language (cf. Hos 2:16) intends to
speak about the restoration of the processes of blessing in creation, whereby Israel
is to flourish. Gary Anderson has shown how the recovery of sexual capacity is
emblematic in Israel of the full restoration of joy and volition.[36] Thus the God who
presided over the devastation of creation is the God who now has the power and
the will to cause creation, for the benefit of Israel, to function fully. All the causes
and motivations for the nullification of exile are now forgiven and forgotten (cf. Isa
54:7-8). The world begins again!

The most extreme statement of this capacity for the recovery of creation is Isa
65:17-25, perhaps the most sweeping resolve of YHWH in all of Israel's testimony:

For I am about to create new heavens and a new earth;
the former things shall not be remembered
or come to mind.
But be glad and rejoice forever in what I am creating;
for I am about to create Jerusalem as a joy,
and its people as a delight.
I will rejoice in Jerusalem,
and delight in my people;
no more shall the sound of weeping be heard in it,

or the cry of distress.
No more shall there be in it
an infant that lives but a few days,
or an old person who does not live out a lifetime;
for one who dies at a hundred years will be considered a youth,
and one who falls short of a hundred will be considered accursed.
They shall build houses and inhabit them;
they shall plant vineyards and eat their fruit.
They shall not build and another inhabit;
they shall not plant and another eat;
for like the days of a tree shall the days of my people be,
and my chosen shall long enjoy the work of their hands.
They shall not labor in vain,
or bear children for calamity;
for they shall be offspring blessed by the LORD—
and their descendants as well.
Before they call I will answer,
while they are yet speaking I will hear.
The wolf and the lamb shall feed together,
the lion shall eat straw like the ox;
but the serpent—its food shall be dust!
They shall not hurt or destroy
on all my holy mountain, says the LORD.

This remarkably rich rhetoric suggests that the new creation that comes now, after the resurgence of chaos, warrants a fuller exposition than I can provide here. We may simply and briefly note some aspects of this extravagant promise. First, the poem is a declaration in the mouth of YHWH, who publicly and pointedly claims authority to replicate the initial creation, only now more grandly and more wondrously. This promised action of YHWH is clearly designed to overcome all that is amiss, whether what is amiss has been caused by YHWH's anger, by Israel's disobedience, or by other untamed forces of death. Second, the newness of creation here vouchsafed touches every aspect and phase of life. All elements of existence are to come under the positive, life-yielding aegis of YHWH. Third, the promise in v. 23 may refer to the disability pronounced in Gen 3:16. That is, whatever is amiss in creation will now be restored and made whole, even the most deeply embedded distortions in YHWH's world. Fourth, the culminating verse (on which see also

Isa 11:6-9) indicates that the new creation now promised concerns not only Israel, not only the entire human community, but also all of creation, so that hostilities at every level and in every dimension of creation will be overcome. "All will be well and all will be well."[37]

Creation at YHWH's Behest

Thus creation is seen, as we piece together the testimony, in three seasons:

1. The *season of blessing*, activating YHWH's free sovereignty, devoted to the well-being and productivity of the world. YHWH has the power and the inclination to form a world of life-generating proportion.

2. A *radical fissure* in the life of the world may come about, according to Israel's rhetoric, most often understood as an act of YHWH's angry, sovereign freedom. Creation is not necessary to YHWH, and YHWH will tolerate no creation that is not ordered according to YHWH's intention for life. The world can be lost!

3. In the face of devastating nullification, experienced by Israel in the fissure of its exile, and experienced by human persons in the fissures of "the Pit," it is characteristic of YHWH to work *a radical newness*. Israel's testimony is restrained on YHWH's motivation for this remarkable act of new creation. In Isa 65:17-25, no reason is given; there is only a declaration of lordly intention. In 45:18-19, it is perhaps suggested that creation is in the very character of YHWH. It is not in YHWH's character to be a God who settles for chaos. It is in YHWH's most elemental resolve to enact blessing and order and well-being.

In 62:3-5, where creation language is in the service of Israel's fruitful future, we are closer to receiving a reason for this fresh way of resolve. YHWH had kept silent (*hashah*) and been dormant (*shaqat*, v. 1). We are not told why. Perhaps YHWH was punishing Israel by such withdrawn, neglectful silence. Or perhaps YHWH was so provoked by Israel as to be sulky and ready provisionally to abandon Israel to the cursed situation it had chosen for itself. For whatever reason, YHWH now resolves to speak "for Zion's sake" (62:1). YHWH announces the resurgence of blessing for the sake of Jerusalem. The same language is more fully utilized, for the same reason, in 42:14:

> For a long time I have held my peace,
> I have kept still and restrained myself;
> now I will cry out like a woman in labor,
> I will gasp and pant.

Again we are not told the reason for the silence, but we are told the character of the new speech as YHWH breaks the silence too long kept. YHWH speaks in Isaiah 42 about the restoration of Israel and in Isaiah 62 about the restoration of blessing for Israel. YHWH breaks the chaos-permitting silence "like a woman in labor." This is a birthing surge of energy that wills to be generative. Perhaps it is action out of affection for Israel, like a mother for a child, an irrepressible, indomitable will for the well-being of the child (cf. 49:14-15). Perhaps it is generative energy within the bones and body of YHWH. In either case, what now is asserted is new energy that refuses to leave things nullified and in a state of exile/chaos/death.

The recovery of 42:14ff. is historical and concerns the recovery of Israel. But the rhetoric also concerns action in the reordering of all of creation:

I will lay waste mountains and hills,
and dry up all their herbage;
I will turn the rivers into islands,
and dry up the pools.
I will lead the blind
by a road they do not know,
by paths they have not known
I will guide them.
I will turn the darkness before them into light,
the rough places into level ground.
These are the things I will do,
and I will not forsake them. (42:15-16)

This is a powerful, irresistible, transformative resolve, to be undertaken with a high level of emotional intensity. It is a burst of generativity that is going to change everything and create a newness. This is a God who will not forsake: "I will not forsake them" (42:16); "You shall no more be termed Forsaken" (62:4). In this resolve to new creation, YHWH promises to overcome all forsakenness and abandonment known in Israel and in the world. When creation is abandoned by YHWH, it readily reverts to chaos. Here it is in YHWH's resolve, and in YHWH's very character, not to abandon, but to embrace. The very future of the world, so Israel attests, depends on this resolve of YHWH. It is a resolve that is powerful. More than that, it is a resolve that wells up precisely in *tohu wabohu* and permits the reality of the world to begin again, in blessedness.

The Drama of
Partnership with YHWH

6

M any other things, of course, can be said usefully on these four subjects—Israel, human persons, the nations, and creation. I suggest, nonetheless, that the discussion in the preceding four chapters considers the major aspects of the four subjects in relationship to YHWH. Indeed, even in relationship to YHWH, the materials can be construed and pieced together somewhat differently from the way I have done it. It is my judgment, however, that if one begins with (a) the incommensurability of YHWH's sovereign freedom, (b) mutuality rooted in YHWH's generous pathos-inclined fidelity, and (c) the unsettled, always-to-be-negotiated tension of incommensurate sovereignty and mutual fidelity, something like the above picture is sure to emerge. As a concluding statement on these four partners of YHWH, I will first consider a recurring pattern in the four partners, then a reflection on YHWH as given us in this unsolicited testimony, and finally a reflection on the significance of this witness amid the dominant ideologies of our interpretive venue.

Recurring Pattern in the Partners

It is a temptation and a bane of Old Testament theology to try to thematize or schematize data excessively, and I have no wish to impose a pattern on the material. Because of the character of YHWH, however, I suggest that for each of these partners, the data permit *a dramatic movement:*

Dramatic Movement for YHWH's Partners

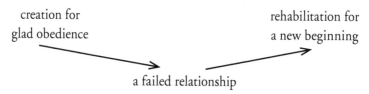

I suggest this pattern only as a rough perspective, which has to be adjusted for each partner; indeed, it needs to be given different nuance in each text. Nonetheless, this drama of brokenness and restoration is the primary ingredient of life with YHWH.

The Pattern with Israel

Israel's life with YHWH is presented in this testimony as:

1. created in love for glad obedience;
2. scattered into exile;
3. restored through YHWH's pathos-filled love for obedience and hope.

If we trace this movement historically, we can see that it roughly correlates with the movement of: (1) early traditions, (2) the prophetic traditions, and (3) the emergence of Judaism.[1] Since we are here concerned with theology of Israel with reference to YHWH, we more appropriately focus on the verbal sentences with YHWH as subject, and not simply on historical eventualities. Thus Israel's life is told as a drama of a people chosen and formed; judged and scattered; gathered, loved, forgiven, and remembered.

The Pattern with Human Persons

I have already observed that human persons, in Israel's unsolicited testimony, are in some way a replication of Israel's own life. Therefore the parallel to Israel does not surprise us. Thus human life, vis-à-vis YHWH, is presented as:

1. created for obedience, discernment, and trust;
2. authorized in the Pit for complaint, petition, and thanksgiving;
3. raised to new life for praise and hope.

It is of particular importance that in tracing human life into the Pit and out of the Pit, we observe that this sequence seems parallel to the creation-sin-redemption pattern of Christian theology—except that it is very different. It is possible to transpose this sequence, which we have found in Israel's testimony, into a doctrinal pattern of creation–fall–redemption. But that is not at all what happens in Israel's testimony. Israel is not consistent in its judgment about how human persons end in the Pit. It never occurs to Israel to reduce entry into the Pit to guilt or anything like "the fall." Israel's way of thinking is much more in medias res, without great explanatory curiosity.

In a second way, Israel's mode of speaking is important. We have noticed that reference to resurrection is very slight in the Old Testament. In the purview of this testimony, it is likely that it is unnecessary and unhelpful to distinguish between the many rescues that occur in life with YHWH and the big one of life after death. All placements in the Pit are face to face with the power of death, and physical death is only an extreme case, different in degree but not in kind from all the other threats to human life. It is characteristically enough in Israel to assert that "the Pit" is a reality, and that when YHWH can be mobilized, the grip and threat of the Pit can be overcome. The truth of human personhood vis-à-vis YHWH is that the human person is not helplessly and hopelessly consigned to the Pit, because the power of YHWH can break the grip of the Pit. It was not necessary in Israel, nor especially useful, to move beyond such metaphorical language, because everyone understood what was being said, especially "Death," who imagined that he controlled the Pit (cf. Hos 13:14).

In one other important way this presentation differs from that of classical Christian theology. The person in the Pit is not to be passive and docile, awaiting the initiative of YHWH. The whole pattern of the psalms of complaint suggests that in the Pit, the human person can and must initiate the process of rescue by shrill protest and insistent hope. It is not possible or appropriate, in the horizon of Israel, to worry about works and grace in such a transaction, because the mutuality of covenanting requires that both parties should be mightily engaged in the demanding, hopeful act of rescue.[2]

The Pattern with the Nations

The situation is not different with the nations as partners of YHWH, as we have seen, both with Israel's near neighbors and with the great imperial superpowers. Thus the nations:

1. are summoned as YHWH's vassals and instruments in the geopolitical process;
2. are punished to nullification in their recalcitrance and arrogant autonomy;
3. are promised new life with reason restored, as they come to terms with YHWH's generous but uncompromising governance.

On this subject Israel speaks with great inventiveness and daring, willing and able to construe the international history of the world in ways congruent with its own life with YHWH.

The Pattern with Creation

Again, the fundamental experience of Israel is writ large in the theme of creation. Creation is:

1. formed and founded in YHWH's generosity as a world of blessing, given within the framework of YHWH's governance;
2. relinquished to the power of chaos and curse when human agents, charged with the well-being of creation, renege on their caretaking responsibility;
3. in newness, according to YHWH's indomitable resolve.

It seems clear that Israel thinks and speaks from its own experience outward. For that reason, however, we do not conclude that Israel "cheated" in articulating creation. In the canonical formation of this testimony, it is YHWH's sovereign fidelity with creation that provides the arena for the life of all the partners, including Israel. Thus we may say that the life of each of these partners is ordered into a drama of brokenness and restoration as shown in the accompanying diagram.

Drama of Brokenness and Restoration for Each of the Partners

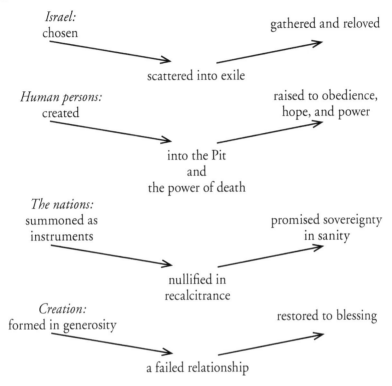

Israel:
chosen

gathered and reloved

scattered into exile

Human persons:
created

raised to obedience,
hope, and power

into the Pit
and
the power of death

The nations:
summoned as
instruments

promised sovereignty
in sanity

nullified in
recalcitrance

Creation:
formed in generosity

restored to blessing

a failed relationship

The unsolicited testimony of Israel yields a drama with profound risk and enormous dynamic, in which none of YHWH's partners have any continuing power of their own. In the end, they are summoned outside themselves, in order to rely on this One whom Israel confesses to be uncompromising in sovereignty, but moved to always new measures of fidelity.

Israel's Articulation of YHWH

My purpose in examining this testimony, in the context of our theological focus, is not primarily to learn something about the partners, though that in itself is a gain. My purpose, rather, is to learn more of Israel's articulation of YHWH. I have said, at the outset of my exposition of this unsolicited testimony, that Israel as a witness had perhaps understood that *speech about these partners is necessary to a proper understanding of YHWH*, because YHWH is always YHWH-in-relation. Thus the drama of brokenness and restoration, which we have suggested for each of the partners, is a telling affirmation of YHWH as articulated in Israel.

Self-giving engagement. YHWH, in authorizing the life of each of these partners, is discerned by Israel as an agent of incomparable power, but one whose incomparable power is not simply for the celebration and enhancement of YHWH's self, but for the generation of a partner. YHWH, by the act of self-giving engagement, evokes partners who can be the objects of YHWH's sovereignty and fidelity. Before the partner exists, YHWH is for the partner in generous ways, creating an arena of blessing.

Rejection of autonomy. YHWH, however, is seen to be uncompromising in the midst of that generosity. None of the partners is finally permitted autonomy. It may be that the partners' character is such that they are not qualified to be autonomous. But the reason given for the rejection of autonomy is characteristically located not in the partner, but in YHWH. YHWH's self-regard is massive, savage, and seemingly insatiable. That self-regard sets boundaries to YHWH's initiatory generosity. Israel does not vex about the oddity of YHWH's readiness to nullify YHWH's own beloved partners. But neither does Israel flinch from acknowledging that YHWH is a jealous God who is capable of irrational destructiveness.

Life-denying fissure. YHWH can be addressed in the life-denying fissure of exile–death–impotence–chaos, to which YHWH's partners seem inevitably to come. This affirmation may be one of the distinctive surprises of YHWH as given in Israel's testimony. To the extent that the fissure is an outcome of YHWH's rejecting rage, or to the extent that it is a result of YHWH's loss of power in the face of the counterpower of death, we might expect that a loss to nullity is irreversible. Thus, "when you're dead, you're dead," "when you're in exile, you're in exile."

YHWH mobilized by cries from the Pit. This unsolicited testimony of Israel, however, moves beyond irreversibility in two stunning affirmations. First, YHWH is inclined toward and attentive to those in the nullity. YHWH can be reached, summoned, and remobilized for the sake of life. Beyond YHWH's harsh sovereignty, YHWH has a soft underside to which appeal can be made. Israel (and we) are regularly astonished that working in tension with YHWH's self-regard is YHWH's readiness to be engaged with and exposed for the sake of the partner.

Second, the mobilization of YHWH in the season of nullity characteristically requires an act of initiative on the part of the abandoned partner. This is classically articulated in the complaints of Israel, subsequently retold in songs of thanksgiving:

> To you, O Lord, I cried,
>   and to the Lord I made supplication:
> "What profit is there in my death,

if I go down to the Pit?
Will the dust praise you?
Will it tell of your faithfulness?
Hear, O LORD, and be gracious to me!
O LORD, be my helper!" (Ps 30:8-10)

I waited patiently for the LORD;
he inclined to me and heard my cry.
He drew me up from the desolate pit,
out of the miry bog,
and set my feet upon a rock,
making my steps secure.
He put a new song in my mouth,
a song of praise to our God.
Many will see and fear,
and put their trust in the LORD. (Ps 40:1-3)

Then they cried to the LORD in their trouble,
and he delivered them from their distress. (Ps 107:6; cf. vv. 13, 19, 28)

This capacity to mobilize YHWH to new activity by cries in the Pit is also
evident in Israel's inadvertent triggering of the exodus by its shrill cry of need and
anguish: "The Israelites groaned under their slavery, and cried out. Out of slavery
their cry for help rose up to God. God heard their groaning, and God remembered
his covenant with Abraham, Isaac, and Jacob. God looked upon the Israelites, and
God took notice of them" (Exod 2:23-25).

The cry may not always be a prerequisite for rescue; YHWH may also take
initiative. The cry is prominent enough, however, to undermine any theological
conclusion about deferential waiting for YHWH's initiative. Thus even in Psalm
40, where the speaker "waits patiently," the waiting is in the context of having cried
out. Israel is not at all deferential, and does not imagine that human persons in
such situations will be deferential. It is in this context that Israel issues its countertestimony against YHWH, in order to mobilize the YHWH of the core testimony
to act characteristically one more time. Thus the God who by incommensurate
sovereignty can rescue from nullity is addressed and reached, precisely by play on
YHWH's available mutuality. YHWH is seen by Israel to be YHWH's variegated
self, precisely in the fissure. Indeed, Israel's faith is formed, generated, and articulated precisely with reference to the fissure, which turns out to be the true place
of life for YHWH's partner and the place wherein YHWH's true character is not

only disclosed, but perhaps fully formed. The reality of nullity causes a profound renegotiation of YHWH's sovereignty vis-à-vis YHWH's pathos-filled fidelity.

The miracle of radical newness. YHWH, who is addressed and reached in the nullity, is known in Israel to be a God willing and able to enact a radical newness for each of YHWH's partners, a newness that the partners cannot work for themselves. This newness is deeply shaped by YHWH's initial acts of sovereign generosity, but it runs well beyond the imagination of those in the nullity. Because this inexplicable, unanticipated newness is the same for all of these partners, it is with good reason that H. H. Schmid has concluded that *creatio ex nihilo*, justification by faith, and resurrection of the dead are synonymous phrases.[3] These phrases are not isolated dogmatic themes. They are, rather, ways in which YHWH's characteristic propensities of generosity are made visible in different contexts with different partners.

Materials for a Metanarrative

This drama of brokenness and restoration is the primary outcome of the transactions between YHWH and YHWH's partners. The work of Old Testament theology, it seems to me, is an articulation of a metanarrative that is a strong contrast to the metanarratives currently available in our society (and in the church, to the extent that the church also partakes of the dominant narratives of society).

I am profoundly ill at ease with the use of the term *metanarrative*, by which I mean simply a more-or-less coherent perspective on reality. I am ill at ease, first, because I am impressed with the plurality, diversity, and fragmented quality of the Old Testament text, and I have no wish to engage in reductionism. Second, I am ill at ease with the term because I take seriously, along with my deconstructionist friends and colleagues, Jean-François Lyotard's suspicion of metanarrative, with its hegemonic potential.[4] For all of that, however, I am impressed with the odd—Yahwistically odd and Jewishly odd—offer of a perspective in these texts that clearly is in profound tension with the regnant metanarratives of our society. I will settle for the judgment that the Old Testament is not a metanarrative but offers the materials out of which a metanarrative is to be construed. I will settle for that, so long as it is recognized that any metanarrative construed out of these materials must include certain claims and awarenesses that cannot be compromised.

I will exposit those nonnegotiable awarenesses in relation to Enlightenment liberalism and in relation to the standard claims of classical Christianity. Vis-à-vis the claims of Enlightenment liberalism, Israel's Yahwistic account of brokenness and restoration may yield several enormously important insistences.

Limitless Generosity at the Root of Reality

At the root of reality is a *limitless generosity* that intends an extravagant abundance. This claim is exposited in Israel's creation texts, sapiential traditions, and hymnic exuberances. This insistence flies in the face of the theory of scarcity on which the modern world is built. An *ideology of scarcity* produces a competitiveness that issues in brutality, justifies policies of wars and aggression, authorizes an acute individualism, and provides endless anxiety about money, sexuality, physical fitness, beauty, work achievements, and finally mortality.[5] It seems to me that, in the end, all of these anxieties are rooted in an ideology that resists a notion of limitless generosity and extravagant abundance.

It is a hard question how literally and how seriously to take Israel's lyrical claims, which Israel itself often did not take seriously. Do these claims mean simply that all humankind should be nice and share, and we will all get along? Do they mean that as we trust abundance, we will learn a kind of joy that does not need so much? Or might they mean, in a venturesome antimodernity, that the genuine practice of trust causes the earth to produce more, so that justice evokes the blessings of the earth? That is the claim of the blessing theology of Lev 26:3-13 and Deut 28:1-14. From the perspective of our several Enlightenment metanarratives, such a claim is outrageous and absurd. But the outrage may at bottom signify nothing more than the totalizing power of the ideology of scarcity. One must depart from the narrative of scarcity in order to host this lyrical affirmation of generosity and abundance, a departure to which Israel was summoned each time it engaged in worship and reflection.[6]

Fissure at the Center of Reality

At the center of reality is a deep, radical, painful, costly *fissure* that will, soon or late, break every self-arranged pattern of well-being. This claim is exposited in the texts of the Deuteronomic tradition, the prophetic lawsuits, the complaint psalms, and the theology of the book of Job. In the Old Testament, no creaturely arrangement survives YHWH's governance unscathed—not mighty Babylon, not the temple of YHWH's presence in Jerusalem, not the beloved Davidic king to whom YHWH has made unconditional promises. The chosen people are forced into exile, people suffer and die, nations and empires fall, and floods come upon the earth. It cannot be helped, and it cannot be avoided.

We have seen, moreover, that Israel's struggle to bear true witness about this reality is complicated and unresolved. Much of the nullity besetting the partners of YHWH comes as a consequence of sin and defiance, as punishment of the sovereign, but there is more. The partner who suffers is often perpetrator, but also sometimes victim. Sometimes the partner is victim of YHWH's negligence, whereby the hosts of the Nihil run rampant in the earth; sometimes the partner is victim of YHWH's mean-spirited irascibility . . . sometimes.

In any case, as perpetrator or as victim or as both, the partner of YHWH must make claim against YHWH. It is in this context that Israel voices its countertestimony. Israel seizes the initiative against YHWH, protests YHWH's hiddenness, unreliability, and negativity. Sometimes—not always—these protests lead to restoration and rehabilitation by the resolve of YHWH.

This insistence on the reality of brokenness flies in the face of the Enlightenment practice of *denial*. Enlightenment rationality, in its popular, uncriticized form, teaches that with enough reason and resources, brokenness can be avoided. And so Enlightenment rationality, in its frenzied commercial advertising, hucksters the goods of denial and avoidance: denial of headaches and perspiration and loneliness, impotence and poverty and shame, embarrassment and, finally, death.[7] In such ideology there are no genuinely broken people. When brokenness intrudes into such an assembly of denial, as surely it must, it comes as failure, stupidity, incompetence, and guilt. The church, so wrapped in the narrative of denial, tends to collude in this. When denial is transposed into guilt—into personal failure—the system of denial remains intact and uncriticized, in the way Job's friends defended the system.

The outcome for the isolated failure is that there can be no healing, for there has not been enough candor to permit it. In the end, such denial is not only a denial of certain specifics—it is the rejection of the entire drama of brokenness and healing, the denial that there is an incommensurate Power and Agent who comes in pathos into the brokenness, and who by coming there makes the brokenness a place of possibility.

The denial precludes participation in the *candor* that assaults the system and that makes newness possible. Israel, of course, knew about the practice of denial. Israel knew how to imagine its own immunity from threat and risk: "As for me, I said in my prosperity, 'I shall never be moved'" (Ps 30:6). In its honest embrace of YHWH, however, Israel did not freeze in its denial, but moved on in a way that made newness a possibility:

> You have turned my mourning into dancing;
> you have taken off my sackcloth

and clothed me with joy,
so that my soul may praise you
and not be silent.
O LORD my God, I will give
thanks to you forever. (Ps 30:11-12)

Israelite Hope versus Enlightenment Despair

At the culmination of Israel's portrayal of reality is a certitude and a vision of newness, a full restoration to well-being that runs beyond any old well-being. This culmination in well-being, assured by the resolve of YHWH, is articulated in the conclusion of most psalms of complaint and in prophetic promises that eventuate in messianic and apocalyptic expectations. Israel's speech witnesses to *profound hope*, based in the promise-maker and promise-keeper for whom all things are possible.

Israel refuses to accept that any context of nullity—exile, death, chaos—is a permanent conclusion to reality. Israel, in such circumstance, articulated hope rooted not in any discernible signs in the circumstance, but in the character of YHWH (based on old experience), who was not a prisoner of circumstance but was able to override circumstance in order to implement promises. This hope is not incidental in Israel's life; it is a bedrock, identity-giving conviction, nurtured in nullity, that YHWH's good intentions have not and will not be defeated. As a consequence, complainers anticipate well-being and praise. Israel awaits home-coming, the dead look to new life, creation expects reordering.

All of this requires confidence in an agent outside the system of defeat. Enlight-enment liberalism, which sets the liberated, self-sufficient human agent at the cen-ter of reality, can entertain or credit no such agent outside the system. Without such an agent who exists in and through Israel's core testimony, there are no new gifts to be given and no new possibilities to be received. Thus, put simply, the alternative to Israelite hope is *Enlightenment despair*. In such a metanarrative, when human capacity is exhausted, all is exhausted. Ultimate trust is placed in human capacity, human ingenuity, and human technology. It is self-evident that such a trust cannot deliver, and so ends in despair, for self-sufficiency is only a whisker away from despair. Such a reading of reality engenders fear and hate, self-hate, and brutality. But Israel, inside its peculiar testimony, refuses such a reading.

I state the contrast as boldly and sweepingly as I know how. The drama of brokenness and restoration, which has YHWH as its key agent, features *generos-ity, candor* in brokenness, and resilient *hope*, the markings of a viable life. The primary alternative now available to us features *scarcity, denial,* and *despair,* surely the ingredients of nihilism.

To be sure, for all its venturesome witness, Israel did not always choose cleanly. Israel accommodated and compromised. It practiced scarcity as much as it trusted generosity. It engaged occasionally in denial, for all its embrace of brokenness. It lived close to despair, for all its resources of hope. The amazing thing, in my judgment, is not that Israel compromised; it is that Israel kept its testimony as sustained as it did amid the pressures and demands of its circumstance. It kept its testimony enough of a coherent assertion that it was able to say, in the voice of YHWH, to itself, to its own children, and to any others who would listen:

> See, I have set before you today life and prosperity, death and adversity. If you obey the commandments of the LORD your God that I am commanding you today, by loving the LORD your God, walking in his ways, and observing his commandments, decrees, and ordinances, then you shall live and become numerous, and the LORD your God will bless you in the land that you are entering to possess. But if your heart turns away and you do not hear, but are led astray to bow down to other gods and serve them, I declare to you today that you shall perish; you shall not live long in the land that you are crossing the Jordan to enter and possess. I call heaven and earth to witness against you today that I have set before you life and death, blessings and curses. Choose life so that you and your descendants may live, loving the LORD your God, obeying him, and holding fast to him; for that means life to you and length of days, so that you may live in the land that the LORD swore to give to your ancestors, to Abraham, to Isaac, and to Jacob. (Deut 30:15-20)

This Deuteronomic assertion, derivative from the vision of Moses, proved durable enough for Israel that in its season of rehabilitation, Ezra could still affirm: "Nevertheless, in your great mercies you did not make an end of them or forsake them, for you are a gracious and merciful God" (Neh 9:31). The choosing between construals of reality is something Israel always had to do again. And the choosing is not yet finished.

Classical Christianity's Tilt toward Closure

A second vision of reality against which the Old Testament may play is the articulation of classical Christianity. Here I will deal much more briefly with the interface and the tension between construals, for on the whole, classical Christianity shares claims with Israel's testimony against Enlightenment liberalism. That is, classical Christianity, like ancient Israel, affirms *generosity* over scarcity, *brokenness* in the face of denial, and *hope* instead of despair. I want to assert only one point that is sharply at issue between these narrative offers. I have repeatedly stressed that Israel deals with an incommensurate God who is endlessly at risk in mutuality. That is, YHWH is seen by Israel to be genuinely dialectical, always on one end of a disputatious transaction that may effect change in YHWH as well as in YHWH's partners. We have seen this profound unresolved already in Exod 34:6-7. We have seen it regularly in the noun-metaphors used for YHWH. Most largely, we have seen this dialectical quality in the juxtaposition of what I have called core testimony and countertestimony. Israel's transactions with YHWH are indeed characteristically open and unsettled.

It appears to me, granting the enormous difference made by a christological center in Christian faith, that the real issue that concerns us in Old Testament theology is this: Classical Christianity is tilted in a transcendental direction, which gives closure to YHWH and to YHWH's relationships with the partners. There may be many reasons for such a closure; perhaps not least is the need of a derivative tradition (Christianity) to substantiate its claim against the precursive tradition (Judaism). For whatever reason, this tendency to transcendental closure compromises the genuinely dialectical quality of Jewish testimony. That compromise, moreover, is of crucial importance for what is possible and what is precluded in our discernment of God, world, and self.[8]

I do not imagine that Christianity in its classical forms will yield much, soon, on this score. But there are hints that as Christianity in the West is increasingly disestablished, and so may distance itself from its Hellenistic-Constantinian propensity, it may move in the direction of its Jewish dimension of genuine unsettlement between YHWH and YHWH's partners. There is no doubt that this drama of brokenness and restoration is shared by Judaism and Christianity. In Judaism, it is a drama of:

exile and homecoming,
death and resurrection,
Pit and rescue, and
chaos and creation.

To that set of categories of discernment, Christianity adds (decisively for its identity) crucifixion and resurrection. That of course is a specific move the Old Testament (and Judaism) do not make. The differential on this point is very great.

What strikes me more, however, is that these traditions are, in the main, agreed. That agreement is the basis for a genuine alternative to the nihilism of the modern world, a nihilism contained in the elimination of this incommensurate, mutual One in the interest of autonomy and self-sufficiency. This testimony of Israel, echoed by Christianity, not only gives different answers—it insists on different questions, wherein the answers offered are perforce thin and tenuous, but not for that reason unuttered. The intramural quarrels in the church, and the ancient alienations between Christians and Jews, are unconscionable, in my judgment, when this lean, resilient tradition stands as a fragile alternative to the embrace of the Nihil. ▬

Notes

Preface

1. Walter Brueggemann, *Theology of the Old Testament: Testimony, Dispute, Advocacy* (Minneapolis: Fortress Press, 1997).

2. Gerhard von Rad, *The Message of the Prophets* (New York: Harper and Row, 1972).

3. The most important articulation of such an organic notion of creation is that of Terence E. Fretheim, *God and World in the Old Testament: A Relational Theology of Creation* (Nashville: Abingdon Press, 2005).

4. I take the term "blowback" from Chalmers A. Johnson, *Blowback: The Costs and Consequences of American Empire* (New York: Metropolitan Books, 2000).

Chapter One

1. See Michael Fishbane, *Biblical Myth and Rabbinic Mythmaking* (Oxford: Oxford University Press, 2003).

2. Morton Smith, "The Common Theology of the Ancient Near East," *JBL* 71 (1952): 135–47; Norman K. Gottwald, *The Tribes of Yahweh: A Sociology of the Religion of Liberated Israel, 1250–1050 B.C.* (Maryknoll, N.Y.: Orbis, 1979), 676–78.

3. The accent upon YHWH's sovereignty is evident in many places, among them the enthronement psalms (Psalms 47, 93, 96–99), the doxologies of Amos (Amos 4:13; 5:8-9; 9:5-6), and the hymns of Isaiah 40–55.

4. Gottwald, *Tribes of Yahweh*, 679–91.

5. On the centrality of these texts, see Walter Brueggemann, *Old Testament Theology: An Introduction* (Nashville: Abingdon, 2008).

6. Gottwald, *Tribes of Yahweh*, 667–709.

7. James A. Sanders, "Adaptable for Life: The Nature and Function of Canon," in *Magnalia Dei: The Mighty Acts of God: Essays on the Bible and Archaeology in Memory of G. Ernest Wright*, ed. Frank Moore Cross, et al. (Garden City, N.Y.: Doubleday, 1976), 531–60, has it just right concerning a "monotheizing tendency."

8. On the move toward polity, see S. Dean McBride, "Polity of the Covenant People: The Book of Deuteronomy," *Int* 41 (1987): 229–44. It is [AQ: do you mean "instructive"?] instinctive that it is the book of Deuteronomy, the most central book for the faith of the Old Testament, that moves toward a polity.

9. Gottwald, *Tribes of Yahweh*, 686–87.

10. Recent scholarship has found rich, alternative analogies to the covenant in the ancient Near East. On the one hand, the bilateral covenant of Sinai (and Deuteronomy) is not unlike the international treaties of the eighth century. On the other hand, the unilateral covenant with Abraham is not unlike the land grant arrangements elsewhere in the ancient Near East. It is important that all of these various social practices can be subsumed under the single term *covenant*.

11. In the book of Deuteronomy, for example, William Moran, "The Ancient Near Eastern Background of the Love of God in Deuteronomy," *CBQ* 25 (1963): 77–87, has long ago shown that "love" pertains to public performance. More recently, Jacqueline E. Lapsley, "Feeling Our Way: Love for God in Deuteronomy," *CBQ* 65 (2003): 350–69, has demonstrated an emotional dimension in these same texts. It is clear that it is a both/and, and we need not and cannot choose one or the other.

12. I use the term "thick" in the way made usable by Clifford Geertz that became available in theological discourse through the work of George Lindbeck, *The Nature of Doctrine: Religion and Theology in a Postliberal Age* (Philadelphia: Westminster, 1984), 115–24.

13. The phrase is from Karl Barth, "The Strange New World within the Bible," *The Word of God and the Word of Man* (New York: Harper & Brothers, 1957), 28–50.

14. There is currently considerable energy in the project of recovering the early christological reading of the Old Testament in the church. See Jason Byassee, *Praise Seeking Understanding: Reading the Psalms with Augustine* (Grand Rapids: Eerdmans, 2007); Robert Wilken, *Isaiah Interpreted by Early Christian and Medieval Commentators* (The Church's Bible; Grand Rapids: Eerdmans, 2007); and Brevard Childs, *The Struggle to Understand Isaiah as Christian Scripture* (Grand Rapids: Eerdmans, 2004).

15. Particular attention should be paid to the recent opening articulated by Dabru Emet, on which see *Christianity in Jewish Terms*, ed. Tikva Frymer-Kensky, et al. (Boulder: Westview, 2000).

16. Martin Buber, *I and Thou* (Edinburgh: T. & T. Clark, 1937).

17. On the pattern of Israel's hymns, see Walter Brueggemann, *Israel's Praise: Doxology against Idolatry and Ideology* (Philadelphia: Fortress Press, 1988), chapter 4.

18. Franz Rosenzweig, *The Star of Redemption* (trans. William W. Hallo; 1970; repr. Notre Dame: University of Notre Dame Press, 1985), 174.

19. Ibid., 176.

20. Ibid.

21. Ibid., 178.

22. Ibid., 180.

23. Ibid., 183.

24. Ibid., 185.

25. Emmanuel Levinas, *Totality and Infinity: An Essay on Exteriority* (Pittsburgh: Duquesne University Press, 1969).

26. Abraham Heschel, *The Prophets* (New York: Harper & Row, 1962).

27. Kazo Kitamori, *Theology of the Pain of God* (Eugene: Wipf & Stock, 1958).

28. Jürgen Moltmann, *The Crucified God: The Cross of Christ as the Foundation and Criticism of Christian Theology* (trans. R. A. Wilson and John Bowden; New York: Harper & Row, 1974), 270, 272.

29. Ibid., 243.

30. George Steiner, *Real Presences* (Chicago: University of Chicago Press, 1989), 225.

31. The dialogical nature of the transaction between God and God's creatures is indicated in the way in which John Calvin begins the *Institutes*. Calvin debates with himself whether to begin with "knowledge of ourselves" or "knowledge of God." Calvin of course opts for the latter in a way that matters enormously, but in principle he acknowledges that he could have begun either way. The difference is not unimportant, but the possibility is worth noting.

32. Rosenzweig, *Star of Redemption*, 232, 233.

33. On the defining accent on gratitude in the life of the world before God, see George W. Stroup, *Before God* (Grand Rapids: Eerdmans, 2004).

34. See Brueggemann, *Israel's Praise*, 89–100.

35. See Claus Westermann, *The Psalms: Structure, Content and Message* (trans. Ralph D. Gehrke; Minneapolis: Augsburg, 1980), 73–83.

36. Special attention should be paid to the recent study of William S. Morrow, *Protest Against God: The Eclipse of a Biblical Tradition* (Hebrew Bible Monographs 4; Sheffield: Sheffield Phoenix Press, 2007), in which he shows that the capacity for protest and complaint was gradually displaced by a call for penance. The shift, so he argues, was in order to protect God's honor and was accomplished by the interpretive elites who had a stake in an uncontested God.

37. Special consideration may be given to Exod 2:23 and the way in which the cry of Israel initiates the narrative of the exodus. More broadly, see James L. Kugel, *The God of Old: Inside the Lost World of the Bible* (New York: Free Press, 2003), 109–36.

38. See Gerhard von Rad, *Old Testament Theology*, vol. 2: *The Theology of Israel's Prophetic Traditions* (trans. D. M. G. Stalker; San Francisco: Harper & Row, 1965), 263–77. It is the merit of von Rad to have organized his two-volume Old Testament theology to feature these promissory oracles as structurally significant for the faith claims of the Old Testament.

39. On the theological intentionality of the Twelve, see Walter Brueggemann, *An Introduction to the Old Testament: The Canon and Christian Imagination* (Louisville: Westminster John Knox, 2003), 209–14, and particularly the citations to Paul House, *The Unity of the Twelve* (JSOTSup 97; Bible and Literature Series 27; Sheffield: Almond, 1990); and James Nogalski, *Redactional Processes in the Book of the Twelve* (BZAW 218; Berlin: de Gruyter, 1993).

40. See Claus Westermann, *Basic Forms of Prophetic Speech* (trans. Hugh Clayton White; Philadelphia: Westminster, 1967).

41. On Israel's complaints that refuse to accept responsibility for the dysfunction, see Fredrik Lindström, *Suffering and Sin: Interpretations of Illness in the Individual Complaint Psalms* (Coniectanea Biblica Old Testament Series 37; Stockholm: Almqvist & Wiksell International, 1994).

42. Because the poetry concerns a failed relationship that may be restored, it is essential that these poets must employ the most intense imagery of interpersonal relationships, those of parent and child and husband and wife; it is now recognized that such usage is deliberately and uncritically patriarchal, but that it nonetheless opens the way for reflection an intensity of wounding and healing.

43. On the covenant formula, see Rolf Rendtorff, *The Covenant Formula: An Exegetical and Theological Investigation* (Edinburgh: T. & T. Clark, 1998). It is quite remarkable that the frequent use of the formula occurs precisely in the exilic period when Israel is preoccupied with the fact of its abandonment by YHWH.

44. On the burden of such innovation, see Samuel Wells, *Improvisation: The Drama of Christian Ethics* (Grand Rapids: Brazos, 2004).

45. Moltmann, *Crucified God*, 272.

Chapter 2

1. Martin Buber and Abraham Heschel have written most eloquently about the inscrutable theological quality of Israel. See Martin Buber, *Israel and the World: Essays in a Time of Crisis* (New York: Schocken, 1948); *On Zion: The History of an Idea* (New York: Schocken, 1973); and *On Judaism,* ed. Nahum N. Glatzer (New York: Schocken, 1967); Abraham J. Heschel, *God in Search of Man: A Philosophy of Judaism* (New York: Farrar, Straus & Cudahy, 1955); and *Between God and Man: An Interpretation of Judaism* (New York: Harper & Row, 1959). Of recent literature the most important and most helpful is Joel S. Kaminsky, *Yet I Loved Jacob: Reclaiming the Biblical Concept of Election* (Nashville: Abingdon, 2007).

2. That is, in the primary claims of the Old Testament, YHWH is never without Israel, and Israel is never without YHWH. Cf. Rudolf Smend, *Die Bundesformel* (Theologische Studien 68; Zurich: EVZ-Verlag, 1963).

3. Erich Voegelin, *Order and History*, vol. 1: *Israel and Revelation* (Baton Rouge: Louisiana State University Press, 1956), has discussed these matters very generally as the interplay of "pragmatic" and "paradigmatic," though by "paradigmatic" he apparently means theological-ideational. David Weiss Halivni, "Response to 'Talmudic Scholarship as Textual Reasoning,'" in *Textual Reasonings: Jewish Philosophy and Text Study at the End of the Twentieth Century,* ed. Peter Ochs and Nancy Levine (Grand Rapids: Eerdmans, 2002), 144–51, uses the term *pragmatic* for early traditions in Israel. By this term he means they "serve the needs of the community of practice," whatever judgment may be made about "historicity."

4. On the relation of the two clusters of material to each other, see R. W. L. Moberly, *The Old Testament of the Old Testament: Patriarchal Narratives and Mosaic Yahwism* (OBT; Minneapolis: Fortress Press, 1992).

5. In Exod 2:23-25 (and characteristically), it is the initiatory cry of need and distress by Israel that evokes and mobilizes YHWH's transformative activity. In this sense the classic notion of divine initiative needs to be kept under criticism. Here it is human cry that evokes the originary action of YHWH. On the cruciality of "the cry" as a theological datum in Israel, see James L. Kugel, *The God of Old: Inside the Lost World of the Bible* (New York: Free Press, 2003), 109–36.

6. James M. Robinson, "The Historicality of Biblical Language," in *The Old Testament and Christian Faith,* ed. Bernhard W. Anderson (London: SCM, 1964), 156.

7. On this term in its political-covenantal dimension, see William L. Moran, "The Ancient Near Eastern Background of the Love of God in Deuteronomy," *CBQ* 25 (1963): 77–87; and more recently Jacqueline E. Lapsley, "Feeling Our Way: Love for God in Deuteronomy," *CBQ* 65 (2003): 350–69.

8. For the classic study that keeps election in a general, liberal framework, reflective of the so-called biblical theology movement, see H. H. Rowley, *The Biblical Doctrine of Election* (London: Lutterworth, 1950). See Kaminsky, *Yet I Loved Jacob.*

9. Good summary statements of recent scholarship may be found in Delbert Hillers, *Covenant: The History of a Biblical Idea* (Baltimore: Johns Hopkins University Press, 1969); Dennis J. McCarthy, *Covenant: A Summary of Current Opinions* (Oxford: Blackwell, 1972); Norbert Lohfink, *The Covenant Never Revoked: Biblical Reflections on Christian-Jewish Dialogue* (New York: Paulist Press, 1991); and especially Ernest W. Nicholson, *God and His People: Covenant and Theology in the Old Testament* (Oxford: Clarendon, 1986).

10. George W. Mendenhall, *Law and Covenant in Israel and in the Ancient Near East* (Pittsburgh: Biblical Colloquium, 1955); Klaus Baltzer, *The Covenant Formulary in the Old Testament, Jewish, and Early Christian Writings* (trans. David E. Green; Oxford: Blackwell, 1971). See also Dennis J. McCarthy, *Treaty and Covenant: A Study in Forms in the Ancient Oriental Documents and in the Old Testament* (rev. ed.; AnBib 21A; Rome: Pontifical Biblical Institute, 1978).

11. Lothar Perlitt, *Bundestheologie im Alten Testament* (WMANT 36; Neukirchen-Vluyn: Neukirchener Verlag, 1969); E. Kutsch, "Gesetz und Gnade. Probleme des alttestamentlichen Bundesbegriffs," *ZAW* 79 (1976): 18–35; and Nicholson, *God and His People*.

12. The classic formulation is that of Walther Eichrodt, *Theology of the Old Testament* (trans. J. A. Baker; 2 vols.; OTL; Philadelphia: Westminster, 1961–67). James Barr, "Some Semantic Notes on the Covenant," *Beiträge zur Alttestamentlichen Theologie: Festschrift für Walther Zimmerli*, ed. Herbert Donner, et al. (Göttingen: Vandenhoeck & Ruprecht, 1977), 37–38, is surely correct in his judgment that the reality of covenant must be recognized as present in the assumed world of Israel, even if the actual word *berit* is a later usage. Speaking of Perlitt's negative conclusion concerning covenant, Barr writes:

> Yet with all the will in the world it is a little hard to believe that the covenant of YHWH with Israel became significant only so late. The sort of analysis that is roughly adumbrated in this article, especially through its implying the existence of syntactical and linguistic, rather than ideological and theological, restrictions on the use of the term *berith*, might possibly suggest other explanations of why this term is not found in certain types of sources. A current of tradition that used *berith* in one kind of linguistic context might use other terminology in another without this being evidence of a basic theological conflict.

13. Moshe Weinfeld, "The Covenant of Grant in the Old Testament and in the Ancient Near East," *Journal of the American Oriental Society* 90 (1970): 184–203, has provided the most compelling notion of unconditional covenant in terms of "land grant." On the dialectic, see David Noel Freedman, "Divine Commitment and Human Obligation," *Int* 18 (1964): 419–31. Jon D. Levenson, *Sinai and Zion: An Entry into the Jewish Bible* (Minneapolis: Winston, 1985), refuses any suggestion of tension or contrast and subsumes the royal (unconditional) covenant under the Mosaic (Torah-based) covenant.

14. In the earlier discussion of covenant, Genesis 15 played a peculiarly important part. See Ronald Clements, *Abraham and David: Genesis 15 and Its Meaning for Israelite Tradition* (SBT 2/5; London: SCM, 1967). Since that time, however, critical assumptions have shifted drastically so that Genesis 15 is not regarded as an early tradition. See Rolf Rendtorff, "Genesis 15 im Rahmen der theologischen Bearbeitung der Vatergeschichte," in *Werden und Wirken des Alten Testaments: Festschrift für Claus Westermann,* ed. Rainer Albertz, et al. (Göttingen: Vandenhoeck & Ruprecht, 1980), 74–81; and John Ha, *Genesis 15: A Theological Compendium of Pentateuchal History* (BZAW 181; Berlin: de Gruyter, 1989).

15. E. P. Sanders, *Paul and Palestinian Judaism: A Comparison of Patterns of Religion* (Philadelphia: Fortress Press, 1977), 75 and passim.

16. On the cruciality of the first commandment for Old Testament theology, see Norbert Lohfink, *Das Hauptgebot: Eine Untersuchung literarischer Einleitungsfragen zu Dtn 5–11* (AnBib 20; Rome: Pontifical Biblical Institute, 1963); Werner H. Schmidt, *The Faith of the Old Testament: A History* (Oxford: Blackwell, 1983); Walther Zimmerli, *The Old Testament and the World* (trans. John J. Scullion; Atlanta: John Knox, 1976); and idem, *Old Testament Theology in Outline* (trans. D. E. Green; Atlanta: John Knox, 1978).

17. This theological perspective has dominated much of the history of interpretation of the love poems. The classic example is the long series of sermons by Bernard of Clairvaux. See

On the Song of Songs (trans. Kilian Walsh and Irene Edmunds; 4 vols.; Kalamazoo, Mich.: Cistercian Publications, 1971–80). Continuing the exegetical trajectory of Bernard, see C. E. Hocking, *Rise Up My Love* (Precious Seeds, 1988), and André LaCocque and Paul Ricoeur, *Thinking Biblically: Exegetical and Hermeneutical Studies* (Chicago: University of Chicago Press, 1998), 235–303. More generally, see Wilfred Cantwell Smith, *What Is Scripture? A Comparative Approach* (Minneapolis: Fortress Press, 1993), 21–44. See the deconstructive interpretation of David J. A. Clines, "Why Is There a Song of Songs, and What Does It Do to You If You Read It?" *Interested Parties: The Ideology of Writers and Readers of the Hebrew Bible* (JSOTSup 205; Sheffield: Sheffield Academic Press, 1995), 94–121.

18. Rabbinic interpreters noted that "do" has priority in the text over "hear."

19. On the dialectic of manifestation and proclamation in Christian theology and liturgy, see David Tracy, *The Analogical Imagination: Christian Theology and the Culture of Pluralism* (New York: Crossroad, 1984), 371–404. Tracy follows the categories of Paul Ricoeur, "Manifestation and Proclamation," *Futuring the Sacred: Religion, Narrative, and Imagination* (Minneapolis: Fortress Press, 1995), 48–67.

20. It is difficult to avoid something like "God's preferential option for the poor" in these texts. On the theme, see Gustavo Gutiérrez, *A Theology of Liberation: History, Politics, and Salvation* (Maryknoll, N.Y.: Orbis, 1988). On the theme of justice, see José Miranda, *Marx and the Bible: A Critique of the Philosophy of Oppression* (Maryknoll, N.Y.: Orbis, 1977), 109–99; Miranda shows that justice in this tradition is not maudlin or romantic in its implementation, but concerns the reality of economic and political life in community. John Barton, *Understanding Old Testament Ethics* (Louisville: Westminster John Knox, 2003), 50–54, has shown that "imitation of God" is a primary way in which Israel characterizes ethics.

21. On possible ideological aspects of Psalm 72, a poem ostensibly about justice, see David Jobling, "Deconstruction and the Political Analysis of Biblical Texts: A Jamesonian Reading of Psalm 72," *Semeia* 59 (1992): 95–127.

22. On this text in Micah, see Marvin Chaney, "You Shall Not Covet Your Neighbor's House," *Pacific Theological Review* 15, no. 2 (1982): 3–13. On systemic dimensions of coveting in prophetic discourse, see D. N. Premnath, *Eighth Century Prophets: A Social Analysis* (St. Louis: Chalice Press, 2003).

23. This has been seen most clearly by Norman K. Gottwald, *The Tribes of Yahweh: A Sociology of the Religion of Liberated Israel, 1250–1050* B.C.E. (Maryknoll, N.Y.: Orbis, 1979). See more generally Michael Walzer, *Exodus and Revolution* (New York: Basic Books, 1985).

24. Samuel Terrien, *The Elusive Presence: Toward a New Biblical Theology* (New York: Harper & Row, 1978), has gone furthest in contemporary scholarship in giving attention to "the tradition of seeing" in the structure and shape of Old Testament theology.

25. Tracy, *Analogical Imagination*, has explored this facet of Christian faith under the twin rubrics of "prophetic" and "mystical," which correspond roughly to "proclamation" and "manifestation." The theme of cultic presence that understands God in sacramental terms (that is, via mystical manifestation) is clearly reflected in these texts, but is largely neglected in Protestant critical scholarship. That neglect seems to have its counterpart in the characteristic preference of Pauline to Johannine New Testament Christianity.

26. When taken canonically, there is no doubt that the tabernacle is presented as an anticipation of the temple of Solomon. By contrast, critical scholarship has generally taken the tabernacle to be a subsequent reflection of the actual temple.

27. On the presence of YHWH in the temple, see Tryggve N. D. Mettinger, *The Dethronement of Sabaoth: Studies in the Shem and Kabod Theologies* (Lund: Gleerup, 1982), 19–37; and Ben C. Ollenburger, *Zion, City of the Great King: A Theological Symbol of the Jerusalem Cult* (JSOTSup 41; Sheffield: Sheffield Academic Press, 1987).

28. See Jon D. Levenson, *Theology of the Program of Restoration of Ezekiel 40–48* (Harvard Semitic Monograph 10; Missoula, Mont.: Scholars Press, 1976).

29. On the "holy one in Israel," see Walter Brueggemann, *Theology of the Old Testament: Testimony, Dispute, Advocacy* (Minneapolis: Fortress Press, 1997), 288–93.

30. On the sociotheological significance of this perspective in the faith of Israel, see Fernando Belo, *A Materialist Reading of the Gospel of Mark* (Maryknoll, N.Y.: Orbis, 1981). See the critical discussion of Israel Knohl, *The Sanctuary of Silence: The Priestly Torah and the Holiness School* (Minneapolis: Fortress Press, 1995).

31. On the "Holiness Code," in addition to Knohl, *Sanctuary of Silence*, see John G. Gammie, *Holiness in Israel* (OBT; Minneapolis: Fortress Press, 1989), 9–44; and Dale Patrick, *Old Testament Law* (London: SCM, 1986), 145–88; and more generally Frank Crüsemann, *The Torah: Theology and Social History of Old Testament Law* (trans. Allan W. Mahnke; Minneapolis: Fortress Press, 1996), 277–327.

32. That is, one cannot determine from the statement of the text whether the words intend a direct, "primitive" experience or a mediated presence through the cultic apparatus. This is a distinction not considered in the text, as it is never considered by the actual practitioners of a cult. Notice how carefully John Calvin, *Commentary on the Book of Psalms* (repr. Grand Rapids: Baker, 1979), 1:253, resists any cultic claim in the words: "*To behold God's face*, is nothing else than to have a sense of his fatherly favour, with which he not only causes us to rejoice by removing our sorrows, but also transports us even to heaven."

33. I make reference to the phrase of Søren Kierkegaard, *Purity of Heart Is to Will One Thing: Spiritual Preparation for the Office of Confession* (New York: Harper & Brothers, 1948).

34. On Job 31, see Georg Fohrer, "The Righteous Man in Job 31," in *Essays in Old Testament Ethics (J. Philip Hyatt, in Memoriam),* ed. James L. Crenshaw and John T. Willis (New York: Ktav, 1974), 1–22.

35. On the peculiar character and role of Israel according to this text, see Martin Buber, *The Kingship of God* (3d ed.; London: Allen & Unwin, 1967).

36. The function recalls the rabbinic phrase taken up by Emil Fackenheim, *To Mend the World: Foundations of Post-Holocaust Thought* (New York: Schocken, 1989). More specifically, see Richard D. Nelson, *Raising up a Faithful Priest: Community and Priesthood in Biblical Theology* (Louisville: Westminster/John Knox, 1993), 39–53 and passim.

37. Hans Walter Wolff, "The Kerygma of the Yahwist" (trans. Wilbur A. Benware), *Int* 20 (1966): 131–58; repr. in Walter Brueggemann and Wolff, *The Vitality of Old Testament Traditions* (2d ed.; Atlanta: John Knox, 1982), 41–66.

38. See Gerhard von Rad, "The Form-Critical Problem of the Hexateuch," *The Problem of the Hexateuch and Other Essays* (trans. E. W. Trueman Dicken; New York: McGraw-Hill, 1966), 66.

39. Wolff, "Kerygma of the Yahwist."

40. Harry M. Orlinsky and Norman H. Snaith, *Studies on the Second Part of the Book of Isaiah* (VTSup 14; Leiden: Brill, 1967).

41. Harry M. Orlinsky, "The So-Called 'Servant of the Lord' and 'Suffering Servant' in Second Isaiah," ibid., 103.

42. It is possible to see all of the Deuteronomic History, Joshua through Kings, as a lawsuit that indicts Israel and points to the exile as the legitimate judgment pronounced on the basis of the indictment. This perspective on the Deuteronomists was suggested by the early work of Gerhard von Rad, *Studies in Deuteronomy* (trans. David Stalker; SBT 1/9; London: SCM, 1953), 74–91. This view is strengthened if we regard Deuteronomy 32 as a model from which the larger history is composed. G. Ernest Wright, "The Law-Suit of God: A Form-Critical Study of Deuteronomy 32," in *Israel's Prophetic Heritage,* ed. Bernhard W. Anderson

and Walter Harrelson (London: SCM, 1962), 26–67, has shown that Deuteronomy 32 is an early poem that is shaped as a lawsuit, and so it is possible to see this linkage between the poem and the history.

43. On the lawsuit in the prophets, see Claus Westermann, *Basic Forms of Prophetic Speech* (trans. Hugh Clayton White; Philadelphia: Westminster, 1967).

44. See Daniel L. Smith, *The Religion of the Landless: The Social Context of the Babylonian Exile* (Bloomington, Ind.: Meyer-Stone, 1989); idem, *A Biblical Theology of Exile* (OBT; Minneapolis: Fortress Press, 2002).

45. Jacob Neusner, *Understanding Seeking Faith: Essays on the Case of Judaism* (Atlanta: Scholars Press, 1986), 1:137–41, has nicely articulated the way in which exile becomes the paradigmatic, definitive mark of Jews, even for those not in exile.

46. On the exile as the "null point," see Walther Zimmerli, *I Am Yahweh*, ed. Walter Brueggemann (trans. Douglas W. Stott; Atlanta: John Knox, 1982), 111–33.

47. See Hans Walter Wolff, "The Kerygma of the Deuteronomic Historical Work" (trans. Frederick C. Prussner), in Brueggemann and Wolff, *Vitality of Old Testament Traditions*, 83–100.

48. See ibid., 91–93, on Deut 4:29-30; 30:1-10; and 1 Kgs 8:33-53.

49. See Nancy C. Lee, *The Singers of Lamentations: Cities under Siege, from Ur to Jerusalem to Sarajevo* (Leiden: Brill, 2002); Tod Linafelt, *Surviving Lamentations: Catastrophe, Lament, and Protest in the Afterlife of a Biblical Book* (Chicago: University of Chicago Press, 2000); and Kathleen M. O'Connor, *Lamentations and the Tears of the World* (Maryknoll, N.Y.: Orbis, 2002).

50. Erhard Gerstenberger, "Der klagende Mensch: Anmerkungen zu den Klagegattungen in Israel," in *Probleme biblischer Theologie: Gerhard von Rad zum 70. Geburtstag*, ed. Hans Walter Wolff (Munich: Chr. Kaiser, 1971), 64–72, has shown that Israel's lament is in fact an act of resilient and determined hope.

51. In a forthcoming book, my colleague Kathleen M. O'Connor will show that both grief and blame are characteristic practices in a community suffering post-traumatic stress syndrome. As in Israel, such communities run a rich and daring emotional gamut.

52. On the translation of this problematic verse, see Delbert Hillers, *Lamentations: A New Translation with Introduction and Commentary* (rev. ed.; AB 7A; New York: Doubleday, 1992), 160–61; O'Connor, *Lamentations and Tears*, 77–79; and Linafelt, *Surviving Lamentations*, 60–61.

53. In the exile, Israel as a displaced community had need of a God who was mobile and not rooted in the temple in Jerusalem. Mettinger, *Dethronement of Sabaoth*, has reviewed the strategies of the Deuteronomic and Priestly traditions in rearticulating YHWH as a mobile God available to the displaced community.

54. On the crucial innovation of these traditions, see Gerhard von Rad, *Old Testament Theology* (trans. D. M. G. Stalker; 2 vols.; San Francisco: Harper & Row, 1962–65), 2:163–77 and passim; and Walter Brueggemann, *Hopeful Imagination: Prophetic Voices in Exile* (Minneapolis: Fortress Press, 1986).

55. On this crucial formula, see the classic study of Ernst L. Dietrich, *Die endzeitliche Wiederherstellung bei der Propheten* (BZAW 40; Giessen: Töpelmann, 1925); and John M. Bracke, "Šûb šebût: A Reappraisal," *ZAW* 97 (1985): 233–44.

56. See Walter Brueggemann, *Genesis* (Interpretation; Atlanta: John Knox, 1982), 75–88, for the suggestion that in the flood narrative of Genesis 6–9, nothing has changed except the inclination of YHWH. The restoration of the earth after the flood is possible not because humanity has changed, but because YHWH has a new inclination driven by pathos.

57. See Walter Brueggemann, "'The Uncared For' Now Cared For (Jer 30:12–17): A Methodological Consideration," *JBL* 104 (1985): 419–28.

58. On the cruciality of this statement for Israel's exilic problem of continuity, see Walter Brueggemann, "A Shattered Transcendence? Exile and Restoration," in *Biblical Theology: Problems and Perspectives*, ed. Steven J. Kraftchick, et al. (Nashville: Abingdon, 1995), 169–82.

59. It is altogether plausible, on the basis of the evidence we have, that Persian imperial policy did indeed effect a reversal of the policy of deportation. In light of that change, however, it is not evident that there was an immediate, wholesale return of Jews from Babylon.

60. Otto Plöger, *Theocracy and Eschatology* (Richmond: John Knox, 1968); Paul D. Hanson, *The Dawn of Apocalyptic: The Historical and Sociological Roots of Jewish Apocalyptic Eschatology* (Philadelphia: Fortress Press, 1975).

61. On the canonizing process in the midst of theopolitical tensions, see Rainer Albertz, *A History of Israelite Religion in the Old Testament Period*, vol. 2: *From the Exile to the Maccabees* (trans. John Bowden; OTL; Louisville: Westminster/John Knox, 1994).

62. On pluralism as a defining mark of Judaism in the period, see Albertz, ibid.; and Michael E. Stone and David Styron, *Emerging Judaism: Studies in the Fourth and Third Centuries B.C.E.* (Minneapolis: Fortress Press, 1989). On the contemporary implications of that pluralism, see Donn Morgan, *Fighting with the Bible: Why Scripture Divides Us and How It Can Bring Us Together* (New York: Seabury, 2007).

63. The tension between obedience and hope as theological reference points trades upon critical judgments, such as those made by Hanson *(Dawn of Apocalyptic)* and Plöger *(Theocracy and Eschatology)*.

64. See Jacob Neusner, *From Politics to Piety: The Emergence of Pharisaic Judaism* (Englewood Cliffs, N.J.: Prentice-Hall, 1973).

65. See James L. Mays, "The Place of the Torah-Psalms in the Psalter," *JBL* 106 (1987): 3–12.

66. On the difficult critical questions concerning this movement of reform, see especially Hugh G. Williamson, *Ezra, Nehemiah* (Word Biblical Commentary 16; Waco: Word, 1985), xxxvi–lii; and Geo Widengren, "The Persian Period," *Israelite and Judaean History*, ed. John H. Hayes and J. Maxwell Miller (OTL; Philadelphia: Westminster, 1977), 489–538.

67. Of particular importance are two recent books by Jon D. Levenson, *Resurrection and the Restoration of Israel: The Ultimate Victory of the God of Life* (New Haven: Yale University Press, 2006), and with Kevin J. Madigan, *Resurrection: The Power of God for Christians and Jews* (New Haven: Yale University Press, 2008). Levenson urges that it is the victory of God in resurrection that assures the restoration of life and the restoration of Israel.

68. On this text, see what has become the decisive discussion in English: Wright, "Law-Suit of God."

69. On this chapter and its symmetrical shape, see David J. A. Clines, "Hosea 2: Structure and Interpretation," *Studia biblica 1978,* ed. E. A. Livingstone (JSOTSup 11; Sheffield: University of Sheffield, 1979), 83–103.

70. On the social reality from which these texts cannot be separated, see Wayne A. Meeks, *The First Urban Christians: The Social World of the Apostle Paul* (New Haven: Yale University Press, 1983).

71. I refer especially to Franz Rosenzweig, *The Star of Redemption* (trans. William W. Hallo; 1970; repr. Notre Dame: University of Notre Dame Press, 1985). See also Eugen Rosenstock-Huessy, ed., *Judaism Despite Christianity: The "Letters on Christianity and Judaism" between Eugen Rosenstock-Huessy and Franz Rosenzweig* (Tuscaloosa: University of Alabama Press, 1969).

72. See James Barr, *The Concept of Biblical Theology* (Minneapolis: Fortress Press, 1999), chapter 18; Leo G. Perdue, *Reconstructing Old Testament Theology: After the Collapse of History* (OBT; Minneapolis: Fortress Press, 2005), chapter 6.

73. Jon D. Levenson, "Why Jews Are Not Interested in Biblical Theology," *The Hebrew Bible, the Old Testament, and Historical Criticism* (Louisville: Westminster John Knox, 1993), 33–61.

74. In addition to the titles of Levenson cited in n. 67, see *Creation and the Persistence of Evil: The Jewish Drama of Divine Omnipotence* (Princeton: Princeton University Press, 1995).

75. On the statement, Dabru Emet, see *Christianity in Jewish Terms,* ed. Tikva Frymer-Kensky, et al. (Boulder: Westview, 2000).

76. See the important discussion, *Contesting Texts: Jews and Christians in Conversation about the Bible*, ed. Melody D. Knowles, et al. (Minneapolis: Fortress Press, 2007).

77. See Susan Handelman, *The Slayers of Moses: The Emergence of Rabbinic Interpretation in Modern Literary Theory* (Albany: SUNY Press, 1982).

78. See Michael Prior, *Zionism and the State of Israel: A Moral Inquiry* (London: Routledge, 1999); idem, *The Bible and Colonialism: A Moral Critique* (Sheffield: Sheffield Academic Press, 1997).

79. For a case study in the use of the biblical rhetoric of domination, see David M. Gunn, "Colonialism and the Vagaries of Scripture: Te Kooti in Canaan (A Story of Bible and Dispossession in Aoteareoa/New Zealand," in *God in the Fray: A Tribute to Walter Brueggemann,* ed. Tod Linafelt and Timothy K. Beal (Minneapolis: Fortress Press, 1998), 127–42. For a study of how the same rhetoric has become shaping for U.S. global ideology, see Christopher Collins, *Homeland Mythology: Biblical Narratives in American Culture* (University Park: Pennsylvania State University Press, 2007).

80. The absence of irony and the capacity for self-criticism in the use of such rhetoric was well understood by Reinhold Niebuhr, *Irony in American History* (New York: Scribner, 1952).

Chapter 3

1. Without much variation or nuance, Walther Eichrodt, *Man in the Old Testament* (trans. K. and R. Gregor Smith; SBT 1/4; London: SCM, 1951), resolves human identity into a mandate of *obedience,* without any countertheme to balance or qualify obedience. In this regard, Eichrodt's reading seems to reflect a rather one-dimensional Calvinism.

2. Emmanuel Levinas, *In the Time of the Nations* (London: Athlone, 1994), 124.

3. My point here is not to underscore the use of masculine terminology by Levinas, but rather to note his insistence that human persons, even non-Israelites, are within the scope of the Torah. The older literature regularly utilizes gendered speech in speaking of human persons.

4. Concerning the destructive alternative of human autonomy, see Abraham Heschel, *Who Is Man?* (Stanford: Stanford University Press, 1966). On the general theme of autonomy, see John S. Macken, *The Autonomy Theme in the "Church Dogmatics": Karl Barth and His Critics* (Cambridge: Cambridge University Press, 1990). Macken shows how Barth moves away from Kant's "turn to the subject." See also Daniel H. Frank, ed., *Autonomy and Judaism: The Individual and the Community in Jewish Philosophical Thought* (Albany: SUNY Press, 1992).

5. The literature is enormous on the notion of "image of God" as a theological theme. Among the more important recent exegetical studies are the following: James Barr, "The Image of God in the Book of Genesis—a Study of Terminology," *Bulletin of the John Rylands University Library of Manchester* 51 (1968–69): 11–26; Phyllis Bird, "Male and Female He Created Them: Genesis 1:27 on the Context of the Priestly Account of Creation," *HTR* 74 (1981):

129–59; Kari E. Borresen, ed., *The Image of God* (Minneapolis: Fortress Press, 1995); Ulrich Mauser, "Image of God and Incarnation," *Int* 24 (1970): 336–56; Gerhard von Rad, *Genesis* (trans. John H. Marks; rev. ed.; OTL; Philadelphia: Westminster, 1972), 57–61; Ellen M. Ross, "Human Persons as Images of the Divine," in *The Pleasure of Her Text: Feminist Readings of Biblical and Historical Texts,* ed. Alice Bach (Philadelphia: Trinity Press International, 1990), 97–116; John F. A. Sawyer, "The Meaning of בְּצֶלֶם אֱלֹהִים ('In the Image of God') in Genesis I–XI," *Journal of Theological Studies* 25 (1974): 418–26; and Krister Stendahl, "Selfhood in the Image of God," in *Selves, People, and Persons: What Does It Mean to Be a Self?,* ed. Leroy S. Rouner (Notre Dame, Ind.: University of Notre Dame Press, 1992), 141–48. The most comprehensive and most helpful discussion of Old Testament usage known to me is that of Claus Westermann, *Genesis 1–11* (German, 1984; trans. John J. Scullion; Continental Commentary; Minneapolis: Fortress Press, 1994), 142–61. Most recently see Richard J. Middleton, *The Liberating Image: The Imago Dei in Genesis 1* (Grand Rapids: Brazos Press, 2005).

6. The bibliography on this issue is enormous. Among the more influential and helpful is Phyllis Trible, *God and the Rhetoric of Sexuality* (OBT; Philadelphia: Fortress Press, 1978), 1–30 and passim.

7. On this question, James Barr, *The Garden of Eden and the Hope of Immortality: The Reid-Tucker Lectures for 1990* (Minneapolis: Fortress Press, 1993), has suggested a radical and significant alternative to the long-established consensus position of Oscar Cullmann.

8. See Walter Brueggemann, "The God of All Flesh," in *"And God Saw That It Was Good": Essays on Creation and God in Honor of Terence E. Fretheim* (WW Sup 5; Minneapolis: Word and World, 2006), 85–93.

9. We are only beginning to notice and appreciate the accent on nonhuman creatures in the creation theology of the Old Testament, largely because of a new ecological awareness. On the animals as God's creatures belonging on the horizon of human responsibility, see especially the work of Douglas John Hall, *The Stewardship of Life in the Kingdom of Death* (Grand Rapids: Eerdmans, 1988); *The Steward: A Biblical Symbol Come of Age* (Grand Rapids: Eerdmans, 1990); and *Imaging God: Dominion as Stewardship* (Grand Rapids: Eerdmans, 1986).

10. So Eichrodt without much nuance or suppleness; see n. 1 above.

11. See Heschel, *Who Is Man?,* 97–98: "Against the conception of the world as something just here, the Bible insists that the world is creation. Over all being stand the words: Let there be! And there was, and there is. To be is to obey the commandment of creation. God's word is at stake in being. There is a cosmic piety in sheer being. What is endures as a response to a command. . . . What I suggest is not that first there is neutral being and then value. Being created implies being born in value, being endowed with meaning, receiving value. Living involves acceptance of meaning, obedience, and commitment."

12. For an impressive review of the matter of human "dominion" in the modern world and its roots in the Bible, see Cameron Wybrow, *The Bible, Baconism, and Mastery over Nature: The Old Testament and Its Modern Misreading* (American University Studies, series 7, vol. 112; New York: Peter Lang, 1991). Wybrow in a most helpful way takes issue with the well-known thesis of Lynn White that the Bible provides the basis for an exploitative relation to the earth.

13. Levinas, *In the Time,* 124–25.

14. See James Barr, *Biblical Faith and Natural Theology: The Gifford Lectures for 1991* (Oxford: Clarendon, 1993); and with more disciplined precision, John Barton, *Understanding Old Testament Ethics* (Louisville: Westminster John Knox, 2003), 32–44.

15. On this pivotal chapter in the Old Testament, see Georg Fohrer, "The Righteous Man in Job 31," in *Essays in Old Testament Ethics (J. Philip Hyatt, in Memoriam)*, ed. James L. Crenshaw and John T. Willis (New York: Ktav, 1974), 1–22.

16. Hans Heinrich Schmid has most helpfully exposited the Old Testament notion of an ordering of creation to which human persons must submit and for the maintenance of which they are responsible. His crucial statement in English is "Creation, Righteousness, and Salvation: 'Creation Theology' as the Broad Horizon of Biblical Theology," in *Creation in the Old Testament,* ed. Bernhard W. Anderson (IRT; Philadelphia: Fortress Press, 1984), 102–17. This article is reflective of his two basic studies, which have not been translated into English: *Wesen und Geschichte der Weisheit: Eine Untersuchung zur altorientalischen und israelitischen Weisheitsliteratur* (BZAW 101; Berlin: Töpelmann, 1966); and *Gerechtigkeit als Weltordnung: Hintergrund und Geschichte des alttestamentlichen Gerechtigkeitsbegriffes* (Beiträge zur historischen Theologie; Tübingen: Mohr [Siebeck], 1968). See also Rolf P. Knierim, *The Task of Old Testament Theology: Method and Cases* (Grand Rapids: Eerdmans, 1995), 171–243.

17. Matthew 6:25-31 is completely congruent with this accent on YHWH the Creator who is faithful to human persons; cf. Pss 104:27-28 and 145:15-16. See also Eccl 9:7-9.

18. These themes are at the center of the Christian anthropology proposed by Wolfhart Pannenberg, *Anthropology in Theological Perspective* (trans. Matthew J. O'Connell; Edinburgh: T. & T. Clark, 1985).

19. Levinas, *In the Time,* 125.

20. Ibid., 127–32.

21. See my discussion of Israel's countertestimony in this regard in *Theology of the Old Testament: Testimony, Dispute, Advocacy* (Minneapolis: Fortress Press, 1997), 374–81. There I have situated the psalms of complaint under the larger rubric of "countertestimony." On Israel's belated discomfort at such rhetoric, see William S. Morrow, *Protest against God: The Eclipse of a Biblical Tradition* (Sheffield: Sheffield Phoenix Press, 2007).

22. Abraham Heschel, in a reference now lost to me, writes, "Man is also necessary to God, to the unfolding of his plans in the world. Man is needed; he is a need of God."

23. The practical outcome of this compartmentalization in the contemporary church is that so-called conservatives tend to take careful account of the most rigorous claims of the Bible concerning sexuality, and are indifferent to what the Bible says about economics. Mutatis mutandis, so-called liberals relish what the Bible says in demanding ways about economics, but tread lightly around what the Bible says about sexuality.

24. See my discussion of this pivotal passage, *Theology of the Old Testament,* 215–18 and 269–70.

25. Alfons Deissler, "'Mein Gott, Warum hast du mich verlassen' . . . (Ps 22.2)," *Ich will euer Gott werden* (Stuttgarter Bibel-Studien 100; Stuttgart: Katholisches Bibelwerk, 1981), 99–121.

26. Thus the Shema of Deut 6:4 is at the center of an Old Testament understanding of human personhood. See J. Gerald Janzen, "On the Most Important Word in the Shema," *VT* 37 (1987): 280–300. It is important, however, to remember that *shema'* means "hear" before it means "obey." Paul Ricoeur, in one of his early writings, observes that to listen is to concede that one is not self-made and autonomous. Listening—responding in obedience to another—is recognition that one is derivative and inherently connected to one who has the right to address.

27. Hans Heinrich Schmid, *Gerechtigkeit als Weltordnung,* has shown that justice is not only Sinai-focused in the Old Testament. *ṣedaqah* belongs to the very structure and fabric of creation and must not be violated; see Prov 8:10-21. On the commandments for Gentiles, see David Novak, *The Image of the Non-Jew in Judaism: An Historical and Constructive Study of the Noahide Laws* (New York: Mellen, 1983).

28. See the references to the work of Hall in n. 9 above.

29. Moshe Weinfeld, *Deuteronomy and the Deuteronomic School* (Oxford: Clarendon, 1972), has gone so far as to suggest that the commandment tradition of Deuteronomy is in fact rooted in sapiental instruction. ·

30. It is a complete misunderstanding to reduce the God-human relation in the Old Testament to the practice of a flat, one-dimensional, uncritical obedience. See Dorothee Sölle, *Beyond Mere Obedience: Reflections on a Christian Ethic for the Future* (Minneapolis: Augsburg, 1970); and Stanley Milgram, *Obedience to Authority: An Experimental View* (London: Tavistock, 1974).

31. I use the term *model* because a great deal of scholarship now regards the historical evidence for Solomon as a wisdom figure as minimal if not nonexistent. Nonetheless, as a model for subsequent tradition, Solomon is a powerful force. See Walter Brueggemann, "The Social Significance of Solomon as a Patron of Wisdom," in *The Sage in Israel and the Ancient Near East*, ed. John G. Gammie and Leo G. Perdue (Winona Lake, Ind.: Eisenbrauns, 1990), 117–32; and idem, *Solomon: Israel's Ironic Icon of Human Achievement* (Columbia: University of South Carolina Press, 2005), 104–23.

32. On the role of Joseph as an ambivalent figure of Israelite faith while in the service of the empire, see W. Lee Humphreys, "A Life-Style for Diaspora: A Study of the Tales of Esther and Daniel," *JBL* 92 (1973): 211–23. Worth noting is the negative judgment of Leon R. Kass, *The Beginning of Wisdom: Reading Genesis* (New York: Free Press, 2003), 569 and passim, that the character of Joseph is marked by "Egyptianization."

33. Proverbs is a sustained reflection on the cruciality of human discernment in the practice of human freedom, human responsibility, and human power. Reference should be made to Gerhard von Rad, *Wisdom in Israel* (trans. James D. Martin; Nashville: Abingdon, 1972), as well as James L. Crenshaw, *Urgent Advice and Probing Questions: Collected Writings on Old Testament Wisdom* (Macon, Ga.: Mercer University Press, 1995); and Roland E. Murphy, *The Tree of Life: An Exploration of Biblical Wisdom Literature* (New York: Doubleday, 1990); idem, "The Personification of Wisdom," in *Wisdom in Ancient Israel: Essays in Honour of J. A. Emerton,* ed. John Day, et al. (Cambridge: Cambridge University Press, 1995), 222–33.

34. See my own foray into this subject matter in Walter Brueggemann, *In Man We Trust: The Neglected Side of Biblical Faith* (1973; repr. Eugene: Wipf & Stock, 2006). This study was early in the scholarly recovery of wisdom, and would now need to be stated somewhat differently.

35. On trust as a theme in the discernment of humanness, see Deissler, "Mein Gott," 111–13; Hugo Goeke, "Die Anthropologie der individuellen Klagelieder," *Bibel und Leben* 14 (1973): 14–15; and Horst Seebass, "Über den Beitrag des Alten Testaments zu einer theologische Anthropologie," *Kerygma und Dogma* 22 (1976): 52.

36. Erik H. Erikson, *Identity and the Life Cycle* (New York: Norton, 1980), 57–67.

37. Gerhard von Rad, *Holy War in Ancient Israel* (trans. and ed. Marva J. Dawn; Grand Rapids: Eerdmans, 1991), 101–14, has situated Israel's notion of faith in the context of holy war, that is, the readiness to trust YHWH when Israel is helpless and has no resources to face the threat in which it finds itself. Von Rad, moreover, proposed that faith from such a context of threat is then transposed in the prophetic tradition of Isaiah so that it becomes a more sophisticated theological motif, but does not lose the concrete reference of its origin. On the usage in Isaiah, see Gerhard von Rad, *Old Testament Theology* (trans. D. M. G. Stalker; 2 vols.; New York: Harper & Row, 1962–65), 2:174.

38. Notice that while *baṭaḥ* is used in v. 1, *'emet* is used in v. 3.

39. This is the counterpoint to Israel's core testimony about YHWH who sustains and intervenes. The functioning human person, as envisioned by Israel, is one who trusts in YHWH's faithful sustenance and intervention and on that basis lives freely. The focus is evident in

Isaiah 36–37, for the Assyrians did not reckon with YHWH as a decisive and particular force in the common history of Judah. They did not know, moreover, about Israel's readiness to act on the basis of trust in YHWH.

40. See Deissler, "Mein Gott," 109–11; and Erhard Gerstenberger, "Der klagende Mensch: Anmerkungen zu den Klagegattungen in Israel," in *Probleme biblischer Theologie: Gerhard von Rad zum 70. Geburtstag*, ed. Hans Walter Wolff (Munich: Chr. Kaiser, 1971), 64–72.

41. The basic study is that of Claus Westermann, *Praise and Lament in the Psalms* (trans. Keith R. Crim and Richard N. Soulen; 2d ed.; Atlanta: John Knox, 1981). Geo Widengren, *The Akkadian and Hebrew Psalms of Lamentation as Religious Documents: A Comparative Study* (Uppsala: Almqvist & Wiksell, 1937), has shown that Israel's complaints draw on a vast background of such religious practice. The most recent comprehensive study of this genre and practice of faith is Patrick D. Miller, *They Cried to the Lord: The Form and Theology of Biblical Prayer* (Minneapolis: Fortress Press, 1994).

42. Erhard Gerstenberger, "Jeremiah's Complaints: Observations on Jer 15:10–21," *JBL* 82 (1963): 405 n. 50, has helpfully distinguished between "complaint" (*Anklage*) and "lament" (*Klage*): "A lament bemoans a tragedy that cannot be reversed, while a complaint entreats God for help in the midst of tribulation." Israel characteristically engages in complaint, not lament.

43. Fredrik Lindström, *Suffering and Sin: Interpretations of Illness in the Individual Complaint Psalms* (Stockholm: Almqvist & Wiksell International, 1994).

44. Claus Westermann, "The Role of the Lament in the Theology of the Old Testament" (trans. Richard N. Soulen), *Int* 28 (1974): 25 and passim (repr. in *Praise and Lament*, 264–65 and passim), has nicely contrasted the characteristic practice of Christian piety (which is in a mood of submissiveness and docility) with Jewish piety (which characteristically does not shrink from protest of a most vigorous kind).

45. See Miller, *They Cried to the Lord*, 86–114; and Deissler, "Mein Gott," 113–15.

46. On motivations, see Miller, *They Cried to the Lord*, 114–26. The motivations offered for YHWH's actions in time of need are of various kinds, some of which are not congruent with "innocent" Christian piety. That is, in addition to confessions of sin and statements of need and trust, Israel also seeks to motivate YHWH to act by appealing to YHWH's honor, vanity, and risk of shame (e.g., Num 14:13-16). I take it that the willingness of Israel to appeal to such risky motivations is a measure of the urgency of the petition. It is not possible or necessary to tone down such motivations to conform to a kind of "pure faith," for the Old Testament is not engaged in "pure faith," and no amount of Christian romanticism can make it so. Israel is engaged in faith that must live honestly in the midst of an unfair and threatening world.

47. Patrick D. Miller, "Prayer as Persuasion: The Rhetoric and Intention of Prayer," *WW* 13 (Fall 1993): 362. Miller nicely summarizes the range of motivations that seek to persuade God to be present and to act in transformative ways. These include appeal to YHWH's faithfulness, YHWH's reputation, Israel's protestation of innocence, and Israel's readiness to praise YHWH. Israel's prayers are permeated with such speech, indicating the urgency of persuasion and defining the dynamic between the two partners in the exchange.

48. In a daring assertion, Karl Barth, *Prayer* (50th anniversary edition; Louisville: Westminster John Knox, 2002), 13, writes: "God is not deaf, but listens; more than that, he acts. God does not act in the same way whether we pray or not. Prayer exerts an influence upon God's actions, even upon his existence."

49. Gerald T. Sheppard, "Theology and the Book of Psalms," *Int* 46 (1992): 143–55; and "Enemies and the Politics of Prayer in the Book of Psalms," in *The Bible and the Politics of Exegesis: Essays in Honor of Norman K. Gottwald on His Sixty-Fifth Birthday,* ed. David Jobling, et al. (Cleveland: Pilgrim, 1991), 61–82. While there may be an element of politics in the

complaint, as Sheppard suggests, it also must be insisted that the prayers are indeed prayers addressed to God, anticipating an active response. On the theological seriousness of the psalms as prayers, see Harold Fisch, *Poetry with a Purpose: Biblical Poetics and Interpretation* (Bloomington: Indiana University Press, 1990), 104–35.

50. The response of YHWH to the complaints of Israel is perhaps to be understood in terms of salvation oracles. On that genre and practice, see the basic study of Joachim Begrich, "Das priesterliche Orakel," *ZAW* 52 (1934): 81–92; the critical assessment of the theory by Edgar W. Conrad, *Fear Not Warrior: A Study of 'al tira' Pericopes in the Hebrew Scriptures* (BJS 15; Chico, Calif.: Scholars Press, 1985); and Miller, *They Cried to the Lord*, 135–77.

51. See my comments on thank offering, in which I have proposed that this is the most elemental act of worship and faith in Israel, in *Theology of the Old Testament*, 126–30; and see Miller, *They Cried to the Lord*, 179–204.

52. The several works by Gerstenberger cited earlier suggest the actual social practice and context of the drama. It is to be insisted, following Harold Fisch, that the complaint of Israel and the ensuing drama are not merely cathartic (though they are that), but the process is genuinely relational and transactional. Israel proceeds in the deep conviction that YHWH is indeed engaged in the process. Thus it will not do to interpret these prayers according to modern notions of autonomy, which is as close as Elisabeth Kübler-Ross, *On Death and Dying* (London: Tavistock, 1970), can come to a parallel. The real claim of prayer is affirmed in the comment by Barth, *Prayer*, 23: "Prayer is not only *directed* to God (one is not talking to one's self), but it *reaches* God. God hears. God answers. God allows prayer to affect and move him." In *Church Dogmatics*, vol. 3/3: *The Doctrine of Creation* (Edinburgh: T. & T. Clark, 1960), 285, Barth writes: "His sovereignty is so great that it embraces both the possibility, and as it is exercised, the actuality that the creation can actively be present and cooperate in His overruling."

53. See James W. Jones, *Contemporary Psychoanalysis and Religion: Transference and Transcendence* (New Haven: Yale University Press, 1993); W. W. Meissner, *Life and Faith* (Washington, DC: Georgetown University Press, 1987); and Mary Lou Randour, *Exploring Sacred Landscapes: Religious and Spiritual Experience in Psychotherapy* (New York: Columbia University Press, 1993). More generally on the development of complex human interiority, see Charles Taylor, *Sources of the Self: The Making of Modern Identity* (Cambridge: Harvard University Press, 1989); William S. Schmidt, *The Development of the Notion of Self: Understanding the Complexity of Human Interiority* (Lewiston, N.Y.: Mellen, 1994); and S. E. Hormuth, *The Ecology of the Self* (Cambridge: Cambridge University Press, 1990).

54. The classic theory is that of D. W. Winnicott, *The Maturational Processes and the Facilitating Environment: Studies in the Theory of Emotional Development* (New York: International Universities Press, 1965). Winnicott's important concepts that bear upon our theme concern an elemental omnipotence and the emergence of "false self" where omnipotence is not practiced. It is my judgment that complaint addressed to YHWH can be understood as Israel's moment of "omnipotence." Further, it is my judgment that because Christian practice has denied people this dimension of piety, the church inclines to produce "false selves" who cannot be honest before God and so must "fake it" with God. As a derivative study, see Walter Brueggemann, "The Costly Loss of Lament," *JSOT* 36 (1986): 57–71.

I do not believe that biblical faith ever has an enduring alliance with any theory of personality. Nonetheless in the present range of available personality theories, I believe that object relations theory now articulates the formation and maintenance of humanness in ways that are peculiarly congruent with Israel's covenantal, transactional notion of self. See Michael St. Clair, *Object Relations and Self Psychology* (Monterey, Calif.: Brooks/Cole, 1986).

Moving away from Freud's notion of self as a conundrum of internal conflicts, object relations theory has proposed that the formation of self is situated in an ongoing relation with a real person (that is, a real object, not a figment of imagination, hence the term "object relations"), most often the mother or someone who performs mothering functions. A key insight of this theory is that in its youngest days and weeks, the infant must experience omnipotence vis-à-vis its mother—must have the sense that the mother exists solely for the child, who is then able to exult fully and celebrate a sense of self with his or her own needs and wants. Such an experience of omnipotence requires the mother's total attention to the child, and permits the beginning of the formation of a strong sense of self.

Alternately, if the mother cannot cede self fully to the child, the child quickly learns to fake it, to please and manipulate the mother in order to satisfy the child's wants. Such a faking procedure produces a "false self," who is never able to be honest but must always pretend, and so develops a capacity for (unrecognized) duplicity between genuine want and need and what is permitted with the mother. Thus everything about emotional health depends on the mother as a strong agent who willingly becomes "useful" to the child for the sake of the child. Other important theorists pertinent to this discussion (in addition to Winnicott) are Otto Kernberg, Heinz Kohut, and W. Ronald Fairbairn.

Of course, it is a long move from a "good enough" mother to the self in relation to a "good enough" YHWH. It occurs to me, nonetheless, that complaint and petition whereby the speaker can be fully honest before YHWH and expect YHWH to accept the self so expressed requires a strong sense of self on the part of the petitioner; it also requires, with equal urgency, a God who can cede initiative and authority in the transaction to the petitioner who speaks imperatives to YHWH and so enjoys an instant of omnipotence. Thus in Israel's practice such prayer belongs to a healthy self. Such a transaction is not to be understood as mere psychology, but theologically depends on a God who is sovereign (like a "good enough" mother), but who in the instant of prayer invites and welcomes omnipotence in the voice of the petitioner.

In my judgment, this matter of omnipotence before YHWH in prayer relates to healthy believers before YHWH. If one must always please God (like always pleasing mother), one learns to fake it and so become a "false self" vis-à-vis YHWH. I suggest that in its characteristically flat articulation of God as omnipotent, the church has unwittingly done much to nourish believers to be false selves. The predictable consequence, now so evident, is church persons who are inordinately moralistic in an insistence that others should please God in the same undifferentiated way they have learned to do.

55. In addition to Gerstenberger, "Der klagende Mensch," see the definitive work of Jürgen Moltmann, *Theology of Hope: On the Ground and Implication of a Christian Eschatology* (German, 1967; trans. James W. Leitch; Minneapolis: Fortress Press, 1993). Moltmann has shown that hope is not one theme among many in Christian theology, but is the foundation for everything. For Old Testament theology, it is important that Moltmann depends on the Old Testament scholarship of Albrecht Alt and Gerhard von Rad in making this judgment.

56. On praise as the "ceding of self," see Walter Brueggemann, "Praise and the Psalms: A Politics of Glad Abandonment," in *The Psalms and the Life of Faith,* ed. Patrick D. Miller (Minneapolis: Fortress Press, 1995), 112–32; and idem, "The Daily Voice of Faith: The Covenanted Self," *Sewanee Theological Review* 37 (Easter 1994): 123–43.

57. The relationship between praise and thanksgiving is a delicate and tricky one. In a most influential way, Westermann, *Praise and Lament*, 25–30, has tended to collapse the two into one. Nonetheless, he regards praise as much more important and dynamic, for he understands thanks as being more calculating and quid pro quo. Against Westermann, Harvey H. Guthrie, *Theology as Thanksgiving: From Israel's Psalms to the Church's Eucharist* (New York: Seabury, 1981), 12–30, inclines to regard thanksgiving as more elemental than praise, and therefore as more at the core of a practice of faith. While the tension between the positions

of Westermann and Guthrie is not easily resolved, the question that concerns them both is of enormous importance.

58. On the theological significance of praise, see Daniel W. Hardy and David F. Ford, *Praising and Knowing God* (Philadelphia: Westminster, 1985). Hardy and Ford (pp. 20, 142) speak of praise as the "jazz factor" of the Christian life. The image is a suggestive one, for it bespeaks the fact that life rooted in biblical faith, Jewish or Christian, in generous surrender (a) has a regular cadence to it, (b) pushes forward into newness, and (c) allows for newness and radical variation amid the reliable cadences. My own experience of the cruciality of praise is highlighted by a presentation of what I thought was a Calvinist accent on praise as the foundation of Christian life. In response, the great Roman Catholic bishop Rembert G. Weakland observed to me that my comments concerning praise were completely Benedictine in orientation. Aside from certain code words, traditions as distinct as Benedictine and Calvinist recognize this foundation for faithful living.

59. Relinquishment here is to be understood first of all as liturgical, symbolic, and emotional. But such a practice has an inevitable and unavoidable counterpart in socioeconomic and political relinquishment; on this see Marie Augusta Neal, *A Socio-theology of Letting Go: The Role of a First World Church Facing Third World Peoples* (New York: Paulist Press, 1977).

60. Self-denial is fraudulent and pathological unless one has arrived at a self that can be willingly ceded and surrendered. Without such a self to give, self-denial is likely simply a refusal to live one's life.

61. See Seebass, "Über den Beitrag," 47–53.

62. See n. 54 above on Moltmann's appeal to the Old Testament in his systematic formulation.

63. See Erhard Gerstenberger, *Der bittende Mensch: Bittritual und Klagelied des Einzelnen im Alten Testament* (WMANT 51; Neukirchen-Vluyn: Neukirchener Verlag, 1980); and "Der klagende Mensch." More broadly, see Walther Zimmerli, *Man and His Hope in the Old Testament* (SBT 2/20; London: SCM, 1971).

64. On this aspect of the notion of "knowledge of YHWH," see Herbert B. Huffmon, "The Treaty Background of Hebrew *yāda'*," *BASOR* 181 (1966): 31–37; and Herbert B. Huffmon and Simon B. Parker, "A Further Note on the Treaty Background of Hebrew *yāda'*," *BASOR* 184 (1966): 36–38.

65. This is the accent made by Hans Walter Wolff, "Wissen um Gott bei Hosea als Urform von Theologie," *Evangelische Theologie* 12 (1952/53): 533–54. See also Dwight R. Daniels, *Hosea and Salvation: The Early Traditions of Israel in the Prophecy of Hosea* (BZAW 191; Berlin: de Gruyter, 1990), 111–16.

66. Martin Buber, *Meetings* (La Salle, Ill.: Open Court, 1973), suggests ways in which human transactions are themselves occasions for "presence."

67. On this psalm and its distinct testimony, see Martin Buber, *Right and Wrong* (London: SCM, 1952), 34–52; J. Clinton McCann, "Psalm 73: A Microcosm of Old Testament Theology," in *The Listening Heart: Essays on Wisdom and the Psalms in Honour of Roland E. Murphy*, ed. Kenneth Hoglund (JSOTSup 58; Sheffield: JSOT Press, 1987), 247–57; and Brueggemann, *Psalms and Life of Faith*, 203–10.

68. On the textual problem in v. 1, see Ernst Würthwein, "Erwägungen zu Psalm 73," *Wort und Existenz: Studien zum Alten Testament* (Göttingen: Vandenhoeck & Ruprecht, 1970), 163–71. More generally see Walter Brueggemann and Patrick D. Miller, "Psalm 73 as a Canonical Marker," *JSOT* 72 (December 1996): 45–56.

69. The notion of desire as a core aspect of the life of faith was especially appreciated by Augustine, who distinguished it in subtle ways from lust. For a thoughtful discussion of the problem in Augustine, see Margaret R. Miles, *Desire and Delight: A New Reading of Augustine's*

Confessions (New York: Crossroad, 1992). In this context, also recall Johann Sebastian Bach's great "Jesu, Joy of Man's Desiring."

70. Claus Westermann, *Elements of Old Testament Theology* (trans. Douglas W. Stott; Atlanta: John Knox, 1978), 106–7, has shrewdly seen that Josh 5:12 stands at the end of the wilderness period of Israel, which began with the giving of free bread in Exodus 16. Thus Exodus 16 and Joshua 5 bracket the time in Israel's normative narrative when the abundance of YHWH was driven out by the scarcity of coveting. It is not accidental, I assume, that the narrative of coveting in Joshua 7–8 follows so quickly after Israel arrives in the promised land. There is something odd and insidious about the fact that *having* makes persons greedier. Thus the reception of gifts from YHWH makes for a circumstance of scarcity, precisely when gifts should locate persons and communities amid God's abundance. This odd turn of matters is well documented in statistics about affluence and the corresponding loss of generosity.

71. It is characteristic of Israel's way of speaking that the word *death* is fluid and never precise in its meaning. In the psalms of complaint, when used as a synonym for *pit*, the term *death* seems close to mythological connotations in which death is not far removed from Mot, the Canaanite god of death. But the term also refers to physical expiration. Sometimes, moreover, the term can mean either or both at the same time. It is crucial for Israel not to be too precise. See Walter Brueggemann, "Death, Theology of," *Interpreter's Dictionary of the Bible, Supplement,* ed. Keith Crim (Nashville: Abingdon, 1976), 219–22; and idem, *Praying the Psalms* (Cascade Books; Eugene, Or.: Wipf & Stock, 2007), 39–48.

72. Jon D. Levenson, *Resurrection and the Restoration of Israel: The Ultimate Victory of the God of Life* (New Haven: Yale University Press, 2006). See Mitchell Dahood, *Psalms,* vol. 1: *1–50: Introduction, Translation, and Notes* (AB 16; Garden City, N.Y.: Doubleday, 1965), 33, 91, 252–53; Nicholas J. Tromp, *Primitive Conceptions of Death and the Nether World in the Old Testament* (BibOr 21; Rome: Pontifical Biblical Institute, 1969); and Robert Martin-Achard, *From Death to Life: A Study of the Development of the Doctrine of the Resurrection in the Old Testament* (Edinburgh: Oliver & Boyd, 1960). It is entirely cogent that Isa 52:13—53:12 may be cited as a third text where such a claim is to be recognized.

73. Gary A. Anderson, *A Time to Mourn, a Time to Dance: The Expression of Grief and Joy in Israelite Religion* (University Park: Pennsylvania State University Press, 1991), has shown how joy is related to creation, procreation, and the power for life that is concretely enacted in the community through birth and reproduction. Kevin Madigan and Jon D. Levenson, *Resurrection: The Power of God for Christians and Jews* (New Haven: Yale University Press, 2008), 111–17, have shown how birth is "the functional equivalent" of resurrection.

74. Thomas C. Oden, *Care of Souls in the Classic Tradition* (Philadelphia: Fortress Press, 1984), has traced the way in which the vocabulary of pastoral care shifted from theological references to psychological references in the twentieth century.

75. Walter Brueggemann, "The Transformative Agenda of the Pastoral Office," *Interpretation and Obedience: From Faithful Reading to Faithful Living* (Minneapolis: Fortress Press, 1991), 161–83.

76. Recent scholarship, such as the commentaries of Carol E. Newsom, "The Book of Job," *New Interpreter's Bible,* ed. Leander E. Keck (13 vols.; Nashville: Abingdon, 1994–2004), 4:317–637; and Samuel E. Balentine, *Job* (Smyth & Helwys Commentary; Macon, Ga.: Smyth & Helwys, 2006), have attempted to see the book whole and to see its various parts as elements of a larger artistic intentionality. This represents an important departure from the older critical analysis that dissected the book.

77. Walter Brueggemann, "Psalms and the Life of Faith: A Suggested Typology of Function," *Psalms and Life of Faith,* 3–32.

78. On the term from Paul Ricoeur, "second naiveté," see Mark I. Wallace, *The Second Naiveté: Barth, Ricoeur, and the New Yale Theology* (Macon, Ga.: Mercer University Press, 1990). On the book of Job in relation to models for faith and life, see Walter Brueggemann, "The Third World of Evangelical Imagination," *Interpretation and Obedience,* 9–27. Job's interaction with God is "not fully resolved or free of pain," and can never be, because Job's children remain lost (cf. 1:18-19; 42:13-16).

79. The character Job could be tested with the eight markings for humanness noted in the discussion above.

80. See Paul Ricoeur, *The Symbolism of Evil* (Boston: Beacon, 1969), 252–60.

81. Ernst Bloch, *Atheism in Christianity: The Religion of the Exodus and the Kingdom* (New York: Herder and Herder, 1972), 84–122.

82. See particularly the rendering of Abraham as "the knight of faith" by Søren Kierkegaard, *Fear and Trembling, Repetition* (Princeton, N.J.: Princeton University Press, 1983), 9–23.

83. Jon D. Levenson, *Creation and the Persistence of Evil: The Jewish Drama of Divine Omnipotence* (San Francisco: Harper & Row, 1988), 149–56.

Chapter 4

1. On the structure and function of the genealogies, see Marshall D. Johnson, *The Purpose of Biblical Genealogies with Special Reference to the Settings of the Genealogies of Jesus* (Society for New Testament Studies Monograph Series 8; Cambridge: Cambridge University Press, 1969); and Robert R. Wilson, *Genealogy and History in the Biblical World* (New Haven: Yale University Press, 1977).

2. On the cruciality of the Noah covenant for the scope of biblical theology, see Patrick D. Miller, "Creation and Covenant," in *Biblical Theology: Problems and Perspectives,* ed. Steven J. Kraftchick, et al. (Nashville: Abingdon, 1995), 155–68.

3. The important exception in this pericope is vv. 25-27 and the curse of Canaan.

4. To take "scattering" as a curse is a consensus position. See Bernhard W. Anderson, "The Tower of Babel: Unity and Diversity in God's Creation," *From Creation to New Creation* (OBT; Minneapolis: Fortress Press, 1994), 165–78, for an alternative interpretation that suggests that the scattering is also a positive good.

5. The same verb is used for Israel and for the nations. See Deut 4:27; 28:64; Jer 9:16; 13:24; 18:17.

6. For a reading of this psalm that focuses on its apparent ideology, see David J. A. Clines, "Psalm 2 and the MLF (Moabite Liberation Front)," *Interested Parties: The Ideology of Writers and Readers of the Hebrew Bible* (JSOTSup 205; Sheffield: Sheffield Academic Press, 1995), 244–75.

7. On the royal psalms, see the older but reliable brief study of Keith R. Crim, *The Royal Psalms* (Richmond: John Knox, 1962); and Hans-Joachim Kraus, *The Theology of the Psalms* (German, 1986; trans. Hilton C. Oswald; Continental Commentary; Minneapolis: Fortress Press, 1992), 107–23.

8. On the relation of Psalms 1 and 2, see Patrick D. Miller, *Interpreting the Psalms* (Philadelphia: Fortress Press, 1986), 87–93; idem, "The Beginning of the Psalter," in *The Shape and Shaping of the Psalter,* ed. J. Clinton McCann (JSOTSup 159; Sheffield: Sheffield Academic Press, 1993), 83–92; and in the latter volume: David M. Howard Jr., "Editorial Activity in the Psalter," 52–70; Gerald H. Wilson, "Understanding the Purposeful Arrangement of Psalms in the Psalter," 42–51; idem, "Shaping the Psalter," 72–82.

9. The "seven nations" function as an ideological cipher referring to those who resist or impede the intention of YHWH for Israel, who must therefore be destroyed. It is not possible

to identify either the seven nations or a time when there may have been seven such nations together.

10. Jon D. Levenson, "Is There a Counterpart in the Hebrew Bible to New Testament Antisemitism?" *Journal of Ecumenical Studies* 22 (1985): 242–60, makes the compelling suggestion that just as Christians rapaciously superseded Jews in their use of the Hebrew Bible, so in the Old Testament the Israelites practice the same kind of negation of the nations who preceded them in the land.

11. This antithesis is true on any of the available theories of Israel's "conquest." The precise meaning of the phrase varies with the different theories of conquest.

12. On the meaning and function of the notion of *ḥerem* in ancient Israel, see Susan Niditch, *War in the Hebrew Bible: A Study in the Ethics of Violence* (New York: Oxford University Press, 1993), 28–77; and Philip D. Stern, *The Biblical [ED: H should have underdot] Herem: A Window on Israel's Religious Experience* (BJS 211; Atlanta: Scholars Press, 1991). It is especially worth noting that in 1 Samuel 15, Saul is fully expected, in the terms of the narrative, to implement *ḥerem* against the Amalekites, but in 1 Samuel 30 David does not execute it, nor is the practice on the horizon of that narrator. On this distinction in the expectations of Saul and of David, see Brueggemann, *Theology of the Old Testament,* 369–70.

13. Notice should be taken of Isa 56:3-8, with its inclusive statement that oddly abrogates the Torah provision of Deut 23:2-8. See Herbert Donner, "Jesaja LVI 1-7: Ein Abrogationsfall innerhalb des Kanons—Implikationen und Konsequenzen," in *Congress Volume: Salamanca, 1983,* ed. J. A. Emerton (VTSup 36; Leiden: Brill, 1985), 81–95.

14. The role of Israel as one who blesses the nations comes under the rubric of the promises of YHWH, on which see Brueggemann, *Theology of the Old Testament,* 168–69. Claus Westermann, "The Way of Promise through the Old Testament" (trans. Lloyd Gaston and Bernhard W. Anderson), in *The Old Testament and Christian Faith,* ed. Bernhard W. Anderson (New York: Herder and Herder, 1969), 200–224, has explored the way in which the themes of *blessing* and *promise* are linked in the Genesis texts.

15. Hans Walter Wolff, "The Kerygma of the Yahwist" (trans. Wilbur A. Benware), *Int* 20 (1966): 131–58; repr. in Walter Brueggemann and Wolff, *The Vitality of Old Testament Traditions* (2d ed.; Atlanta: John Knox, 1982), 41–66. See also Gerhard von Rad, "The Form-Critical Problem of the Hexateuch," *The Problem of the Hexateuch and Other Essays* (trans. E. W. Trueman Dicken; New York: McGraw-Hill, 1966), 65 and passim; and Claus Westermann, *Genesis 12–36: A Commentary* (trans. John J. Scullion; Continental Commentary; Minneapolis: Augsburg, 1985), 146 and passim.

16. On a theology of mission toward the nations, see Exod 19:5-6, the blessing theme in Genesis, and Isa 42:6-7, 49:6-9. In a close study of the form and grammatical structure of Gen 12:1-3, Patrick D. Miller, "Syntax and Theology in Genesis xii 3a," *VT* 34 (1984): 472–75, has demonstrated that the ultimate purpose of Abraham's departure at the behest of YHWH is so that the nations may be blessed. Miller has shown, moreover, that the statement on curse is not symmetrical to the statement of blessing and is not a part of the purpose of the journey.

17. There is no doubt that Genesis provides an alternative to a dominant harsh ideology. It is of immense importance, however, that this more generous alternative is evident not only in Genesis, but also in Deuteronomy, that is, in the heart of the harsh ideology. It is recognized that Edom is derived from "Esau your brother," in both narrative (Deut 2:1-8) and command (23:7-8). Moab and Ammon, kinsmen of Israel by Lot, are also given more generous treatment (2:8-25). See Patrick D. Miller, "God's Other Stories: On the Margins of Deuteronomic Theology," *Israelite Religion and Biblical Theology: Collected Essays* (JSOTSup 367; Sheffield: Sheffield Academic Press, 2000), 592–602. It is clear that even in Deuteronomy, something other than a flat, violent dismissal of the nations is on the horizon of Israel.

18. On Psalm 67, see Walter Brueggemann, "The 'Us' of Psalm 67," in *Palabra, Pordigio, Poesia: In memoriam P. Luis Alonso Schökel, S.J.,* ed. Vincente Collado Bertomeu (Rome: Editrice Pontificio Instituto Biblico, 2003), 233–42.

19. This generosity with the Torah, that is, making it available to the nations, is in deep tension with Deut 4:7-8, where Torah is prized as the distinctive property of Israel. In Zech 8:20-23, see a different perspective on the nations vis-à-vis Israel. There the nations are required and expected to recognize "that God is with you" (that is, Israel).

20. On the oracles against the nations, see Norman K. Gottwald, *All the Nations of the Earth: Israelite Prophecy and International Relations in the Ancient Near East* (New York: Harper & Row, 1964); and Paul R. Raabe, "Why Prophetic Oracles against the Nations?" in *Fortunate the Eyes That See: Essays in Honor of David Noel Freedman,* ed. Astrid B. Beck, et al. (Grand Rapids: Eerdmans, 1995), 236–57. Most helpful for theological interpretation of "YHWH and the nations" is the discussion of John Goldingay, "Jeremiah and the Superpowers," in *Uprooting and Planting: Essays on Jeremiah for Leslie Allen,* ed. John Goldingay (London: T. & T. Clark, 2007), 59–77.

21. See Walter Brueggemann, "Patriotism for Citizens of the Penultimate Superpower," *Dialog* 42, no. 4 (2003): 336–43.

22. Klaus Koch, *The Prophets,* vol. 1: *The Assyrian Period* (Minneapolis: Fortress Press, 1983), 70–76; *The Prophets,* vol. 2: *The Babylonian and Persian Periods* (Minneapolis: Fortress Press, 1984), 71, 171, and passim.

23. On motivations for the oracles against the nations, see Graham I. Davies, "The Destiny of the Nations in the Book of Isaiah," in *The Book of Isaiah: Le Livre d'Isaïe,* ed. Jacques Vermeylen (Bibliotheca ephemeridum theologicarum lovaniensium 81; Leuven: Leuven University Press, 1989), 93–120.

24. Walter Harrelson, *The Ten Commandments and Human Rights* (OBT; Philadelphia: Fortress Press, 1980), 173–201, links the Helsinki Accords to the Decalogue.

25. On this theme, see Donald W. Gowan, *When Man Becomes God: Humanism and Hubris in the Old Testament* (Pittsburgh: Pickwick, 1975).

26. John Barton, *Amos's Oracles against the Nations: A Study of Amos 1.3—2.5* (Society for Old Testament Studies Monograph Series 6; Cambridge: Cambridge University Press, 1980), has shown that the reasons for condemnation of the nations are not narrowly Yahwistic, but pertain "to a human convention held to be obviously universal . . . a common ethos" (2, 45).

27. See Walter Brueggemann, "Pharaoh as Vassal: A Study of a Political Metaphor," *CBQ* 57 (January 1995): 27–41.

28. It should be noted that in the list of superpowers that are under criticism in these oracles, the several Hellenic powers are not, for the most part, dealt with. In the later texts they are treated, as in the book of Daniel, under the cipher of Nebuchadnezzar, or in rhetoric that is not explicit but that moves toward transhistorical, apocalyptic imagery. This, however, represents no less an intense theological concern with these powers, but only a general move of Judaism toward apocalyptic rhetoric.

29. Thus in Jeremiah 43–44, a return to Egypt is portrayed as the end of the *Heilsgeschichte* that began in the emancipation of Israel from Egypt. With the return to Egypt, Israel has now come full circle from bondage to freedom with YHWH and back to bondage. See Richard E. Friedman, "From Egypt to Egypt: Dtr¹ and Dtr²," in *Traditions in Transformation: Turning Points in Biblical Faith,* ed. Baruch Halpern and Jon D. Levenson (Winona Lake, Ind.: Eisenbrauns, 1981), 167–92.

30. On the presentation of Egypt as a transhistorical force that disrupts creation, see Terence E. Fretheim, "The Plagues as Ecological Signs of Historical Disaster," *JBL* 110 (1991): 385–96; and, more generally, idem, *Exodus* (Interpretation; Louisville: John Knox, 1991).

31. Fretheim, "Plagues as Ecological Signs," 393.

32. I say "all," but of course the Exodus narrative poignantly notes that Israel is an exception. See Exod 9:4, 6, 26; 11:7.

33. Ellen Davis, "'And Pharaoh Will Change His Mind . . .' (Ezek 32:31)," paper read at Society of Biblical Literature, 1993.

34. Jürgen Kegler, "Zu Komposition und Theologie der Plagenerzählungen," in *Die Hebräische Bibel und ihre zweifache Nachgeschichte: Festschrift für Rolf Rendtorff*, ed. Erhard Blum, et al. (Neukirchen-Vluyn: Neukirchener Verlag, 1990), 55–74, has suggested that in the later strata of the plague cycle of the Exodus narrative, "Egypt" is to be understood as a coded reference to Babylon.

35. In the geopolitical horizon of the Old Testament, Assyria is the inevitable counterpart to Egypt. Sometimes Assyria is specifically intended when it is named, at other times it appears to be a cipher for whatever northern superpower threatens Israel.

36. On these texts, see Brevard S. Childs, *Isaiah and the Assyrian Crisis* (SBT 2/3; London: SCM, 1967); and Christopher Seitz, *Zion's Final Destiny: The Development of the Book of Isaiah: A Reassessment of Isaiah 36–39* (Minneapolis: Fortress Press, 1991).

37. On the ideological struggle with Babylonian policy in the book of Jeremiah, see Christopher R. Seitz, *Theology in Conflict: Reactions to the Exile in the Book of Jeremiah* (BZAW 176; Berlin: de Gruyter, 1986); and John Hill, *Friend or Foe? The Figure of Babylon in the Book of Jeremiah* (Leiden: Brill, 1999).

38. See Walter Brueggemann, "At the Mercy of Babylon: A Subversive Rereading of the Empire," *JBL* 110 (1991): 3–22. On the cruciality of Shaphan and his family for this interpretive enterprise, see Oded Lipschits, *The Fall and Rise of Jerusalem: Judah under Babylonian Rule* (Winona Lake, Ind.: Eisenbrauns, 2005) 84–92.

39. On this text, see Alice Ogden Bellis, *The Structure and Composition of Jeremiah 50:2—51:58* (New York: Mellen, 1994); and Martin Kessler, *Battle of the Gods: The God of Israel versus Marduk of Babylon: A Literary/Theological Interpretation of Jeremiah 50–51* (Assen: Van Gorcum, 2003).

40. See Walter Brueggemann, *Finally Comes the Poet: Daring Speech for Proclamation* (Philadelphia: Fortress Press, 1989), 111–42.

41. See Jon L. Berquist, *Judaism in Persia's Shadow: A Social and Historical Approach* (Minneapolis: Fortress Press, 1995).

42. See Lisbeth S. Fried, "Cyrus the Messiah? The Historical Background to Isaiah 45:1," *HTR* 95 (2002): 373–93.

43 On Persian policy as a reversal of Babylonian policy, see Daniel L. Smith, *The Religion of the Landless: The Social Context of the Babylonian Exile* (Bloomington, Ind.: Meyer-Stone, 1989).

44. On the large panorama of the nations in the book of Daniel, see Martin Noth, "The Understanding of History in Old Testament Apocalyptic," *The Laws in the Pentateuch and Other Studies* (trans. D. R. Ap-Thomas; London: Oliver & Boyd, 1966), 194–214.

45. It is evident that this rehabilitation is not in hand but is anticipated.

46. On this text, see Walter Brueggemann, "'Exodus' in the Plural (Amos 9:7)," in *Many Voices, One God: Being Faithful in a Pluralistic World*, ed. Walter Brueggemann and George W. Stroup (Louisville: Westminster John Knox, 1998), 15–34.

47. Nothing has changed geopolitically, even in the present state of Israel. Israel is positioned, even now, so that it must pursue defense and peace on two fronts to the north and to the south. In contemporary political reality, moreover, the northern front is characteristically less stable and more problematic.

NOTES TO CHAPTER 4-5

199

48. The book of Jonah is an important exception to both of these statements: (a) There is an evident motivation in Nineveh's repentance, and (b) there is an allusion to YHWH's passion in 4:2, with reference to YHWH's steadfast love and compassion.

49. James L. Kugel, *The God of Old: Inside the Lost World of the Bible* (New York: Free Press, 2003), 109–36, has detailed the way in which YHWH is the God who hears cries.

50. Donner, "Jesaja LVI 1-7," 81–95.

51. Paul M. Kennedy, *The Rise and fall of the Great Powers: Economic Change and Military Conflict from 1500 to 2000* (New York: Random House, 1987); Douglas Johnston and Cynthia Sampson, *Religion: The Missing Dimension of Statecraft* (Oxford: Oxford University Press, 1994).

52. Zygmunt Bauman, *Modernity and Holocaust* (Cambridge, Eng.: Polity Press, 1991). See also Richard Rubenstein, *After Auschwitz: History, Theology, and Contemporary Judaism* (2d ed.; Baltimore: Johns Hopkins University Press, 1992).

53. On this insensitive and arrogant claim for the United States, see Francis Fukuyama, *The End of History and the Last Man* (New York: Free Press, 1992). Happily in more recent days Fukuyama has largely distanced himself from his earlier outrageous judgment.

54. See Fareed Zakaria, *The Post-American World* (New York: Norton, 2008), who calls attention to the powers that "come after" the United States. The prophetic tradition knows that there is always another power to "come after."

Chapter 5

1. Reductionism in church theology in a conservative, fundamentalist way has been especially noted by Mark A. Noll, *The Scandal of the Evangelical Mind* (Grand Rapids: Eerdmans, 1994). While his analysis pertains to the reductionism of the right, the same may be said of the left in church theology, on which see Stephen Sykes, "Authority in the Church of England," *Unashamed Anglicanism* (Nashville: Abingdon, 1995), 163–97. Moreover, Jon D. Levenson, *Creation and the Persistence of Evil: The Jewish Drama of Divine Omnipotence* (San Francisco: Harper & Row, 1988), has noted a like reductionism in Jewish theology, with reference to Yehezkel Kaufmann. On creationism and its confusion of categories, see Langdon B. Gilkey, *Creationism on Trial: Evolution* (Minneapolis: Winston, 1985).

2. I speak of "human home" because that seems to be how the issue is articulated in Israel's testimony. It is self-evident that creation is a home for all creatures, including nonhuman creatures. See Ps 104:14-23 and, negatively, Eccl 3:18-20.

3. There are dissenters to this opinion, most recently James McKeown, *Genesis* (Two Horizons Old Testament Commentary; Grand Rapids: Eerdmans, 2008), 19.

4. See Levenson, *Creation and Persistence of Evil*, 5.

5. See Claus Westermann, *Creation* (trans. John J. Scullion; Philadelphia: Fortress Press, 1974), 49; and Walter Harrelson, *From Fertility Cult to Worship: A Reassessment for the Modern Church of the Worship of Ancient Israel* (Garden City, N.Y.: Doubleday, 1969).

6. This text is often cited as a basis for natural theology, whereby creation itself "reveals" YHWH. See James Barr, *Biblical Faith and Natural Theology: The Gifford Lectures for 1991* (Oxford: Clarendon, 1993), 85–89; and Rolf P. Knierim, *The Task of Old Testament Theology: Substance, Method, and Cases* (Grand Rapids: Eerdmans, 1995), 322–50. It is to be noted, nonetheless, that the utterance of the psalm is on the lips of Israel. Without Israel's awed doxology, the testimony of "nature" is not direct or explicit. I will not say it is mute, but in any practical way, this witness depends upon Israel.

7. The same patriarchal utilization of women is articulated in royal garb in Ps 45:12b-17.

8. See the review of the theme of dominion by Cameron Wybrow, *The Bible, Baconism, and Mastery over Nature* (New York: Peter Lang, 1991). See also Norbert Lohfink, "'Subdue the Earth?' (Genesis 1:28)," *Theology of the Pentateuch: Themes of the Priestly Narrative and Deuteronomy* (trans. Linda M. Maloney; Minneapolis: Fortress Press, 1994), 1–17.

9. Claus Westermann, *Blessing in the Bible and the Life of the Church* (trans. Keith Crim; OBT; Philadelphia: Fortress Press, 1978), 39.

10. H. H. Schmid, *Gerechtigkeit als Weltordnung: Hintergrund und Geschichte des alttestamentlichen Gerechtigkeitsbegriffs* (Tübingen: Mohr [Siebeck], 1968); and Knierim, *Task of Old Testament Theology*, 86–122.

11. See the definitive discussion on "deed-consequence" by Klaus Koch, "Is There a Doctrine of Retribution in the Old Testament?" in *Theodicy in the Old Testament*, ed. James L. Crenshaw (IRT; Philadelphia: Fortress Press, 1983), 57–87. Koch's categories are important for the argument developed by Schmid, *Gerechtigkeit als Weltordnung.*

12. On the centrality of creation in the worship of Israel, see Bernhard W. Anderson, *Creation versus Chaos: The Reinterpretation of Mythical Symbolism in the Bible* (Philadelphia: Fortress Press, 1987), 78–109; and Harrelson, *From Fertility Cult to Worship*, 81–152.

13. On this text, see Patrick D. Miller, "The Blessing of God: An Interpretation of Numbers 6:22-27," *Int* 29 (1975): 240–50; and Michael Fishbane, *Biblical Interpretation in Ancient Israel* (Oxford: Clarendon, 1985), 329–34.

14. Westermann, *Blessing in the Bible*, 103–20, has commented on the distinction between blessing that is present in all of creation and blessing as it is mediated institutionally. Sigmund Mowinckel has urged the cult as a generative, constitutive force for blessing. See, derivatively, Walter Brueggemann, *Israel's Praise: Doxology against Idolatry and Ideology* (Philadelphia: Fortress Press, 1988), 1–28.

15. See Peter J. Kearney, "The P Redaction of Exod 25–40," *ZAW* 89 (1977): 375–87; and Joseph Blenkinsopp, *Prophecy and Canon: A Contribution to the Study of Jewish Origins* (Notre Dame: University of Notre Dame Press, 1977), 54–69.

16. The seven speech units are Exod 25:1—30:10; 30:11-16; 30:17-21; 30:22-33; 30:34-38; 31:1-11; and 31:12-17.

17. In addition to the uses of the term *finish* in Gen 2:4 and Exod 39:32 and 40:33, see Josh 19:49-51. As Blenkinsopp observes, the uses assert the intentional parallel of creation, tabernacle, and land distribution.

18. In the discussion that follows, I am informed by the exposition of Levenson.

19. Levenson, *Creation and Persistence of Evil*, 47.

20. Ibid., 232.

21. Ibid., 26, 233.

22. Karl Barth, "God and Nothingness," *Church Dogmatics*, vol. 3/3: *The Doctrine of Creation* (Edinburgh: T. & T. Clark, 1960), 289. To be sure, Barth will not finally leave nothingness beyond God's providential sovereignty, as does Levenson. Nonetheless, Barth recognizes the depth and seriousness of this recalcitrance toward God.

23. Levenson, *Creation and Persistence of Evil*, 12.

24. See Anderson, *Creation versus Chaos*, 144–70; and Barth, *Church Dogmatics*, vol. 3/1: *The Doctrine of Creation* (Edinburgh: T. & T. Clark, 1958), 107 and 352ff.

25. On the serpent as the adumbration of Satan, see Paul Ricoeur, *The Symbolism of Evil* (Boston: Beacon, 1969), 255–60.

26. Terence E. Fretheim, "The Plagues as Ecological Signs of Historical Disaster," *JBL* 110 (1991): 385–96.

27. Fredrik Lindström, *Suffering and Sin: Interpretations of Illness in the Individual Complaint Psalms* (Stockholm: Almqvist & Wiksell International, 1994).

28. Levenson, *Creation and Persistence of Evil,* 17, refers to Leviathan in this passage as God's "rubber ducky."

29. See the comment of Fretheim, "Plagues as Ecological Signs," 391–92.

30. On these curses, see Delbert R. Hillers, *Treaty-Curses and the Old Testament Prophets* (BibOr 16; Rome: Pontifical Biblical Institute, 1964); and F. C. Fensham, "Maledictions and Benedictions in Ancient Near-Eastern Vassal-Treaties and the Old Testament," *ZAW* 74 (1962): 1–19.

31. See H. Graf Reventlow, *Das Amt des Propheten bei Amos* (FRLANT 80; Göttingen: Vandenhoeck & Ruprecht, 1962), 75–90.

32. On this text, see Walter Brueggemann, "The Uninflected *Therefore* of Hosea 4:1-3," in *Reading from This Place,* vol. 1: *Social Location and Biblical Interpretation in the United States,* ed. Fernando F. Segovia and Mary Ann Tolbert (Minneapolis: Fortress Press, 1995), 231–49.

33. The phrase is from Levenson, *Creation and Persistence of Evil,* 5.

34. Bernhard W. Anderson, "From Analysis to Synthesis: The Interpretation of Genesis 1–11," *JBL* 97 (1978): 31–39.

35. See Isa 54:9-10, where the same narrative is turned to be an assurance specifically to Israel. On the text, see Walter Brueggemann, "A Shattered Transcendence? Exile and Restoration," in *Biblical Theology: Problems and Perspectives,* ed. Steven J. Kraftchick, et al. (Nashville: Abingdon, 1995), 169–82.

36. Gary A. Anderson, *A Time to Mourn, a Time to Dance: The Expression of Grief and Joy in Israelite Religion* (University Park: Pennsylvania State University Press, 1991), 82–97 and passim.

37. The phrase is from Julian of Norwich, *Showings* (New York: Paulist Press, 1978).

Chapter 6

1. It is instructive that (a) early traditions and (b) prophetic traditions constitute the primary scheme of Gerhard von Rad for his *Old Testament Theology* (trans. D. M. G. Stalker; 2 vols.; New York: Harper & Row, 1962–65). It is important, given Christian supersessionist tendencies, that von Rad's scheme does not allow for emerging Judaism as a distinct component of Old Testament theology. Von Rad does not have in purview Judaism as a force for theological rehabilitation after exile.

2. On the defining importance of the cry as a theological datum in Israel, see James L. Kugel, *The God of Old: Inside the Lost World of the Bible* (New York: Free Press, 2003), 109–36.

3. H. H. Schmid, "Rechtfertigung als Schöpfungsgeschehen: Notizen zur alttestamentlichen Vorgeschichte eines neutestamentlichen Themas," in *Rechtfertigung: Festschrift für Ernst Käsemann,* ed. Johannes Friedrich, et al. (Göttingen: Vandenhoeck & Ruprecht, 1976), 403–14.

4. Jean-François Lyotard, *The Postmodern Condition: A Report on Knowledge* (Minneapolis: University of Minnesota Press, 1984).

5. M. Douglas Meeks, *God the Economist: The Doctrine of God and Political Economy* (Minneapolis: Fortress Press, 1989), has shrewdly and compellingly analyzed the function of the myth of scarcity.

6. The departure from the narrative of scarcity (on which see Isa 55:22-13) is liturgical and symbolic, but finally is economic and political. See Marie Augusta Neal, *A Socio-theology of Letting Go: The Role of a First World Church Facing the Third World Peoples* (New York: Paulist Press, 1977).

7. This rationality has been well exposited by Jacques Ellul, *The Technological Society* (trans. John Wilkinson; New York: Knopf, 1964). In *Propaganda: The Formation of Men's Attitudes*

(trans. Konrad Kellen and Jean Lerner; 1965; repr. New York: Vintage, 1973), Ellul has also explored the power of advertising to promote and sustain the unexamined values of that rationality. As advertising is largely a practice of denial supported and sustained by technology, see the ominous analysis of Ernst Becker, *The Denial of Death* (New York: Free Press, 1973).

8. Edward T. Oakes, *Patterns of Redemption: The Theology of Hans Urs von Balthasar* (New York: Continuum, 1994), especially 72–78, 277–99, has suggested that in contemporary Roman Catholic theology, Urs von Balthasar, for all his deep conservatism, indicates an openness to the possibility that this dialectic may indeed be present in the very character of God. Oakes suggests that Urs von Balthasar is more receptive to this than is Karl Rahner, for all the apparent openness of the latter.

Scripture Index

Author Index

178n25, 186n2, 187n13, 188(nn 19, 20)
Linafelt, Tod, 184(nn 49, 52)
Lindbeck, George, 178n12
Lindström, Fredrik, 78, 146, 179n41, 190n43,
    200n27
Lipschits, Oded, 198n38
Lohfink, Norbert, 180n9, 181n16, 200n8
Lyotard, Jean-François, 170, 201n4

M

Macken, John S., 186n4
Madigan, Kevin J., 185n67, 194n73
Martin-Achard, Robert, 194n72
Mauser, Ulrich, 187n5
Mays, James L., 185n65
McBride, S. Dean, 178n8
McCann, J. Clinton, 193n67
McCarthy, Dennis J., 180n9, 181n10
McKeown, James, 199n3
Meeks, M. Douglas, 201n5
Meeks, Wayne A., 185n70
Meissner, W. W., 191n53
Mendenhall, George W., 24, 181n10
Mettinger, Tryggve N. D., 182n27, 184n53
Middleton, Richard J., 187n5
Miles, Margaret R., 193–194n69
Milgram, Stanley, 189n30
Miller, Patrick D., 190(nn 41, 45–47), 191(nn
    50, 51), 193n68, 195(nn 2, 8), 196(nn 16,
    17), 200n13
Miranda, José, 182n20
Moberly, R. W. L., 180n4
Moltmann, Jürgen, 10–11, 17, 85, 179(nn 28,
    29), 180n45, 192n55, 193n62
Moran, William L., 178n11, 180n7
Morgan, Donn, 185n62
Morrow, William S., 179n36, 188n21
Murphy, Roland E., 189n33

N

Neal, Marie Augusta, 193n59, 201n6
Nelson, Richard D., 183n36
Neusner, Jacob, 184n45, 185n64
Newsom, Carol E., 194n76
Nicholson, Ernest, 24, 180n9, 181n11
Niditch, Susan, 196n12
Niebuhr, Reinhold, 186n80
Nogalski, James, 179n39
Noll, Mark A., 199n1

Noth, Martin, 198n44
Novak, David, 188n27

O

Oakes, Edward T., 202n8
O'Connor, Kathleen M., 184(nn 49, 51, 52)
Oden, Thomas C., 194n74
Ollenburger, Ben C., 182n27
Orlinsky, Harry, 38, 183(nn 40, 41)

P

Pannenberg, Wolfhart, 188n18
Parker, Simon B., 193n64
Patrick, Dale, 183n31
Perdue, Leo G., 186n72
Perlitt, Lothar, 24, 181n11
Plöger, Otto, 49, 185(nn 60, 63)
Premnath, D. N., 182n22
Prior, Michael, 186n78

R

Raabe, Paul R., 197n20
Rad, Gerhard von, 74, 177n2 (preface),
    179n38, 183(nn 38, 42), 184n54, 187n5,
    189(nn 33, 37), 196n15, 201n1
Randour, Mary Lou, 191n53
Rendtorff, Rolf, 179n43, 181n14
Reventlow, H. Graf, 201n31
Ricoeur, Paul, 145, 182n17, 188n26, 195n80,
    200n25
Robinson, James, 20, 180n6
Rosenstock, Eugen, 185n71
Rosenzweig, Franz, 6–8, 11–12, 54–55,
    178(nn18–24), 179n32, 185n71
Ross, Ellen M., 187n5
Rowley, H. H., 180n8
Rubenstein, Richard, 199n52

S

Sampson, Cynthia, 135, 199n51
Sanders, E. P., 25, 181n15
Sanders, James A., 178n7
Sawyer, John F. A., 187n5
Schmid, Hans Heinrich, 141, 170, 188(nn 16,
    27), 200n10, 201n3
Schmidt, Werner H., 181n16
Schmidt, William S., 191n53
Seebass, Horst, 189n35, 193n61
Seitz, Christopher R., 198(nn 36, 37)

CPSIA information can be obtained
at www.ICGtesting.com
Printed in the USA
LVHW020720020921
696302LV00015B/251